Speaking of Silence

Christians and Buddhists on the Contemplative Way

Edited by SUSAN WALKER

T0204856

PAULIST PRESS • NEW YORK • MAHWAH

Contributors

Tenshin Anderson
Sister Benedetta
Tessa Bielecki
Lodrö Dorje
Jack Engler
Joseph Goldstein
Thomas Hopko
Thomas Keating
The Dalai Lama
Judith Lief
William McNamara
Reginald Ray
Eido Shimano
David Steindl-Rast
Tai Situpa
George Timko
Chögyam Trungpa
John Yungblut

To
two great spokesmen
of spiritual renewal in this age:
Thomas Merton and
Chögyam Trungpa

Library of Congress Cataloging-in-Publication Data

Speaking of silence.

    Papers originally presented at Naropa Institute
conferences.
    Bibliography: p. 319
      1. Spiritual life—Comparative studies—Congresses.
2. Contemplation—Comparative studies—Congresses.
3. Christianity and other religions—Buddhism—Congresses.
4. Buddhism—Relations—Christianity—Congresses.
I. Walker, Susan. II. Naropa Institute.
BL624.S658 1987   248.3'4   87-9207
ISBN 0-8091-2880-2 (pbk.)

Published by Paulist Press
997 Macarthur Boulevard
Mahwah, New Jersey 07430

Printed and bound in the
United States of America

Father Merton's visit to Southeast Asia took place when I was in Calcutta....I had the feeling that I was meeting an old friend, a genuine friend. In fact, we planned to work on a book containing selections from the sacred writings of Christianity and Buddhism. We planned to meet either in Great Britain or in North America. He was the first genuine person I met from the West. After meeting Thomas Merton, I visited several monasteries in Great Britain, and at some of them I was asked to give talks on meditation, which I did....I was very impressed and moved by the contemplative aspect of Christianity, and by the monasteries themselves. Their lifestyle and the way they conducted themselves convinced me that the only way to join the Christian tradition and the Buddhist tradition together is by means of bringing together Christian contemplative practice with Buddhist meditative practice.

CHÖGYAM TRUNGPA

from an address to the Naropa Institute Conference on Christian and Buddhist Meditation, August 9, 1983

Chögyam Trungpa is a completely marvelous person. Young, natural, without front or artifice, deep, awake, wise. I am sure we will be seeing a lot more of each other....I've had the idea of editing a collection of pieces by various Buddhists on meditation etc., with an introduction of my own....I must talk to Chögyam Trungpa about this today.

THOMAS MERTON

from entries dated October 20 and 22, 1968 in *The Asian Journal*

Contents

Part One: Tradition: A Way of Speaking

1 The Way of Christ

2 Buddha's Way

3 Renewal, Transmission, and Change

Part Two: Comparing Ways

4 *God and Emptiness*

5 *Views of Self and Ego*

6 *Sin, Suffering, and Virtue*

7 *Prayer and Meditation*

Part Three: Everyday Journey

Foreword

James Finley

Interreligious dialogue is a complex phenomenon. It is multi-dimensional and multi-faceted, with theological, ethical, philosophical, sociological, and historical implications. And yet, the talks and conversations you are about to read are not intellectually complicated or intricate. That is because this book is not actually about Buddhist-Christian dialogue—although it is an example of it.

To help attune you to what you are about to read, let us suppose for a moment that you are a Christian seeker who has just spent a month in solitude. It has been a month of silence and fasting, with long hours of prayer. Your retreat has now ended, and the first person you will meet is a Buddhist. That Buddhist has also just completed a month-long retreat. Your meeting has been prearranged, and the one ground rule you have agreed upon is this: neither will say anything that does not resonate with and come out of the experience of the search.

The two of you begin your meeting by walking down a path together. You might walk on for a long time before either of you says anything. That silence itself would be significant. Within it would be a mutual, intuitive recognition of the other's presence. Each of you would be giving a nonverbal, noncognitive witness to the other's search. This recognition, or awareness, would be preeminently simple, because it wouldn't be composed of anything. There would be nothing to agree or disagree with. And then, after walking on in this way for some time, you would begin to speak.

This kind of nonverbal recognition is the key for how to approach this book. If you enter into this meeting between Christianity and Buddhism in that way, the talks and discussions you read will make sense. If you try to approach it in any other way, such as with a particular doctrinal stance or scholarly perspective, the real message will be lost. You will miss it. These articles have come out of speech that is faithful to the search. They capture that speech, and therefore they resonate for each person who is willing to listen. That is the beauty of this book.

Now, if you are a Christian, you may ask, "What about belief? How

1

can I resonate with the experience of someone who doesn't believe in Jesus, or, for that matter, who doesn't believe in God—at least not in the way I usually understand belief in God? Doesn't belief matter, or does it simply get swept away into all this silence?" This question recalls an interesting observation I made when reading these talks, which is that nowhere does a speaker water down his or her own tradition for the sake of dialogue. Never is there any sense of compromise. On the other hand, neither does one speaker try to convince the other person. You don't sense that he or she is privately thinking, "Do yourself a favor and see it my way." This is because the speakers understand the truth that, in the order of sameness and difference, sameness is real and difference is real.

If I am a Christian, I will typically choose another Christian to be my spiritual director. The sameness of our belief is important to me. I am counting on my spiritual director to represent and hand down the beliefs of the community. Likewise, if the person I am walking with down the path is not a Christian, that difference is also real. I don't have to pretend he is a Christian; I don't have to try to make him into a Christian. But if sameness or difference is the basis for my meeting with that other person, we are locked into that order. We will never go beyond it; there will be no escape.

The kind of meeting we are talking about here is not a meeting in the order of sameness and difference. It is a meeting in the order of God. God is beyond all sameness and beyond all difference, or, to say the same thing another way, he is the infinite ground of all that is the same and the infinite ground of all that is different. In him, all sameness and all difference is one.

It is in the order of God that we are able to see the unity of the contemplative path. In this dialogue, we are not looking for theological unity, because theology is in the order of sameness and difference. Theology is in the realm of the rational: it knows by comparing one thing to another thing and then coming to a conclusion. Here we are concerned with another kind of unity, which is the unity of the contemplative way. Where is this unity to be found? It is in the compassion of those who walk it. It is in their humility, integrity, and in their non-impositional conviction. It is a unity that in no way denies the order of sameness and difference. Rather, it acknowledges and reveres all sameness and all differences as such, because it speaks with the wisdom of knowing that that order is not the ultimate order.

Editor's Note

This book began as a stack of verbatim transcripts documenting the five annual conferences on Christian and Buddhist Meditation that were hosted by Naropa Institute in Boulder, Colorado between 1981 and 1985. The transcripts included over forty individual presentations, sixteen panel discussions, and a number of behind-the-scenes interviews and working sessions. This raw material—totalling over two thousand pages of double-spaced text—has been sorted, rearranged, trimmed, and refined many times on its way to its present shape.

I don't really know why I ever embarked on this editing project. It wasn't because I had the right scholastic background or experiential overview, either Christian or Buddhist. Growing up, I belonged to the Anglican Church of Canada, but, although I generally enjoyed going to the Sunday services, my interest and participation faded well before adolescence. When I became spiritually restless during my college years, I turned to books on Eastern mysticism and to a Gurdjieffian-style guru I met in Montreal. After a period of being tossed about, both psychologically and geographically, by this powerful and charismatic individual, I became frustrated by the lack of a consistent, well-rooted spiritual tradition and found myself once again looking to Christianity. I visited many church communities, but found the services and leadership to be superficial, and in some cases even condescending or manipulative. In 1975, I attended a seminar by the Venerable Chögyam Trungpa Rinpoche and started reading his books. I began a daily practice of meditation and, within the following year, took Refuge Vows with a lama of the Sakya school of Tibetan Buddhism. Six years later, I found myself studying and practicing with the Vajradhatu community in Boulder, Colorado and working at Naropa Institute. By 1981, when I attended the first Christian-Buddhist conference, my interest in Christianity had dwindled to a minor curiosity. I was too eagerly and actively soaking up the Buddhist teachings and practices around me to even pay much attention to other Buddhist schools and teachings—let alone to Christianity. With such little intellectual and experiential preparation, I was probably one of the most wide-eyed members of the audience at that first Naropa Institute conference in 1981.

Perhaps it was because of my naivete that I began this project: Having never heard Christianity presented with such unassuming profundity, humanness, and humor, I was taken by surprise. I was also enthused to hear Buddhism articulated in so many diverse ways while still remaining consistently true to my experience of meditation. Moreover, these Christians and Buddhists were actually talking to each other, and obviously enjoying each other's company very much. Somehow, all of this must have left a big impression on me, for the next thing I knew I was collecting transcripts. After two more conferences I announced to my fellow staff members that I had begun a project: I would compile and edit some of the transcripts into a book. Most people thought it was a good idea; a few conference participants had even donated money toward a small fund to be set aside for such a publication. At the time, I envisioned the final product to be an in-house publication of "conference papers."

In 1984 I took the transcripts to the ten-week Vajradhatu seminary which was being held in the Bedford Springs Hotel in rural Pennsylvania. In the morning I chanted Buddhist liturgies and meditated; in the afternoon I retreated to my small attic room to work. With the afternoon sun coming through one small dingy window, I read, reread, and indexed the transcripts. I also began to read some of the books on the conference reading list, especially those recommended by the Christian faculty: The Cloud of Unknowing, the Philokalia, the Ascent of Mount Carmel, books by Thomas Merton and William Johnston. During many of these afternoons, I experienced the breathless exhilaration of letting myself fall into the magical power of a spiritual tradition other than the one to which I was by now so deeply committed and devoted. I was finally discovering the contemplative side of Christianity; ironically enough, my Buddhist practice had led me to it. In fact, it was probably my Buddhist practice that allowed the words I was hearing and reading to penetrate so deeply. By the end of seminary, my editorial interest in the Christian-Buddhist dialogue had been replaced by a much more intimate involvement with the material. My project was beginning to lead me beyond my initial ideas about what I was doing or why. All I had to do, it seemed, was to follow along.

As my background reading progressed, and I realized that the conference transcripts were speaking out of sound traditional doctrine and therefore didn't contribute any radically new ideas to the Christian and Buddhist literature that was already available, I began to wonder whether the enthusiasm with which I had begun had more personal than universal significance, and whether the time and effort required to consolidate and publish the transcripts was justifiable. However, I soon began to cross paths with many people, both Christian and Buddhist, who were keen to read the transcripts and who encouraged me to continue. Through them, I became more aware of the larger context of the conferences: the on-going, vigorous contemplative renewal within Christianity and the yearn-ing among Western Buddhists to reconnect with and appreciate the true potency of the religion that has been so instrumental in shaping our Western psyche and culture.

Although the ideas in the transcripts are not new, the movement to bring Christian and Buddhist spirituality into direct contact with each other, for the sake of their mutual benefit, continues to be revolutionary. It is revolutionary not only as a social phenomenon; it is also personally revolutionary. Each one of us who has embarked on a contemplative path must go through the process of realizing that the way to nurture our re-spective traditions in the midst of a spiritually-cynical society is not by holding on more tightly—which may be the first impulse—but by open-ing up, letting go, and extending beyond our personal and religious iden-tities.

By the end of 1984, I had drafted a first outline for a Table of Con-tents. I began to excerpt and rearrange the transcripts according to the themes that had been recurrent in the discussions, both as concerns that were shared by both traditions, and as doctrinal descriptions that stood out in apparent contradiction when the two religions were placed along-side one other. During this planning phase, it was obvious that not every-thing, nor everyone, could be included. I selected and pruned according to my original thematic outline, focusing on a central "cast of characters" that the reader could reasonably get to know and recognize as distinctive personalities representing distinctive traditions. As a result, a number of conference speakers, and certainly a large number of talks and panel dis-cussions, have been omitted. This was necessitated by the practical de-mands made by such a large body of material and does not reflect the relative merit of what was or wasn't incorporated. In particular, most of the material that was included comes from the first three conferences, which occurred during the book's planning stage.

One day after I was well on the way to completing a first draft of the manuscript, I was rereading through the 1983 transcripts when I was taken aback to hear my teacher, Trungpa Rinpoche, say that he and Thomas Merton had once planned to work together on a book "containing selections from the sacred writings of Christianity and Buddhism." (I have documented their respective comments in the opening epigraphs.) Although this collaboration was never realized because of Thomas Merton's sudden and tragic death a few months later, in December, 1968, I cannot help but feel that their intention to bring together these two contemplative traditions has in some way remained alive, and that this book is one of the long-term expressions of that intention. Certainly Trungpa Rinpoche's ongoing interest in this dialogue has provided the "atmosphere of inspiration and blessings" out of which the conferences and this book have born, and perhaps that atmosphere is the closest I could come to explaining why I ever did begin, and had the confidence to continue, this project. I would therefore like to take this opportunity to thank him for his unwavering and uncompromising devotion to the renewal of spiritual values and for his unceasing kindness and wisdom as a spiritual director.

Secondly, I would like to thank all the other conference presenters in this book for so patiently and willingly responding to my requests to review and revise my often-clumsy and sometimes-humorous editorial blunders. For the record, they have all confirmed that they did indeed say what "I said they said" in the present draft—or at least that they would have said it, given the chance. I am especially grateful to His Eminence the Tai Situpa Rinpoche for so generously responding to my request for a calligraphy for this book.

I would also like to extend a thank-you to the friends who have encouraged me through my "dark nights" and distracted moments along the way. Foremost in this category is my husband, Timothy. Perhaps a gesture of gratitude to the author's or editor's spouse is sometimes an expected formality; in this case, however, it is definitely well-deserved. Special thanks also go to Martha Bonzi, Bill McKeever, Richard Bock, and John Hart; to Carolyn Gimian and Larry Mermelstein for their editorial advice with respect to Trungpa Rinpoche's and Situ Rinpoche's contributions; to assistants Matthew Bloomfield, Janine Randoll, and Eileen Heaney; to Hal Richman for the use of his computer; and to all the people who helped with the often-tedious job of transcribing the conference tapes verbatim.

Finally, the Naropa Institute staff must be thanked for being sufficiently visionary and energetic to host the Christian-Buddhist conferences year after year. In particular, Judith Simmer Brown and Mary Edwards, along with their assistants, have been consistently dedicated and tireless in this respect.

Style

Traditions which by definition value and respect their particular distinctiveness, color, and conventions do not easily conform to a "standard of style." In this book I have tried to maintain a middle way between consistency and diplomacy. I have been pulled back and forth by the tendency to capitalize in Christian writing (although this trend has been modified in more recent years) and the tendency toward lower case in Buddhist writings (especially when rendered into English by Buddhist translators); by the tendency for long strings of honorific titles in Vajrayana Buddhism and the aversion for any titles at all among Quakers, Vipassana teachers, and many post-Vatican II Catholics; by the editor's tendency to document references and cite English-language sources and many of the contributors' tendency to freely translate and paraphrase from original texts. In the end, there is little real logic to some of the conventions I have adopted, beyond an overall loyalty to the University of Chicago Press's Manual of Style and a leaning toward the preferences of the contributors. In some cases, consistency in capitalization has been sacrificed for the purpose of communicating a particular emphasis or subtlety of meaning. With a few exceptions, quotations from the Bible are from the Revised Standard Version.

Titles and Abbreviations

The contributors' names as they appear in the by-lines at the beginning of each article include their formal titles. In the conversations, names appear in the form they usually used when addressing each other: "Brother David," "Father Timko," "Mother Tessa," "Situ Rinpoche," "Eido Roshi," etc. Although Father Thomas Keating was sometimes addressed as "Father Thomas" and Father William McNamara as "Father William," their last names have been used throughout in order to avoid possible ambiguity or inconsistency.

Following is a brief explanation of titles and abbreviations:

C.S.C.L   Community of Sisters of the Church. An Anglican order.

H.E.   His Eminence. A title of respect, in this case referring to one of the four main lineage holders of the Kagyu school of Tibetan Buddhism.

H.H.   His Holiness. A title of respect, in this case referring to the head of one of the four main lineages of Tibetan Buddhism.

Loppon   Tibetan for head master or teacher.

O.C.D.   Order of the Carmelites of the Discalced Fathers. A Catholic monastic order.

O.C.S.O.   Order of the Cistercians of the Strict Observance. A Catholic monastic order, commonly known as "Trappists."

O.S.B.   Order of Saint Benedict. A Catholic monastic order.

Rinpoche   A Tibetan title of respect (literally Precious One) used when addressing Tibetan Buddhist tulkus, or reincarnated lineage holders.

Roshi   A title of respect used when addressing Zen masters.

Ven.   Venerable. A title of respect.

Glossary

In one sense, this entire book is a glossary, in that it is an attempt to develop and define a particular spiritual terminology: one that transcends sectarian and religious boundaries.

Most foreign words that appear in this book have been rendered understandable by their context; in other cases they are defined in chapter-end notes. The word "contemplative," which has specific meanings in both Christianity and Buddhism, in this book refers to the nonconceptual, experiential dimension of spirituality.

Acknowledgments and Copyright Notices

"The Song of Devotion and Longing" by Khakhyap Dorje and one verse of "The Song of Lodrö Thaye" from *The Rain of Wisdom,* translated by the Nalanda Translation Committee under the direction of the Venerable Chögyam Trungpa, Rinpoche, copyright 1980 by Chögyam Trungpa.

Background:
Contemplative Dialogue
at Naropa Institute

Reginald Ray

When the Venerable Chögyam Trungpa Rinpoche first suggested
that Naropa Institute initiate a program of interreligious "contemplative
studies," our response was hesitant. As Buddhists just beginning to find
our way around Buddhism, we thought we had left Christianity and Judaism behind for good. As is typical of new converts, we shared a resistance and lack of curiosity toward other religions, and especially toward
those with which we had grown up. For the next two years, therefore, the
contemplative studies project remained just an idea.

In 1978, Rinpoche raised the matter once again, and this time, in
spite of our uncertainties, we decided to go ahead. Actually, by then we
were beginning to feel more at home in our newfound Buddhism, and
the idea of interacting with other contemplative traditions started to seem
an intriguing, if somewhat intimidating, prospect. We began by planning
an annual summer conference devoted to dialogue between the contemplative traditions of Buddhism and Christianity.

The Contemplative Emphasis

From the outset, there was consensus among conference planners
that we wanted to explore the living flame of spiritual or "contemplative"
experience in our two traditions. From our viewpoint, this is what is most
fundamental in the religious life, the wellspring that nourishes the great
traditions. And it is the contemplative path that most directly brings
about human self-confrontation and spiritual transformation and serves
as the gateway to the ultimate object of spiritual longing.

This decision to explore our respective contemplative traditions was
to have far-reaching effects on the conferences and on our experience of
dialogue. For one thing, we soon found that our meetings were taking us
far beyond the realm of polite, theoretical conversations about Buddhism

11

and Christianity, and that we had embarked on a shared journey into new territory.

An important element of our conferences was the atmosphere that surrounded and permeated them, established by our contemplative subject matter, the meditation hall where we met, the superlatively accomplished faculty, and the twice-daily meditations of everyone involved with the conferences. Interestingly enough, even in the short time that we spent together each summer, we experienced an atmosphere similar to the one might encounter around Buddhist temples, Christian contemplative centers, or other places where a lot of meditation or prayer has gone on: an atmosphere of quiet, not simply as an absence of noise, but as a genuine stillness that one recognizes as fundamental. This environment was helpful, for it provided directness and clarity and encouraged everyone to present themselves as they were.

Spiritual Journey

The study of the contemplative traditions was the context for something immediate and intimate, namely, for the ongoing spiritual journey of each one of us. From one viewpoint, we were all at the conference to pursue a traditional end: the exploration and nurturing of our own spiritual lives as Christians or as Buddhists. Beyond this, as the conferences progressed, we gradually discovered that we were engaged in a mutual and intimately personal journey. This was generally unexpected; after all, we belonged to very different traditions. In our culture, we are used to thinking that this creates spiritual separation, even antagonism. Don't we usually think that the further another tradition is historically and doctrinally removed from us, the less relevant it is to our lives?

Through our dialogue, we discovered that exploration of the spiritual life with members of a very different faith might in fact be a situation of exemplary power. We began to discover, for example, that we shared a common sense of obstacles in the spiritual life: the danger of staleness in oneself and one's tradition and of the self-satisfaction and smugness that mask true spirituality. Those of us who participated in the conferences found that in dialogue with the "other," whatever dogmatism and closed-mindedness we had brought with us were uncovered. The resulting exposure—painful, humbling, and sometimes humorous—couldn't have been more positive, for it opened the way for increased self-aware-ness and communication.

This communication was often unexpectedly heartfelt. In particular we began to sense that we Christians and Buddhists were on the same journey. Not a similar journey, but the same journey. We share the same longing for the ultimate and yearning for fundamental transformation; we rely upon the great contemplatives, past and present, of our respec-tive traditions; and we see community to be fundamental, even as it iron-ically highlights the solitary nature of the spiritual journey. We also found that many of our deepest insights were provoked by or came from the other: Christians experienced over and over that they learned about what is true and ultimately real from Buddhists, and Buddhists learned likewise from Christians.

To indicate just how radical this experience could be, I recall the comment of a Buddhist staff member who had attended a Catholic Mass, held in the Buddhist shrine hall one morning: "I have been meditating for fourteen years, I received *abhisheka*[1] several years ago, and I have had a lot of experience with the Vajrayana Buddhist liturgies. When I at-tended the Mass, I didn't expect anything. I just thought I would join in. Through the course of the Mass, I noticed the tone of the room shift sub-tly but definitely. I saw a "softening" and clearing of the atmosphere and a relaxation and warmth grow on people's faces, Buddhists as well as Christians. It was very moving. It was the same kind of magical transfor-mation that I experience in our liturgies and meditation. In Christian terms, this morning's Mass made salvation real and immediate for all of us."

Community

Another theme expressed in our meetings was that of community. In a sense, all of us were participants in something much bigger than the idea of a "conference" would suggest. We gradually discovered that the normal boundaries between the sects within each of our traditions, and between Buddhism and Christianity themselves, were dissolving into a larger "something." This larger enterprise bound us into a single "com-munity of believers" that for many of us was quite unexpected in its strength and intimacy. I frequently heard comments, particularly from the conference faculty and staff, to the effect that they often felt more in common with these contemplatives of the other faith than with many people within their own religion. Were these statements of apostasy? I feel they were not, but were rather reflections of the depth, genuineness, and conviction of each person's faith. It seemed that it was just this depth of experience that gave one the insight and the confidence to feel this way, and to say so.

A Paradigm for Dialogue

The Naropa Institute conferences encouraged us toward daring and wholehearted dialogue. It became clear that we need to see the dogmatic insistence on the unapproachable "superiority" of any given faith as a spiritual obstacle. Beyond this, we have to face the possibility that turning one's back on other traditions may be, in this age, to turn one's back on the ultimate object of one's own faith. It may be that what Father Thomas Keating calls the "Ultimate Mystery"—which calls us through all our spiritual longing and for which our spiritual lives exist—is speaking to us with particular potency through the voice of the other faith.

This experience of encountering the Ultimate Mystery through another faith represents a kind of death, for in that experience we have to let go of our religion as personal possession, security, and identity. In the conferences, such a death was met by each of us with anxiety, with fear, and with resistance; yet, truth has a way of being insistent, and it was not the kind of experience one could ultimately refuse. In this death, one sensed God (or Buddha) proclaiming his transcendence and defeating any self-interested attempts to own him, even with one's religion. As Father William McNamara said, the Terrible Good is not to be tamed!

Nevertheless, we found that death is not the end of the story, for out of such defeat one finds one's own tradition re-awakened with new freshness and vigor. Often as not, the radical extent of our communication with the other tradition leads us to see depth in aspects of our traditions that were before taken for granted. We discover hidden or underplayed elements that begin to call us. We find new ways to articulate old truths that perhaps have lost their voice. Sometimes we discover strengths in our tradition that had previously been invisible. In general, we gain new confidence to go ahead with our spiritual lives.

Thus the experience of the conferences suggest that what formerly separated us—our difference of faiths—is now precisely that which can strengthen us and unite us as religious people. He or she from the other faith, whom we had dismissed as being irrelevant to our religious lives, turns out to be the long-lost spiritual friend.

Such experiences should not be misinterpreted as asserting the "unity of religions," an assertion which plagues many projects of contemporary dialogue. Certainly Buddhism and Christianity are different and distinct traditions, with different cultural contexts, histories, theologies, and methodologies, and often with divergent concerns. In light of our experiences at Naropa Institute, such differences are to be acknowledged, retained, and even celebrated as affirmations of the dignity and integrity of each tradition, and as the precondition that alone makes possible this kind of contemplative dialogue. Here, as elsewhere, it would seem, the more one is willing to be who one is, the more deeply and intimately one can communicate with the other.

Another potential misunderstanding is that the Naropa Institute conferences are trying to create, or should try to create, a new religion: some sort of grand amalgamation of traditions. Quite to the contrary, the interchange has been so powerful precisely because we are committed to our respective traditions and have no desire to be otherwise. Moreover, as noted above, the outcome of our experience is renewed conviction and, more than that, experience, of the depth and validity of our traditions. The more deeply committed and experienced we are within our traditions, the more confidently and fully we can enter into dialogue. And we come out of the encounter more fully Christian and more fully Buddhist—and, one hopes, less arrogantly so. One feels more appreciative and confident of one's own faith, and certainly less dogmatic, and therefore more "at home."

How do the Naropa Institute conferences fit into the larger conversation going on between Buddhism and Christianity? Obviously, the experience of these conferences does not supplant other forms of Buddhist-Christian dialogue, be it theological encounter, academic collaboration, institutional cooperation, or dialogue at the congregational level. Each style of encounter performs an essential function within the overall economy of the current dialogue between Buddhism and Christianity. For example, theological encounter highlights areas of theological misunderstanding and helps traditions become informed about each other's viewpoints. By investigating and comparing history and dogma, dialogue on the academic level lays the groundwork of facticity that is necessary to successful dialogue. Institutional cooperation enables traditions to see how they can cooperate in joint projects in a positive and productive way and fosters mutual understanding among those who set policies and guide the traditions at an institutional level. And congregational interchange allows for mutual awakening and nourishment at the grassroots level, which, among other things, encourages those involved in more specialized forms of dialogue. It is within this overall context that the Naropa Institute contemplative conferences make their special contribution.

The Naropa Institute style of dialogue is distinct from the others mentioned above; however, it has important implications for each of them. For example, although not primarily theological in intent, and therefore not systematic in that sense, by pointing to the "place" where dogma and boundaries do not exist, the conferences shed fresh light on some of the major doctrinal questions confronting Christianity and Buddhism. Thus, we discover that the theism of Christianity and the nontheism of Buddhism, which seem to be opposed theological perspectives, appear within the context of contemplation as the two traditions' distinctive ways of attempting to deal with the same issue of "transcendence" in religious experience.

Although not primarily academic in nature, the interchanges at Naropa Institute revealed the need for academic exploration of some neglected areas of religious history, particularly in the area of contemplative Christianity and Buddhism. Not only do we, as professionally-engaged Christians and Buddhists, know little about each others' traditions; we also know surprisingly little about the contemplative traditions of our own faiths.

Although not aiming at institutional cooperation, our encounters suggest perspectives from which such cooperation could be entered into with less paranoia and more mutual trust. The insight that we Christians and Buddhists are in some way engaged in the same project of spirituality suggests that our working together on the institutional level is not only a politically wise and effective way to confront the world's problems, but is perhaps also a religious necessity for each of us. Doesn't a vision of spiritual brotherhood call to be translated onto the institutional level?

And although not aimed at intercongregational conversation, our dialogue revealed the intense longing for openness, exploration, and communication that is often felt at the congregational level in both Buddhism and Christianity—a longing that can partially be fulfilled in the dialogical situation.

In its place within the current Christian-Buddhist dialogue, and in its implications for other forms of dialogue, the Naropa Institute conferences call for a return of religious people and of religions to their roots and their source: to direct spiritual experience. And they call for a return to the primary mode of access to that experience: to the great contemplative traditions. If we can respond to this call, we may look with hope and good cheer to an expected "eschaton" of renewal and regeneration among the world's religions.

The Naropa Institute conferences also have definite implications for the contemporary relationship among religions. Life within religious traditions has always been characterized by diversity: of lifestyle (monastic, eremetic, and lay); of cultural context and local history; of liturgical color; and of doctrinal emphasis. At the best of times, the tendency toward orthodoxy which exists within every tradition has accommodated considerable diversity, viewing it as a reflection of its own resourcefulness and richness of expression. Today, as in the past, we face a situation of diversity, except that it has become much more extreme and challenging. In our contemporary world, we need to find a way to talk about the Ultimate Mystery that is not purely biased to one or another religion, and we need to develop a sense of community among all spiritual people, whatever their tradition. Thus, on the one hand, we must work to maintain the integrity and health of individual religions in their theological, liturgical, and community lives. At the same time, as a parallel effort, we must strive to develop meta-theological, meta-community, and perhaps even meta-liturgical forms wherein the great religions, in tact and in all their power, are at the same time seen and experienced as members of a common spiritual enterprise.

This will be no simple task, because we must find the middle way between the two extremes of abandoning concern for the integrity of our respective traditions and rigidly insisting on past definitions and approaches. It is on this issue that the Naropa Institute conferences have something to say, for they suggest a context and an approach that may provide the methodology by which this goal can be accomplished.

This is one final implication of the Naropa Institute conferences: this time, not for religious dialogue, but for modern-day communication and understanding. Today, more than ever before in human history, all of us are confronted on a daily basis with differences of race, nationality, culture, and belief. These differences could be a cause for offense, as they most often have been in the course of history. Or they could be viewed in an entirely different way, as invitations to step beyond the identities that we each have and to enter into a place where communication is penetrating and genuine, and from which we emerge, again and again, with a larger view of who we are and what it means to be human.

The Naropa Institute conferences proclaim that such an approach to differences is not only possible, but can be experienced as exciting, enlivening, and deeply satisfying. What is possible for the four hundred or so people who attend these conferences each year is surely possible on a much larger scale.

Background Note:
1. *Abhisheka* is a form of Vajrayana Buddhist initiation, which in this case takes place after a substantial amount of meditative training, and which qualifies the practitioner to perform advanced liturgies.

Part One

Tradition:
A Way of Speaking

A religious tradition—with its images, symbols, and sacred writings—is a way of speaking. It speaks about the experience that comes out of silence.

Through tradition there is continuity: each generation inherits the language of the past. There is also change: language interacts with time and cultural context, and it is brought up to date by human revelation.

1

The Way of Christ

The Church gives us not a system but a key; not a plan of God's city, but the means of entering it. Perhaps someone will lose his way because he has no plan. But all that he will see, he will see without a mediator, he will see it directly, it will be real for him; while he who has studied only the plan risks remaining outside and not really finding anything.[1]

GEORGE FLOROVSKY

Standing on Holy Ground

David Steindl-Rast O.S.B.

None of us would have any interest in learning about any form of spirituality if we hadn't had some experience of wonderment and of ultimate belonging in the world. Perhaps this experience was just fleeting. If you tried to communicate it, you might find yourself saying something like, "For a moment I lost myself. I was listening to music, and I just lost myself." In the *Four Quartets,* T. S. Eliot speaks of being "lost in a shaft of sunlight." But at the same time—and this is the paradox—you could say that at those moments when you lost yourself, you were also more truly yourself than at any other time. At the moment when you lose your little self, you find your true self, your full self. In his autobiography, *To Leave Before Dawn,* Julian Green recalls such a moment from his adolescence:

> I was lying on my back when, all of a sudden, a feeling of indescribable happiness swept over my whole being. It seemed as though the threats that weighed on the world no longer existed, that all sadness had suddenly ended, and that, in a deep and complete security, everything blossomed into joy. . . . I did not think of God, I thought of nothing, to speak truthfully, I did not think, I forgot who I was.[2]

Self-forgetfulness, which brings us to the very center of our being, is associated with the Biblical concept of heart. The heart is where we are fully alive, fully aware, fully ourselves, and at the same time it is where we are fully united with all others and with God. As Christ says in the New Testament, "He who loses his life for my sake will find it" (Matt. 10:39). The heart is the place where the human and the divine are simply one. For most of us this type of experience is elusive, yet it is the only means we have of touching who we really are, and of finding our true anchorage in life. So naturally the desire springs up to live that way always: to always be in touch with the very center of one's being. That is the desire underlying every spiritual path. It is not to say that we should try to cling to those experiences that are fleeting; obviously that would be futile. But the question becomes, how can we put ourselves into a frame of mind that will lead us to live life in its fullness? Out of that question every path springs, and in the case of the Benedictine path, it was in response to that question that Saint Benedict wrote a Rule of life. "Rule" is not used here in this sense of rules and regulations. The word *rule* comes from the Greek term *canon*, which originally meant "trellis." The Rule of Saint Benedict is a trellis which supports a life of mindfulness, a life lived in fullness.

The Rule was written in the sixth century. At that time, Christian monasticism was only three hundred years old, but it had already become rather decadent; and so Saint Benedict introduced a set of guidelines in the form of a little book, a Rule for how to conduct monastic life. By the high Middle Ages, most of the monasteries in the West followed his Rule.

In The Rule of Saint Benedict is a passage that says we should always be on guard, living in a state of continual suspense with death always before our eyes.[3] Awareness of death is a key point in understanding the Benedictine path. Now, it may seem somewhat macabre to deliberately reflect on death, but it is in no way meant to be so; on the contrary, the remembrance of death is what can make us more and more alive. In this passage, the word "suspense" suggests something suspended, as if a sword were hanging on a very thin thread over our heads. That image should wake us up, not scare us; it is exactly the opposite of fear. The awareness of death has nothing to do with fear, except perhaps that it is a way of overcoming it. Death is the horizon of who we are, against which each experience is silhouetted. It is like writing on a blackboard with white chalk. If we aren't aware of that horizon, we can never really see or appreciate whatever is standing in the foreground. When we are aware, we naturally feel a sense of wonderment that things are as they are. I recently spent some time at Tassajara Monastery where I met a little three-and-a-half-year-old philosopher. She was walking around with the air of someone who had just made an important discovery, pointing to everything she saw, and saying, "What if it were different?" It is such a basic question. And of course the greatest difference would be, what if it wasn't here at all? When we apply that question to ourselves, we understand that everything is totally gratuitous. To feel this gratuity against the background of the possibility of not being here at all is the beginning of the spiritual path. When I read The Rule of Saint Benedict for the first time, the passage about death struck a deep and familiar chord in me, and I thought, "Oh yes, that is what I have always wanted in my life: I want to live in such a way that I can stand up to that challenge." So it has a special importance for me, personally. But the awareness of death also holds its own place in the monastic tradition in general. Many sundials in the old monasteries bear the inscription *memento mori:* remember that you will die. But there are also some that say *memento vivere:* remember to live. And there is really no difference between these two admonitions.

If you have ever visited a monastery of any tradition, you have seen that it is something like a laboratory, a controlled environment in which everything is geared toward the pursuit of mindfulness. The theological superstructure may vary, but the cultivation of mindfulness is always the common element. In a Benedictine monastery, the Rule is what shapes time and place. Everything is designed and arranged in order to help you be present, to be where you are.

It seems that people are often disappointed when they first come to live in a monastery. Everyone expects to be taught some kind of spirituality, but instead they are taught that when you take off your shoes, you should put them parallel to each other, and not pigeon-toed. You should close doors behind you and learn the proper way to walk and to eat. At first novices might think, "All this must be for beginners. I will wait until the real thing comes along." But that *is* the real thing. Those little acts all help to make us mindful. Everything is arranged in a particular way, so that we will be present where we are. In the Benedictine monastery this principle is also expressed by the arrangement of buildings, which has been remarkably stable through the centuries. All buildings point to a center, and in that center stands the church. In the case of the Monastery of Mount Savior, where I live, the church is an octagonal building, and at the very center of that is the altar.

When you first come to the monastery, you think that there are many activities in the course of a day: you work, you study, you sleep, you eat. And all these different activities are in different places. You also go to church more frequently than you used to and stand around the altar with the others and read or chant. Then after a while your picture changes, and you think of yourself standing with the others around the altar, occasionally going out to do something or other because it needs to be done. But basically you are always standing there, by the altar. After awhile comes a third phase, when you see yourself always at the center, and the altar is no longer that important: it is just a symbol. When you stand at the kitchen stove, that is the center, that is the altar. And when you lie on your bed, then your bed becomes the altar. You are always standing on holy ground. In the well-known Biblical passage, Moses sees the burning bush, and the presence of God calls out to him, "Put off your shoes from your feet, for the place on which you are standing is holy ground" (Exod. 3:5). The rabbis interpret this not so much as a warning to Moses that he should take off his shoes because that particular ground is holy, but rather that the shoes are made out of the skin of animals, and represent something dead or foreign between our feet and the ground on which we stand. Wherever we take off our shoes, we will realize that we have been standing on holy ground.

All of monastic life is an effort to take off our shoes. Of course, it is not necessary to live in a monastery in order to live this life. In fact, there are many lay people who are vastly more alive than monks. Nevertheless, the monastic environment is explicitly geared, through the arrangement of space and time, toward helping us become more alive. All the bells, gongs, and drums in a monastery are there to remind us: this is the moment, this is the moment. Saint Benedict says that at the very first sound of a bell a monk should drop everything and go toward whatever it is the time to be doing. He shouldn't even stop to dot his "i's" if he is in the middle of writing a letter, but he should just get up and go. In the *Four Quartets,* T. S. Eliot calls this "time, not our time." To act when it *is* time is different from doing something when we feel like it. A task for all of us is to attune ourselves to time which is not *our* time. Time is not something that we can hang on to; it is a gift we receive moment by moment. Eliot introduces here the image of the Angelus bell. This bell was traditionally rung in monasteries at sunrise, at noon, and at sunset, to indicate that the monks were about to meet for prayer. It was rung loudly enough so that people in the houses and villages surrounding the monastery could also hear it. Then they would join the monks in prayer. You may have noticed that those are special times even for the birds and for the monkeys who climb up into the trees. They start singing and yelling as the sun rises and also when it sets. And then at high noon all of creation is quiet. It is something like a miniature eclipse. Everything becomes absolutely still and quiet. These times of the day, at least, are marked out in every tradition as special moments of mindfulness: sunrise, high noon, and sunset. They are unrepeatable, unique moments. The sun is not going to set twice; you cannot bring it back. The show won't be repeated because you were not ready for it.

In a Benedictine monastery, time and place are ordered in a way that helps us to be alert, mindful, and always present. Present to what? Present to that word which comes out of the silence. In order to bring this somewhat abstract-sounding statement into our own experience, we have to learn to listen. That is one of the great tasks in monastic life in general, and in particular, I would say, in the mindfulness discipline of Benedictine spirituality. We have to learn to listen. And that means, of course, not only to listen to scriptures or to what our abbot tells us, but to listen unconditionally, always, in every situation, with our hearts.

In the First Book of Kings the prophet Elijah went to the mountain of God and stood there, hoping that God's presence would be renewed and would become available to him. After some time a great storm arose, but God was not in the storm. Then a terrible earthquake shook the land, but God was not in the earthquake. Next a burning fire passed by Elijah, but God was not in the fire. And finally, there was a still, small voice of silence. And when Elijah heard this he hid his face, because he knew he was in the presence of God.

Obedience, as it is practiced in the Christian tradition, means learning to tune in and to listen to God's word; in fact *obaudire* means "to listen thoroughly." The Biblical expression is, "to listen with circumcised ears." On the first pages of Genesis, God says: "Let there be light." And there was light. He says, "Let there be a firmament." And there was a firmament. And so on, with all the elements of the world. Everything we come across is a word of God. And not only every *thing* but every person and every situation is another spelling-out the eternal word of God which speaks to us.

When we first make an effort to listen, we will probably become aware of a lot of background static which is preventing us from hearing. It is just like the noise we hear on a little transistor radio when we try to tune in to a distant station: a nearby radio station is making so much noise that all we hear is a lot of static. For us, the nearby station is the loud voice of our selfish desires, hopes, fears: our selfishness in other words. Because ego makes so much noise, we need a way to get rid of its static, and the way we do that is by handing over our self-will to someone else. We give over our self-will to someone in whom we trust, and we vow to do whatever that person tells us to do. This takes place within a special set of circumstances, and with particular rules to the game. It is somewhat like putting an arm that has been injured into a sling. The goal, of course, is not to have that arm in a sling for the rest of one's life: we want to eventually take the arm out and use it again. In the same way, monastic obedience is not the goal *in se*. Otherwise at the end of a life of obedience we would be marionettes, mindlessly following someone else's instructions. The real goal is to learn how to tune in to God's word, which tells us what we need to do in any given situation. The goal of obedience is to find meaning in life. When we find something totally meaningless, we say that it is absurd. This is interesting linguistically, because the Latin root *absurdus* means "out of tune." The meaning we seek is not of anything in particular, but meaning which is ultimate, meaning within which we can rest. The heart is restless until it finds that within which it can rest.[4] The heart, the innermost center of one's being, is like a needle on a compass. It is always restless until it is perfectly oriented toward magnetic north, which is the direction we call God. Our senses are involved in this quest for meaning. In the context of Christian spirituality, the word is made flesh because God speaks to us through our senses. For most of us, our senses are terribly neglected. For example, there are many people for whom there exist only two smells: good and bad. What an impoverished mentality that is! God didn't need to bother creating so many different smells if all we are capable of appreciating is good or bad. Actually, there are no bad smells at all: there are only good smells that happen to be in the wrong places!

Take a moment to imagine a fresh spring day. What smells come to mind? Perhaps you think of wet pavement, or grass, or the smell of a certain place you like to go. Write these down for yourself, and then make a similar list for each of the other seasons. Soon you will become aware of all the tremendous varieties and possibilities there are. And later, some time when you are a little depressed or bored, you can look through your list again, and read it as a litany of praise to what life has given you in the past. Appreciation of that richness is an important part of spirituality in Benedictine life, because we know, in our heart of hearts, that God speaks to us through everything. And in the Christian context, he has only one message, only one thing to say, which is, "I love you." It is an inexhaustible message, which therefore has to be spelled out forever and ever. Think of lovers. They have nothing else to say except, "I love you." Yet, they never tire of hearing it from each other. We never say, "Well, I told you that twenty-five years ago, dear. Do you really want to hear it again?" We never come to the end of our spiritual life, because we never finish experiencing all the many different ways in which God says, "I love you." Every time we taste or hear or feel something new, we discover a different way, which is untranslatable in any other experience or language. When we hear thunder, that is something unique. And when we hear rain, God is speaking in an entirely different language. If we have never experienced it, we just don't know it. There is no other way but to listen to the rain. Life is just too short to learn all these many languages. But it is never too late to begin opening ourselves and tuning in.

I would like to conclude with a little key word which ties together all these many elements of Benedictine life. It is a master key which simplifies things enormously. All that I have been discussing so far is contained within the word *gratefulness*. "Grate-fulness" has two parts. First of all, there is the *gratuitousness* of everything there is. It is the sense of wonderment that things exist at all. When we cultivate gratefulness, we cultivate wonderment. Everything is gratuitous. We haven't made it. We haven't earned it, even if we have worked hard. Everything is a gift. And the second aspect of gratefulness is the *fullness* of our response. It is a response from the heart, because only in our heart of hearts are we fully present, fully ourselves, and fully in touch with God, who is closer to us than we are to ourselves. We might think that gratitude is something passive: to be grateful, you just say "thanks." But that is not the idea here. Other languages express it more powerfully. In Latin, it is *gratias agere*, which means "to *give* thanks," "to *act* gratefully."

Within every situation, the gift of gifts is opportunity. We are grateful not for the situation itself, but for the fact that we have been given the opportunity to do something in response: to speak out, to act, or to suffer. To suffer is always the last thing we can do, and we always have the opportunity to do it willingly. If we suffer *with* the grain, rather than just being pulled along against the grain, then we experience the passion of suffering, which is also a response to the fullness of each moment.

In the very center of Catholic spirituality, we find the eucharist, the Lord's Supper. "Eucharist" means thanksgiving. The sacramental celebration of thanksgiving extends into every part of daily life. The eucharist is a ritual which symbolizes the experience of God's life within us. In Christian theology, and above all in monastic theology, God is Giver.

Therefore God can be called Father, Mother, Life-Giver, Giver of all Things. Everything that comes to us is a gift from the Ultimate Giver, whom the Bible calls God. The ultimate gift is the Son, our true, God-given self. God is manifest now, the unmanifest is made manifest. The word comes out of the silence, and the Son gives himself back to the Father in thanksgiving. But the spirit of thanksgiving is God's own Spirit, the Holy Spirit. Thus through thanksgiving we can enter the very life of God, who is the very life of our lives. Through gratefulness, we enter into that prayer of thanksgiving in which the Son continuously gives thanks to the Father in the Spirit. That is the essence of prayer. Prayer itself is God's life within us, God's great dance. When we allow that life to come to ever greater fullness, we become more and more alive, and we begin to live the life of prayer. It is no longer prayer *within* one's life, but a life that is *itself* prayer. That is ultimately the aim of Benedictine monasticism.

The Temptations of Antony

Thomas Keating O.C.S.O.

Christian monastic life was first propagated in Egypt, during the decline of the Age of Martyrdom, which finally ended with the Edict of Milan in 312. According to *The Life of Antony*, written by Saint Athanasius in the mid-fourth century, the total dedication expressed by the ideal of martyrdom could also be expressed through the monastic lifestyle, which Antony called a "martyrdom of conscience." This message inspired thousands of people, who withdrew to the Egyptian and Syrian deserts in imitation of Antony. In the course of the following two hundred years, monks developed a monastic wisdom out of their experience of the desert. What they learned and practiced was then distilled, through the genius of Benedict of Nursia, into a Rule of life which has survived to this day. Monastic centers gradually spread throughout Europe, becoming a powerful civilizing influence during the Dark Ages. By the eleventh century, they had developed an outstanding humanistic culture and were known for their architectural achievements, elaborate ritual, Gregorian chant, and the art of copying and illuminating manuscripts. But the mon-

RULE OF SAINT BENEDICT

The English translation of the Prologue begins:

*Listen carefully, my son, to the master's instructions, and attend to them with the ear of your heart. This is advice from a father who loves you; welcome it, and faithfully put it into practice. The labor of obedience will bring you back to him from whom you had drifted through the sloth of disobedience. This message of mine is for you, then, if you are ready to give up your own will, once and for all, and armed with the strong and noble weapons of obedience to do battle for the true King, Christ the Lord. . . . *[5]

This page is from a collection of monastic rules, *Regulae Monasticorum*, printed in Venice by Johannes Emericus de Spira on April 13, 1500, for Lucantonio Giunta. Courtesy of the Annmary Brown Memorial, Brown University, Providence, Rhode Island.

astic lifestyle itself had become off-balance. A group of monks, later known as Cistercians, decided that the original purity of Benedict's Rule had become diluted. In their view, everything had become too grandiose. They wanted to return to the contemplative practice of the early monks: to their simplicity of lifestyle, to their silence and solitude, and to their emphasis on manual labor.

According to the Benedictine Rule, the three main activities of monks are: *lectio divina,* that is, the reading, listening, and responding to the word of God expressed in scripture; celebrating the gift of divine life through the liturgy; and supporting the community through manual labor. These three occupations form a tripod upon which the monastic program rests. If one leg is missing, the lifestyle becomes lopsided and could even collapse. The reforming Cistercians aspired to return to the original inspiration of Benedict, and they succeeded for at least 150 years. In the seventeenth century, after a gradual period of decline, a reform of the Cistercians occurred in the French monastery of La Trappe. Present-day Cistercians, who are the inheritors of that reform, are often called "Trappists." In recent times, Thomas Merton is the best-known member of the order.

The contemplative training in the Cistercian tradition begins with the development of a personal (that is, fully responsible) self. That may sound like an astonishing statement to spiritual seekers who are trying hard to get rid of the darned thing! In any case, the goal of the first phase of Christian practice is not the destruction of one's ego identity; it is its healthy development. Self-consciousness is in fact the greatest accomplishment of human evolution to date. It is what distinguishes us from earlier, more primitive levels of consciousness. We could say that the human family is sitting at the midpoint of its evolution. We have evolved from the state of preconscious hominoids into full self-conscious human beings, with the destiny to move toward still higher levels of consciousness. We are literally crucified between heaven and earth. We can't go up, and we can't go down. We cannot return to the security of *un*self-consciousness that the beasts enjoy. They can have a great time wagging their tails and being what they are. We, on the other hand, have the potential to experience union with the Ultimate Mystery. But without the conscious experience of that union, we are confronted by the sense of alienation from God and the consequent feelings of guilt. Thus self-consciousness, which in actual fact is a magnificent step on the path of evolution, ironically places us in the most vulnerable position imaginable. Animals do not experience separation from God. But we *think* that we are separated from him, and so we are terrified to the roots of our being.

The personal love of Christ is crucial at this point. It addresses our deep, human existential insecurity, our sense of being alone and alienated in a potentially hostile universe, and it offers us the divine assurance of our basic goodness. To be loved is the only way we can become fully alive as human beings. The personal love of Christ for us gives us the motivation to respond and to grow as persons. The personal self is the gift which we must ultimately surrender to God. But first we must have that gift, before we can offer it.

Contrary to some popular notions, Christ did not go through his passion, death, and abandonment by the Father so that we would never have to do any work ourselves. To be a Christian means to do what Christ did as well as what he said. A classical example of someone who followed Christ is Saint Antony. Because Athanasius's *Life of Antony* has been the source of inspiration for literally all monastic life for the past 1500 years, I will use it here as a point of departure for describing the classical monastic teaching relating to the various phases of the spiritual journey: how to overcome the temptations of the world, the flesh, and the devil.

Antony's story begins on a farm in lower Egypt, where he was born and raised. He was a shy and retiring young man, sheltered from the harsher side of life. But, as happens to everyone in this world, he was eventually thrown out of the family nest. When he was about eighteen years old, his parents both died, leaving him with the care of his younger sister and the family property. Antony had been thinking about the ascetic life. One day he entered a church and heard the gospel proclaimed. When one has learned how to listen to the word of God, it speaks to the heart. So it was on that day. Antony heard Christ addressing him with the same words that sincere seekers have heard down through the ages: "If you would be perfect, go, sell what you possess and give to the poor, and you will have treasure in heaven" (Matt. 19:21). It was an invitation to renounce his property, his family, and his own will and to take refuge in Christ. When someone takes up that invitation, they have no idea where it may lead.

After Antony heard those words, he could not bear to keep the farm. He sold it, holding back only a small portion to take care of his sister's needs. But this God of ours is rather relentless. The next time Antony went into the church, he heard the words, "Do not be anxious about tomorrow" (Matt. 6:34). Once more he felt the two-edged sword of the word of God go straight to his heart. He went out, sold everything, and placed his sister with some holy nuns who were living as a community and serving the poor. Then he set off to pursue the ascetical life.

What followed was the springtime of Antony's spiritual life. He visited the holy men in his area and imitated the virtues of each:

> He observed the graciousness of one, the earnestness at prayer in another; studied the even temper of one and the kindheartedness of another; fixed his attention on the vigils kept by one and on the studies pursued by another; admired one for his patient endurance, another for his fasting and sleeping on the ground; watched closely this man's meekness and the forbearance shown by another; and in one and all alike he marked especially devotion to Christ and the love they had for one another.[6]

Antony exercised his ascetical practices with such discretion and sweetness that no one was jealous of him. He refrained from those competitive spiritual adventures which are the hazard of enthusiastic beginners. The text, with a certain sardonic humor, then states:

> But the Devil, the hater and envier of good, could not bear to see such resolution in a young man, but set about employing his customary tactics also against him.

And so, just as God had a plan for Antony, the adversary also had a plan. Who was this adversary? Admittedly, most of our troubles come from ourselves. But when a certain temptation goes on for weeks and months, and there appears to be no escape, it seems likely that there is a demon sticking his finger into the pie.

At any rate, when the consolations of the initial stage of the spiritual journey have slowly or abruptly begun to fade, the old weaknesses begin to resurface. Little by little, as the defense mechanisms that prevent us from thinking about the darker side of our personality are reduced, whatever has been lurking in the unconscious begins to emerge. Meanwhile, the demon is sizing us up to see what kinds of bait will lure us away from our resolution. He knows that if we persevere in our practice, we will inevitably reach our goal. And so he tries, by enticing us with particular thoughts, to prevent us from doing so.

The demon first tried to convince Antony to desert the ascetic life by putting memories of the old farm into his mind. We can imagine Antony sitting in his hut on an especially hot day, recalling the lovely cool breezes coming off the Nile. The thought came to him: "Antony, if you stay here, you are never going to see that beautiful property again."

The demon next summoned the memory of his relatives: "If you stay in this place, you may never see your loved ones. Even if you do, there will be long intervals when you won't see them." With this, Antony began to feel a little homesick and lonesome.

The demon then evoked the lure of money: "If only you had stayed home, you would be a junior executive by now; you would have your own Mercedes." Instead, all Antony had was a wretched bicycle to peddle around with.

The demon next suggested the delights of eating and drinking. Antony had never hung out in ice cream parlors, let alone bars. But all of a sudden, he started thinking of those tasty crocodile burgers down by the Nile. He thought: "If only I could have one now!"

It was not so much particular thoughts gliding by, one by one, that seemed so attractive. The demon dwelt upon the circumstances of Antony's life, stirring up feelings of nostalgia. He played soft background music to remind Antony of the good times of the past. The composite set of images was so concrete that it reached out in a tantalizing way for his assent. The whole purpose of these poignant memories and attractions to his former lifestyle was to dislodge Antony's resolution.

Antony was a determined young man, and none of this masterful manipulation of images and emotions made any great impression on him. As fast as the memories came up, he let them go. When the demon saw that he couldn't catch Antony with worldly or selfish bait, he tried something more refined and noble. The insidious thought came: "What have you done? Your little sister, whom you put with those gloomy, horse-faced nuns, is utterly miserable. They are too severe. You must leave immediately and rescue her!"

This kind of temptation can take a myriad of forms. After being in solitude for a few weeks, the novice may suddenly get the bright light: "I am needed in the world. I must go out and convert my old friends. Now at last I know just what to say to them. . . . "

Another train of thought might be: "My mother is eating her heart out. I'm her only child. She will commit suicide if I don't hurry home."

I had a most loving grandma, who in her old age lived with a nurse in an apartment in New York. One day I received a letter from her which said, "I tell my nurse that if my grandson won't come home, would you please throw me out the window." Now, how would you like to read that on one of your darkest days? At those times, you'd just as soon give up the whole trip!

Or again: "My old flame is heartbroken. How can I delay returning to her?" Actually, she has met a wonderful guy, is about to get married, and hasn't given you a second thought. But you don't even consider such a possibility when the mind is flooded with images of her tear-struck, pleading face. In all these instances, the question arises: "How can I justify causing so much suffering to the people who love me?" One's motivation is profoundly challenged. This is the point where superficial attractions to the path are sifted out and where secondary motives, such as an attraction for sacred music, the religious habit, certain people, and the thought of a lifelong home in the country, all fall away. Temptations confront one's conscience with the realistic consequences of one's choice.

In the case of Antony, when positive attractions to return to his former lifestyle failed to dislodge him from his set purpose, the demon suggested negative feelings about the ascetic life. He said to Antony: "You'll never be able to survive your practice. It's too hard. It may be all right for a week, but how do you expect to keep this up for months, a year, thirty years—or maybe even sixty or seventy?" In earlier times, monks, like the population in general, did not live to a great age. It was said that at the monastery of La Trappe, newcomers could count on being dead within five to eight years. One can commit oneself to almost anything for a few years, if one is then sure to pass to one's eternal reward. The factor of longevity in our day makes most contemporary candidates think twice about becoming Trappists. No doubt the demons are on hand to remind them that if they make final vows, they are not going anywhere for the rest of their lives. To live in the same place with the same people for the whole of one's life is a staggering proposition! It is equivalent to handing God a blank check with your signature at the bottom of it.

Antony overcame all these temptations of worldliness with three basic tools. The first was resolution. This is the determination to remain on the path no matter what may happen, no matter how long the journey may take, and no matter what the obstacles may be. The second was continuous prayer during times of temptation. And the third was trust in Christ. By exercising those three instruments, Antony was also able to triumph over the temptations of the flesh and the devil.

The next trial is called by Athanasius the "temptation of the flesh." This temptation took the form of an upsurge of sexual energy. Antony had previously led a life of complete innocence in this regard. The demon determined to soften up his resistances. As in modern warfare, where paratroopers are dropped behind enemy lines to soften up the opposition, the demon suggested thoughts about the delights of sexual activity. He reminded Antony of how much he had missed while growing up and of how useful it would be to have some experience in this area. Antony resisted these thoughts with his prayers. Next the demon stirred up sexual feelings. These became so intense that even Antony's friends perceived the struggle going on between them. Then one night, in order to deceive him, the demon came disguised as a seductive woman, and Antony felt the desires of his sexual energy as "burning oil." If you have ever tried to put out a fire of burning oil, you can imagine the distress of this young man, who was trying to devote all his natural energies to the spiritual path. What was Antony's response? He thought of the nobility of the soul and of Christ taking upon himself all the struggles and temptations of the human condition.

The demon presented a final temptation: "Antony, you are tired. You have done your best. Why don't you just give in?" Antony responded by thinking of the fires of hell. Notice the wisdom of this strategy. It was not a matter of stirring up the emotion of fear, which would have been counterproductive, but of introducing the image of a different kind of fire. The thought of the pain of physical fire helped Antony to neutralize the fire of sexual desire that was burning out of control. Once again, with his usual determination, continuous prayer, and trust in Christ, Antony came through unscathed.

Immediately the demon changed his tactics and began fawning upon him: "Antony, you are not like other people. Whenever I tempted them as I have tempted you, they gave in easily, or after a little while. But you resisted to the end!" This is the insidious temptation to spiritual pride, the temptation to attribute to one's own efforts that which is God's free gift. Antony firmly rejected the demon's false praise. Only then does Athanasius state, "This was Antony's first victory over the Devil." All the virtues in the world are useless if one takes credit for what one has succeeded in doing only with God's help. Antony, quoting the scriptures, said, "Not I, but the grace of God that is in me" (Gal. 2:20).

After a period of peace and calm, Antony determined to set off for the tombs. In the cultural condition of that time, the tombs were generally regarded as the chief hangout of the demons. This is clear evidence that Antony was taking the initiative in the spiritual combat. He engaged a friend to accompany him to the tombs and to lock him in, thus closing off every avenue of escape. This incursion into their territory infuriated the demons, and that night they beat him into unconsciousness. By chance, his friend came by the next day with bread for him and, finding him half-dead, brought him to the local church and laid him on the floor. His relatives and friends gathered around, praying for his life. After midnight, they started dozing. Antony regained consciousness and asked his friend to take him back to the tombs. The friend carried him to the tombs once again and locked Antony inside, where he lay on the ground, too weak to stand. The demons were astonished at the courage of this man and didn't know what to do with him. The head demon said, "He is going to drive us out of the desert unless we do something. . . . So come, let's all gang up on him!" Athanasius writes:

> It was as though demons were breaking through the four walls of the little chamber and bursting through them in the form of beasts and reptiles. All at once the place was filled with the phantoms of lions, bears, leopards, bulls, and of serpents, asps, and scorpions, and of wolves; and each moved according to the shape it had assumed. The lion roared, ready to spring upon him, the bull appeared about to gore him through, the serpent writhed without quite reaching him, the wolf was rushing straight at him; and the noises emitted simultaneously by all the apparitions were frightful and the fury shown was fierce.

Antony taunted the demons, saying, "If you had any power over me, it would have been enough for just one of you to come. . . . " After many ruses the demons gnashed their teeth, because they knew they were only fooling themselves. The Lord was not forgetful of Antony's struggle.

Antony looked up and saw a "beam of light coming down to him." Suddenly the demons vanished from view, and his pains ceased. He then asked the vision that poignant human question, "Where were you? Why did you not appear in the beginning, to stop my pains?"

The Lord answered, "Antony, I was right here, but I waited to see you in action. And now, because you held out and did not surrender, I will ever be your helper, and I will make you renowned everywhere."

One might object that such encouragement was long overdue. Why must one wait until the trial is over before peace and calm return? Many saints have asked a similar question. Perhaps it is necessary to experience one's existential helplessness before one can trust in Christ without any limit. This is the confidence that leads to divine union, the transforming experience of liberation from the false self, and the establishment of the new self in God.

Bridal Mysticism

Tessa Bielecki

While I was editing *Mystical Passion*, a book written by my spiritual father, William McNamara, I came across this mysterious sentence: "When the support of a creature breaks under us, the only abyss we can fall into is the arms of God." I didn't understand that line, and I hated the awkward wording of it, so I wanted to edit it out. But Father William was visibly disappointed. He said, "Oh no, you can't do that! Just meditate on it and hopefully one day you will understand." So I did. It became a *koan* for me for months and months. And finally I reached a point when I fell far enough into the abyss that I understood the meaning of Father William's words. It is out of that abyss and those arms that I am now sharing with you my experience and understanding of bridal mysticism.

Bridal mysticism is one way to experience God, in the Christian tradition as a whole and in Carmelite mysticism particularly. Because this topic can be so easily misunderstood or even abused, I will begin by giving you a context, in the form of a brief overview of the Carmelite tradition. Though I won't often be referring to Christ himself, he is, of course, the

CHRIST ICON

Courtesy of the Ikonen-Museum, Recklinghausen, Germany

bridegroom in bridal mysticism. I hope that you will recognize him to be the beginning and the end of this presentation, just as he is the beginning and the end of my entire life.

The Carmelite story begins with a mountain: Mount Carmel, which is located in Palestine, near the modern city of Haifa. I continually delight in the fact that our tradition does not take its name from a person, as do so many other Christian traditions, but from a great chunk of rock. Mount Carmel is rich in history, venerable with age, and the confidante of thousands of stories. It was the scene of numerous Biblical incidents and the home of the prophet Elijah. It was on this mountain that the first Carmelite hermits went to live.

But Mount Carmel is not only geographical and historical; it is also metaphysical and trans-historical. In the *Ascent of Mount Carmel,* for example, John of the Cross outlines the purgative way in terms of climbing this mountain. He describes our path as taking us straight up the face of the mountain; we do not choose the circuitous side paths, which would be easier to travel but would take longer. Carmelites are mountain climbers who go by way of the straight path. Thus Mount Carmel is the homeland of the heart for every Carmelite. For years I said that it personally didn't matter whether I ever literally saw it or not. But as time has passed, I have come to realize that it does matter to me very much. I hope that one day I actually set foot on that sacred ground.

Mount Carmel is located in the midst of the desert, and Carmelites are not only mountain climbers; we are also desert rats. The spirituality of the Carmelite tradition is to be equally found in the silence, solitude, and simplicity of the desert. As the prophet Hosea said, "I will espouse you, lead you into the desert, and there I will speak to your heart." Our journey is an arduous trek through purgation into paradise. We have to be like the ancient Jewish people. The Book of Exodus is a great allegory for the path of our own spiritual lives: we have to pass from the desert into the promised land. The desert experience begins with the free and deliberate decision to suffer and ends with the uproariously happy surprise of being in harmony with the universe, in the glory of God's presence, and in love with all that is. Of course, going into the physical desert helps our journey tremendously, and in fact our community in southern Colorado is deliberately situated in the geographical desert. But not everyone can journey to the physical desert, so we need other alternatives. To enter into silence, for example, is to enter into the desert.

Just as Eido Roshi once described a Zen monk as one who moves his cushion to the edge of a precipice, I would say that a Carmelite monk is one who moves his cushion to the desert. Part of the pervading atmosphere of that desert is death. In our monastic vows of poverty, celibacy, and obedience, we anticipate death. The vow of poverty, like death, strips us of all our material possessions; celibacy anticipates the fact that "in heaven" we will not marry; and obedience, like death, substitutes God's will for our own self-will. Before Vatican II, every Carmelite monastery had a human skull sitting on the central dining table. Most people find such a presence uncomfortable, if not morbid, and most of my community thinks it would be extremely odd. At first I also felt this way, but now I think I would love to continue this tradition. Instead, we have a number of animal skulls displayed in our hermitage. When you walk through the desert, you can't help but find dried bones—beautiful bones whitened and bleached by the sun. I have been collecting them for years and have hung them along one wall in the diningroom. So we do have this reminder of the centrality of death, which is also a reminder of life. The spirit of the desert is this confrontation with death, from which we draw radical consequences for life fully lived.

Just as physicality of place is crucial in our tradition, so are the people who make up our long and colorful history. The first figure to enter the scene is the prophet Elijah, who appears abruptly in Jewish history, sometime during the ninth century. The Bible gives us absolutely no introductory information about him: All of a sudden, there is Elijah standing before Ahab. And Elijah says, in the opening of the seventeenth chapter of the Book of Kings, "The Lord God lives, before whom I stand." According to Father William, these words comprise the shortest and most effective autobiography ever written. They remain a charter for all contemplatives ever since, and particularly for Carmelites, who regard Elijah as their spiritual father. Elijah's statement points dramatically to the reality of God himself. The primary fact of Elijah's existence and personal identity is that the Lord God lives. Elijah shows us that the contemplative must be God-conscious and not self-conscious. We see him not so much as a person, but as an august event: he is the ravages of a tornado, the eye of a storm, the place where lightning strikes. Elijah's symbol is fire. Again and again, in the Book of Kings, Elijah calls down fire onto the top of Mount Carmel.

The person we call Our Lady of Mount Carmel also plays a crucial role for us because she provides the necessary feminine balance. Mary appeared to Elijah as a vision which came to him as he sat on top of Mount Carmel, looking out over the Mediterranean Sea. He saw a cloud rising over the sea, "no bigger than a man's hand." Carmelites later interpreted this experience as a vision of Mary, the Mother of God. The cloud is an apt symbol for the feminine, because only through the cloud, which is Mary, can we bear to look upon the majesty and radiance of Christ. At his ascension, Christ departs in clouds, and he is to come again riding on the clouds of heaven.

The first evidence that hermits were living on Mount Carmel dates back to 1155 A.D. Very little is known about these hermits. We don't know whether they were literate or illiterate, whether they were knights or soldiers, clergy or lay people. The important point, very simply, is that they lived on Mount Carmel in the tradition of Elijah and dedicated to Our Lady. The sole purpose of their lives was prayer and contemplation, and their Rule, in a nutshell, was this: We are called to meditate day and night on the law of the Lord, unless engaged in some other just occupation. "Law" in this case does not merely mean the Ten Commandments, but also the law that is written in the universe: the law in our hearts, the natural law, the cosmic law.

At that time there was a resurgence of eremitical life throughout Europe, partly because the monastic life had become overly complicated, involving the administration of enormous abbeys and estates. Therefore the eremitical life also became a recognized and valid part of society: there were layfolk, knights, soldiers, monks, canons . . . and hermits. People understood and appreciated who they were and why they lived as they did. This is indeed a far cry from the way it is today! Now it is hard enough to be a monk and be considered a valid part of society; it is even harder if you are a hermit. The hermits continued to live on Mount Carmel for a little over a hundred years, until they were forced into Europe through persecution by Saracens and other Middle Eastern peoples. Because of the religious climate in Europe at that time, they found it necessary to conform to the prevailing monastic lifestyle, which was socially active. By doing so, the Carmelites sacrificed their special identity as hermits and lost their emphasis on contemplation. My own community, the Spiritual Life Institute, is an attempt to recapture what has been lost over the centuries and to return to that primitive Carmelite ideal. We strive to live the way these original twelfth-century hermits lived, as a *new expression* of an ancient tradition.

Another significant event in the evolution of the Carmelite tradition was the appearance of Teresa of Avila and John of the Cross in sixteenth-century Spain. Just as Elijah is the spiritual Father of Carmel, and Mary is the spiritual Mother, we refer to Saint Teresa as our Holy Mother and John of the Cross as our Holy Father. Teresa, with the help of John, brought the Carmelites back to an emphasis on contemplation and founded the Discalced ("barefoot") Order. To give you some feeling for buoyant Teresa's personality, one of her greatest prayers was, "God, deliver me from sour-faced saints!" One story describes Teresa riding in a little cart along the back roads of Spain during a torrential downpour. The cart broke down in the mud, and everything was a terrible mess. Christ spoke to her, saying, "Teresa, this is the way I treat my friends." Teresa, who was on very intimate terms with Christ, responded, "No wonder you have so few!" John of the Cross, on the other hand, is best known for his more ascetic and sober personality, and of course for the spiritual direction of the *Ascent of Mount Carmel* and *Dark Night of the Soul.*

Teresa and John did not go to live on Mount Carmel, and they did not move into the wilderness. They did not go into the physical desert. Instead they tried to actualize the eremitical life in the midst of urban Europe. Personally, I have always been spooked by the grille and veils that characterize the Carmelite monasteries of women founded by Saint Teresa, and I have always questioned the value of strict "cloister." But I think it is important to remember that these features, many of which have been modified since Vatican II, were part of Teresa's plan to lead her nuns and friars to the heights of Carmelite contemplation. She wanted to return to the silence, solitude, and simplicity of the ancient Carmelite ideal.

The first stage of the Carmelite journey is the Purgative Way, which is also known as "the dark night of the soul." This dark night is divided into two parts: the dark night of the senses and the dark night of the spirit. These are then further divided into the active and passive night of the senses and the active and passive night of the spirit. When we set out on our path, we are full of self: self-righteousness, self-consciousness, self-importance. We also have a lot of good feelings about what we are doing, which in our community we call "sensible consolation." But when we enter the stage of purgation it all goes: no more good feelings, no more consolation, no more clear ideas about God. We are purged of all our self-centeredness and weaned away from the baby food of the spiritual life. Many people I know who have left the priesthood and the religious life have done so because they were perilously caught in the dark night, but didn't know it. They were unable to see their experience as a sign and necessary stage of progress in their spiritual lives. John of the Cross said during this stage you find relief in absolutely nothing. There is no consolation of any kind. You can't even raise your mind and heart to God. There is a very real sense not only that God is "displeased," but that he is utterly "cruel." It is impossible to exaggerate how intense this psychological suffering can be. The entryway into the dark night, and the beginning of this horrible purgation in our prayer life, is characterized by the passover from meditation to contemplation.[7]

If someone were to ask me, as Brother David and Eido Roshi were recently asked, to identify the meeting ground of East and West, I would suggest that one place it may be found is in the dark night: the void, the abyss, the emptiness, the nothingness. *Nada* is the Spanish word for "nothing" and *nada* is the heart of John of the Cross' whole teaching. That is why our hermitage in Colorado is called "Nada" and the one in Nova Scotia is called "Nova Nada"—"new nothing" or "nothing new."

During the second stage, the Way of the Proficient, or the Illuminative Way, we gain a real foothold on the path. We become less self-centered and more God-centered. We enjoy a certain fellowship with God, although he still seems to be a separate entity. The final goal of all Christian mysticism is union with God, which can be described through any number of relationships: we might relate to God as child to father, friend to friend, or disciple to master. In the Carmelite tradition, the most common type of relationship is between spouse and spouse, bride and bridegroom. The feminine dimension of the Godhead, which in the Christian tradition is called Wisdom, unites with God through Jesus, in all his human masculinity. Although bridal mysticism is known to all mystical Christian traditions, the Carmelites, and specifically John and Teresa, have been the most vocal and articulate in describing it. In the Illuminative Way we begin to experience spousal union, but it is not until the third stage that we actually enter into spiritual marriage.

In the Way of the Perfect, or the Unitive Way, God is no longer separate; the self has been transformed into God. This union is so great, so close, and so intimate that the soul, or as we could say the "bodyperson," seems to be God, and God seems to be the soul. Now, the experience of God on any level is difficult to describe, and at the higher levels description becomes almost impossible. Anyone who experiences this kind of union with God is generally reluctant to talk about it and would prefer to remain silent. But, thank goodness, John and Teresa have spoken about it for the sake of others. For example, in a beautiful series of poems called "Romances," John of the Cross describes Christmas as a wedding, a wedding of God and man, divine and human, matter and spirit:

> When the time had come
> For Him to be born
> He went forth like the bridegroom
> From his bridal chamber,
>
> Embracing His bride,
> Holding her in His arms,
> Whom the gracious Mother
> Laid in a manger.[8]

Carmelite descriptions of spiritual marriage are astonishingly reminiscent of the human marriage between man and woman. In fact, the love between man and woman is the most intense of any human experience, and this is the metaphor the mystics have chosen to describe their very intimate union with God. Thus the soul is the bride, God himself is the bridegroom, and to go to prayer is to enter the bridal chamber, the marriage bed. John of the Cross writes elaborately about the intimacy of this spiritual embrace: "Joyfully and festively, she practices the arts and games of love as though in the palace of her nuptials." In my experience, breathing itself is part of the life of prayer—though perhaps this is even more the case in Eastern religions. But what I am most accustomed to in my tradition is not my own breath, but the breath of God. And if you've ever slept with someone you love, such as your mother, lover, child, friend, or even your cat or dog (these last two being the only options I have!), you know the ecstasy of listening to the beloved breathe. In his *Living Flame of Love*, John says, "In your sweet breathing filled with good and glory, how tenderly you swell my heart with love."

Despite the ecstasy of his experience, in characteristic fashion John writes with restraint about the bosom of the beloved and the kiss in which the soul actually kisses God. Saint Teresa, on the other hand, in her *Conceptions of the Love of God*, shows absolutely no restraint. Quoting the Song of Solomon, she becomes wild in her descriptions of mystical marriage: " . . . let him kiss me with the kisses of his mouth . . . his fruit is sweet to my taste . . . his breasts are better than wine. . . . " She describes how prayer brings us to the brink of intoxication, and she tells us not to be afraid to drink:

> (God's) will is that she (the bride) shall drink, and become inebriated with all the wines that are the storehouse of God. Let her rejoice in those joys; let her marvel at His wonders; let her not fear to lose her life through drinking beyond the capacity of her weak nature; let her die in this paradise of delights.[9]

Both Teresa and John talk about "holy inebriation," or "divine intoxication." Teresa describes how the soul, in a state of heavenly inebriation, becomes stupefied and dazed with a holy madness, so that it is completely drenched in countless grandeurs of God. This blessing, she says, is the greatest that can be tasted in life, even if all the delights and pleasures of the world were joined together.

There is no trial in the Purgative Way that does not have a corresponding reward in the Unitive Way. And the reward is so tremendous that one actually forgets how bad the purgation was. According to John of the Cross, no one has endured any tribulation or penance or trial to which there does not correspond a hundredfold of consolation and delight in this life—in *this* life! It is not in the next life, when we "get to heaven," as Christians have been taught for so many generations. We can experience such great delight during this life, not only as verbally promised but also as embodied in the people who have lived in this tradition. This is possible for those who are faithful—and I can't stress this enough—for those who are *faithful*.

From these descriptions we can see that prayer to God is as intimate as making love to a human spouse. That is why such an experience, if it needs to be shared at all, must be done so with utter discretion and supreme reverence. Otherwise we end up with what could be called "spiritual voyeurism" or "Peeping-Tom mysticism." Furthermore, it is impossible for me to describe or to teach a particular technique which will bring someone to this kind of prayer, because the experience of spousal union is utterly gratuitous. It is a pure gift from God and not the result of any one form of meditation and prayer. Therefore you can come to this experience through whatever form of meditation you use, no matter how you pray. Now you can see, I think, why for me and for other people who have some experience of this kind of prayer, it is not a discipline but a delight. We go to prayer because God is there waiting for us and beckoning to us irresistibly.

On our journey we climb the mountain of Carmel. We rest on top of the mountain in the arms of the beloved; but we don't remain there. This is extremely important. Union with Christ is not always expressed as bedchamber ecstasy, no more so than it is in human marriage. It would be an error to think that we could always remain in this state of delight. To become the spouse of Christ means to become the spouse of the suffering servant. What choice have we but to suffer with our spouse and to serve him? This is most graphically expressed in the life of Teresa who, as a sign of her spousal union with God, was given not a ring, but a nail from the cross. In her *Interior Castle*, this is her final lesson to us:

> Do you know when people really become spiritual? It is when they become the slaves of God and are branded with His sign, which is the sign of the Cross, in token that they have given Him their freedom. Then He can sell them as slaves to the whole world, as He Himself was sold.[10]

In conclusion, she says that if we aren't determined about becoming his slave, we aren't making very much spiritual progress. The final expression of spousal union with God is not bed-chamber ecstasy, but the ecstasy of service. We come down from the mountain to share our life and our love with those in the marketplace.

Poem

The following stanzas are by Saint John of the Cross, a mystical theologian and poet who lived in sixteenth-century Spain. According to Saint John's own Pro-

logue, The Spiritual Canticle *was "composed in a love flowing from abundant mystical understanding" and therefore cannot be adequately explained in rational terms. Nevertheless, his line-by-line commentary reveals that the* Canticle *contains a doctrinally precise and systematic description of the stages of the contemplative path.*

In these excerpted stanzas, the bride (soul) first experiences the absence of the Beloved (Christ) and, stirred by longing, sets out in search of him. This is the beginning of the Purgative Way, the "dark night." After practicing austerities, the soul experiences "spiritual espousal," where God reveals his grandeur through "the mountains, and lonely wooded valleys. . . . " This is the beginning of the Illuminative Way. After further preparation, the bride enters the "sweet garden of her desire," which is the Unitive Way of spiritual marriage. The remaining stanzas describe this union and offer praises.

The Spiritual Canticle

Where have You hidden,
Beloved, and left me moaning?
You fled like the stag
After wounding me;
I went out calling You, and You were gone.

Shepherds, you that go
Up through the sheepfolds to the hill,
If by chance you see
Him I love most,
Tell Him that I sicken, suffer, and die.

. . . .

Ah, who has the power to heal me?
Now wholly surrender Yourself!
Do not send me
Any more messengers,
They cannot tell me what I must hear.

All who are free
Tell me a thousand graceful things of You;
All wound me more
And leave me dying
Of, ah, I-don't-know-what behind their stammering.

· ·

My Beloved is the mountains,
And lonely wooded valleys,
Strange islands,
And resounding rivers,
The whistling of love-stirring breezes,

The tranquil night
At the time of the rising dawn,
Silent music,
Sounding solitude,
The supper that refreshes, and deepens love.

· ·

The bride has entered
The sweet garden of her desire,
And she rests in delight,
Laying her neck
On the gentle arms of the Beloved.

· ·

In the inner wine cellar
I drank of my Beloved, and, when I went abroad
Through all this valley
I no longer knew anything,
And lost the herd which I was following.

There He gave me His breast;
There He taught me a sweet and living knowledge;
And I gave myself to Him,
Keeping nothing back;
There I promised to be His bride.

Now I occupy my soul
And all my energy in His service;
I no longer tend the herd,
Nor have I any other work
Now that my every act is love.

. . . .

Let us rejoice, Beloved,
And let us go forth to behold ourselves in Your beauty,
To the mountain and to the hill,
To where the pure water flows,
And further, deep into the thicket.

And then we will go on
To the high caverns in the rock
Which are so well concealed;
There we shall enter
And taste the fresh juice of the pomegranates.

Where You will show me
What my soul has been seeking,
And then You will give me,
You, my Life, will give me there
What You gave me on that other day:

The breathing of the air,
The song of the sweet nightingale,
The grove and its living beauty
In the serene night,
With a flame that is consuming and painless.[11]

JOHN OF THE CROSS

Life's Newness

Thomas Hopko

The philosopher Friedrich Nietzsche once accused Christians of always referring to other people's sweat and blood. Well, I confess to you that this is what I do. I speak from other people's blood. My intention here is to present the voice of the tradition, and not my own.

Eastern Orthodoxy comes, of course, from the Bible; it comes from the experience of Abraham, Isaac, Jacob, and Moses; it comes from the Law, the prophets of Israel, the event of Jesus, and the apostolic church. As a tradition, it began in the eastern half of the Roman Empire, which at that time included parts of the Orient, the Middle East, the Greek lands, and the Slav countries. Orthodox Christianity evolved in isolation from the Christian West, developing its own cultural, spiritual, liturgical, and theological forms. In fact, the separation between Western and Eastern Christianity was well-defined long before the formal schism between the churches in the eleventh century.

Orthodoxy is a tradition which did not know Saint Augustine and which knew neither the Dark Ages nor the scholastic period. It was not the church out of which the Reformation came. On the other hand, many of the saints of the Orthodox Church are common to the Christian heritage of both East and West. Particularly, the Egyptian and Syrian Fathers who influenced the monastic tradition of the West were also the founding Fathers of the spiritual tradition within Eastern Christianity. We trace our heritage in an unbroken tradition from those Desert Fathers down through the Fathers of the Byzantine, Slav, and modern Russian Church.

At the same time, it must be said that the Orthodox way is ultimately not a teaching, it is not a technique, it is not the twenty-seven liturgical books or the one hundred fifty volumes of the church Fathers and Mothers. It is the living God within us. In the Gospel of John, Thomas said, "Lord . . . how can we know the way?" Jesus responded with those words which all Christians quote: "I am the way, and the truth, and the life" (John 14:5-6). That which is incarnate in the human life of Jesus of Nazareth is the heart of the Christian faith. "And the Word became flesh and dwelt among us, full of grace and truth. . . . And from his fullness have we all received grace upon grace" (John 1:14-16). Therefore, the life and the light are what Christ is. He *is* the presence of the kingdom.

If we choose to follow this way, where will it lead? The traditional answer is, "to the kingdom of God." But I think it is important to realize, and this is according to Jesus himself, that the way is actually the way to life: "I came that they may have life, and have it abundantly" (John 10:10). "Life" is really just another way of saying "reality," but we are not talking about reality in the intellectual or transcendental sense. We are talking about being fully alive, within a human body. And that is why Jesus Christ is not only the truth and the life, but he is also the resurrection. The word became flesh so that Christ could destroy death, raise the dead, and give new life—not merely at the end of the ages, but here and now. The Orthodox way is a means to rise and conquer the dominion of death. For example, baptism means to die with Christ and then to rise with him in the newness of life. Then we are sealed with the chrism of the kingdom, the gift of God's Holy Spirit. Similarly, the eucharist is not just a memorial of the Last Supper. It is a sacrament of eating and drinking with God, here and now, in the presence of his kingdom. The way is to actualize, in one's own life, what Jesus Christ actualized in his life. He has given us the power and grace, or you could say the possibility, to do so. The result of the way is, in the words of Maximus the Confessor, "to be by grace everything that Christ is by nature." The Fathers also speak about dying before death, and rising before the resurrection, so that we may live the resurrected life now. The following selection from an essay by Vasileios Gondikakis, a contemporary Father and currently abbot of the monastery of Stavronikita on Mount Athos, is an eloquent affirmation of this:

> The Lord did not come into the world merely to make an improvement in our present conditions of life. Neither did He come to put forward an economic or political system, or to teach a method of arriving at psychosomatic equilibrium. He came to conquer death and to bring us eternal life. . . . The Orthodox monk is not simply a "mystic." He is not someone who by employing certain forms of abstinence or certain techniques has arrived at a high degree of self-control or at various ascetic exploits. All these things are only achievements belonging to this present world, unimportant in themselves, incapable of over-

coming death. . . . The true Orthodox is a man raised up, sharing in the Resurrection. His mission is not to effect something by his thoughts, or to organize something by his own capacities, but by his life to give witness to the conquest of death. And this he does only by burying himself like a grain of wheat in the earth.[12]

The word of God is a powerful tool of destruction. Being destroyed is, in a certain sense, what this way is all about. It is about learning how to die. When he listens to the scriptures, the Orthodox lets the word of God work through him, so that it is able to break him apart. The word of God is killing, it is wounding, it is the rock on which all has to be broken. Irenaeus of Lyons, an early Greek Father, said that God has two hands: his Word and his Spirit. To be handled by God is to be taken and smashed, so that the vessel can be recreated.

The Christian has the sacred task of celebrating, in the midst of the church, the salvation of all created things. Thus he reveals the spiritual mission of what is material. At the same time he reveals the tangible existence of what is uncreated and holy. He is one who is totally dedicated to this mystery. In a particular way he is concerned with everyone and everything. He is concerned with the way each thing is situated and ordered, and with how it finds its true place and true beauty within the transfigured universe, within the Divine Liturgy of the salvation of all things. And yet in another way, he is concerned with nothing. The Christian is united with all and yet separated from all. Father Vasileios continues:

It is not my job to build houses or to whitewash them. Nor is it my job to read and write. What is my calling? It is, if possible, to die in God. Then I shall live and be moved by another Power. Then I can do all things freely—dig, organize, read, write— without being attached to anything. . . . When you build in order to build, you are enlarging your tomb. When you write in order to write, you are weaving your shroud. But when you live and breathe seeking always the mercy of God, then an incorruptible garment is woven around you, and you find the sweetness of a heavenly reassurance welling up within you.[13]

When the apostle Peter went out on the day of the Pentecost, he told the people in the streets of Jerusalem that Jesus who had been crucified was risen from the dead and glorified as Lord and Christ. According to the New Testament, the people were "cut to the heart," and a voice came out from the crowd, saying, "What shall we do?" (Acts 3:37). That could be our question. Perhaps we have experienced a moment of coming alive. We come to this tradition, this path, and we ask, "What shall I do?" Peter's answer was, "Repent and be baptized." Nowadays many people think repentance involves quitting smoking and being baptized means going to the nearest church to be doused in water. But repentance, or metanoia, literally means "to change one's mind." It means that you have to be ready to see everything differently. You have to change your entire way, without any agenda or prejudice about what you think ought to happen: "Repent for the kingdom of heaven is at hand." And then the second thing is to be baptized. Baptism is death. "Baptism" in Greek means "to be immersed" and "to die." The baptismal water, according to Saint Cyril of Jerusalem, is the tomb and the womb, the grave and the mother. Jesus Christ himself was baptized in the Jordan River, identifying himself with all of us who are dead and taking on all of the iniquities and corruption of this fallen world.

According to the Fathers, everything depends on what happens when a person first hears that there is a way. The right kind of motivation or faith has to be there. There has to be a willingness to plunge in. In fact, you could sum up the entire tradition by saying that the way depends wholly on the will. As Jesus Christ said, "Where your treasure is, there will your heart be also" (Luke 13:34). What do you really love? You must really want to see reality as it is and therefore be willing to plunge in and do what the tradition demands. Once Abba Lot said to Abba Joseph, "Father, I fast a little. I pray and meditate; I live in peace as far as I can; I purify my thoughts. What else can I do?"

And Joseph stood up and stretched his hands toward heaven. His fingers became like ten flames, and he said, "If you want, you can become all fire."[14] *If you want. . . .*

The true seeker, the one who hungers and thirsts for God, for truth, is already blessed. Beyond that, however, this tradition teaches that a spiritual father or mother is necessary. The question often comes up, "Suppose I haven't found one?" In recent times, especially, the Fathers themselves say that there aren't many around. But they also say that that is no reason to feel that all is lost. Because ultimately God is our interior master. If the heart is pure enough, we will be a *theodidaktos*, one who is taught by God. According to John Climacus, if you really leap into the fire with humility and courage, God himself will be your teacher. Even when we do have a spiritual guide, we are still being taught by God. The guide is there just to keep us on the way. And of course, the Fathers are alive through their writings, and the Lord himself is alive in the midst of the church. Still it is considered that the way could be dangerous without guidance. The devil sits along the sides of the way, trying to divert those who walk by.

When Saint Antony the Great of Egypt saw all the snares the devil had set along the path, he cried out in agony, *"Lord! How can one be saved?"* And he heard a voice which said, "Humility." Obedience is the key to this entire tradition. Through obedience to the other, we cut off our own will, our love of self, which is the cause of every sorrow. We do not *achieve* humility; we allow ourselves to be humbled. We let God, in the person of our spiritual father, humble us. All the other things we may do—prayer, fasting, vigilance—mean nothing without humility. We could just be building our pride, or what Theophan the Recluse calls "spiritual hedonism." That is why, when we set out on the way, we cannot walk upon it just for any reason. What is it that we are really seeking? In traditional Christian language, we might say that we are seeking the will of God. But we don't know what that will is or where it will lead us. In this sense, we are seeking nothing that we can know or imagine before we set off.

A few years ago I was in Greece having dinner with a fellow who had just come back from Mount Athos. He told me about a disturbing sight he had seen there. A gloomy-looking monk had been sitting outside his cell, making weeping sounds. The visitor asked him, "Father, what is the matter?"

The monk replied, "Oh! Everything is bad. I have been on this holy mountain for thirty-eight years and I have not yet achieved pure prayer."

My dinner companion, when telling this story, said, "Now, isn't that sad? This monk has been on Mount Athos all this time, fasting, praying, keeping vigil, not being with women, and he has not yet achieved pure prayer."

Another guest who was at the same table responded, "You know, that is a sad story. The real sadness, however, is that after thirty-eight years on the holy mountain, he still cares about achieving pure prayer!"

You don't go to the holy mountain, or anywhere else, to find pure prayer, and certainly not your own notion of what pure prayer is, or ought to be. You go to discover the will of God, and you receive what he gives, whatever that may be. The intention of true prayer is to be one with God in order to do his will. It is to discover reality and to be present in it. That is all prayer is. It is not for anything else. Even when we recite the Lord's Prayer, the words are not the important thing; it is the intention. We are told that both Theopan the Recluse and Ignatius Brianchaninov forbade the practice of the Jesus Prayer without a director, saying that it could only be done with the blessing of certain elders in the church. When explaining why, Ignatius lamented that many people who practiced it did not succeed in finding the will of God: their only success was that they ruined their lungs.

The monks once asked Abba Agathon, "What is the virtue that requires the greatest effort?" He answered them, "Forgive me, but I think there is no labor greater than that of prayer to God. . . . Whatever good work a man undertakes, if he perseveres in it, he will attain rest. But prayer is warfare to the last breath." Fidelity to prayer, which is very simply keeping the mind and the heart united in God in order to do his will, is the whole content of the way. All obedience, all humility, all scriptures are for that end.

Perhaps it should be stated here that the methods and instructions given in this tradition are the same for monastics as for anyone else. The difference is just in the context. There is an interesting story about this, which comes from the life of Saint Antony. The Lord once led Antony to the home of a physician, where he told Antony he would show him his equal. Antony asked the physician, "What do you do?"

The physician replied, "I heal those who come to me. More than I need I do not take. More than I can use I give to the poor, and all day long I sing the Sanctus in my heart." In the eyes of the Lord, this man was considered equal to Antony the Great. Certainly these days his life could be called a miracle—not only because he sang the Sanctus in his heart all day long, but because, being a physician, he didn't take more than he needed!

So the point is not whether we are in the desert or in the monastery, or whether we are married or unmarried. Nevertheless, not to mislead anyone, I would have to add that the tradition does acknowledge only two manners of existence in the world: to be a consecrated celibate or to be heterosexually, monogamously married. I have sometimes been invited to speak at Vassar College in upstate New York. The last time I was there, my topic was "Heterosexual Monogamous Marriage." I gave a talk on God's passionate, erotic love for the world, and how, in the Orthodox tradition, Easter is the great nuptial celebration of Christ the Bridegroom coming to win his harlot bride. In fact, the whole Bible is about God's mad love affair with us. Then I went on and talked about husband-wife fidelity. When my talk was over, a man in the audience raised his hand and said, "Do you actually believe all that?"

I answered, "Though my name is Thomas, I try! I believe fidelity is a sign of love, obedience, humility, and submission to one another in bringing the kingdom into the world."

He said, "Well, if you ask me, it would take a miracle to pull that off!"

My response was, "Well, at least one person understood my talk today!"

This tradition has a wealth of specific teachings about how to interact with others, how to live one's life, and how not to be led astray. For example, it is said that one should always accept criticism from others as being true. That way, if the accusation was right, you have repented and changed, and if it was wrong, then you have still changed by giving up your self-justification. It is also instructed that one should never attempt to measure progress or to compare oneself with others. Each moment is unique, and one's place on the path cannot be known. As Isaac of Syria said, "If you did find out, it would be a miracle greater than raising the dead."

As for visions and prophecies, they are said to be absolutely nonessential: if you have a vision, doubt it; if you have a dream, don't follow it; if you hear a voice, say it came for the person in the next room—and you will be saved. If it *did* come from God, you will inevitably receive it. But the voice of the devil and the voice of one's own nature speak all the time, and it is easy to be misled.

In order to give some idea of where the Orthodox way leads, I would like to conclude with Father Vasileios's description of one who has traveled this path completely:

> He literally overflows. That is an expression which gives some idea of the truth about him. He has a treasure of inexpressible joy hidden in an earthen vessel, small and fragile. And this joy overflows and spreads all around him, filling his surroundings

with its fragrance. Light shines from his being. His inner rejoicing sometimes goes beyond his endurance, breaks his heart, shows itself in tears and cries and gestures. And whether he speaks or whether he is silent, whether he sleeps or whether he is awake, whether he is present or whether he is absent, it is always the same thing that he says, the same thing that he is, the same grace and the same power. His presence or the memory of him, the feeling that he is near, or simply that he exists, of itself conveys something other, something uncreated, tranquil, penetrating. . . . He is nature and holiness, perfect man and perfect god by grace. He does nothing which is false. He does not make things, he causes things to be begotten and to proceed. He does not speak, he acts. He does not comment, he simply loves. . . . He has gone out of the realm of our habitual reactions. If you strike him, your blows will not reach him; he is beyond them. If you seek him, wherever you are, you will find him beside you. He lives only for you.[15]

Liturgy

The "Blessing of the Baptismal Water" is one section of the Orthodox liturgy "The Service of Holy Baptism."

The blessing begins with a praise ("Great art thou . . . "), which has been abbreviated in this excerpt. The praise affirms that God is "inexpressible, existing uncreated before the ages" and concludes by recalling that he has revealed himself on earth through Christ. Then follows the invocation, which calls the Holy Spirit to enter the water: "Wherefore, O King. . . . " The water is then exorcised of negativity and its power to purify and renew is affirmed. Following this section of the liturgy, the person to be baptized is anointed with the "oil of healing" and then immersed into the water.

The Greek word baptiso means "to immerse." Water is the sacramental vehicle or instrument through which one is immersed into God: into the "name" (i.e. nature) of the Father, the Son, and the Holy Spirit. Through this sacrament, the "old man" dies and the "new man" emerges.

The Blessing of the Baptismal Water

Priest: Great art thou, O Lord, and marvelous are thy works, and there is no word which suffices to hymn thy wonders (recited three times). . . .

For thou, O our God, hast revealed thyself upon earth, and hast dwelt among men. Thou didst hallow the streams of Jordan, sending down upon them from heaven thy Holy Spirit, and didst crush the heads of the dragons who lurked there.

Wherefore, O King who lovest mankind, come thou now and sanctify this water, by the indwelling of thy Holy Spirit (recited three times). . . .

For we have called upon thy Name, O Lord, and it is wonderful, and glorious, and awesome unto adversaries.

The priest then blesses the water by dipping the fingers of his right hand into it and tracing the Sign of the Cross three times. He breathes on the water and says:

Let all adverse powers be crushed beneath the sign of the image of thy Cross.

We pray thee, O God, that every aerial and obscure phantom may withdraw itself from us; and that no demon of darkness may conceal himself in this water; and that no evil spirit which instills darkening of intentions and rebelliousness of thought may descend into it with him (her) who is about to be baptized.

Be do thou, O Master of all, show this water to be the water of redemption, the water of sanctification, the purification of flesh and spirit, the loosing of bonds, the remission of sins, the illumination of the soul, the laver of regeneration, the renewal of the Spirit, the gift of adoption to sonship, the garment of incorruption, the fountain of life. For thou hast said, O Lord: Wash and be clean; put away evil things from your souls. Thou hast bestowed upon us from on high a new birth through water and the Spirit. Wherefore, O Lord, manifest thyself in this water, and grant that he who is baptized therein may be transformed; that he may put away from him the old man, which is corrupt through the lusts of the flesh, and that he may be clothed upon with the new man, and renewed after the image of him who created him: that being buried, after the pattern of thy death, in baptism, he may, in like manner be a partaker of thy Resurrection; and having preserved the gift of thy Holy Spirit, and increased the measure of grace committed unto him he may receive the prize of his high calling, and be numbered with the first-born whose names are written in heaven, in thee, our God and Lord, Jesus Christ.

For unto thee are due glory; dominion, honor, and worship, together with thy Father, who is from everlasting, and thine all-holy, and good, and life-giving Spirit, now, and ever, and unto ages of ages.

People: Amen.
Priest: Peace be with you all.
People: And with your spirit.
Priest: Bow your heads unto the Lord.
People: To thee, O Lord.

Chapter 1: Notes
1. Epigraph: *Bible, Church, Tradition: An Eastern Orthodox View* (Belmont, Mass.: Nordland Publ., 1972), p. 50. This is a paraphrase from Father B. M. Melioransky.
2. Julian Green, *To Leave Before Dawn* (New York: Harcourt, Brace & World, 1967), trans. Anne Green, p. 188.
3. *Mortem cotidie ante oculos suspectam habere:* "Day by day remind yourself that you are going to die." (Chapter 4, verse 47).
4. "Our hearts are restless until they rest in You." (Saint Augustine, *Confessions*.)
5. This manuscript page is from a collection of monastic rules, *Regulae Monasticorum*, printed in Venice by Johannes Emericus de Spira on April 13, 1500, for Lucantonio

Giunta. It is reprinted here courtesy of the Annmary Brown Memorial, Brown University, Providence, Rhode Island.

6. This and subsequent quotations from Antony's life story are from Saint Athanasius, *The Life of Saint Antony,* trans. Robert T. Meyer, in Ancient Christian Writers, No. 10 (Westminster, Md.: The Newman Press, 1950).

7. See Mother Tessa's description of these two stages of prayer in "Long, Loving Look at the Real," in Chapter.

8. Romance No. 9, "The Birth" in *The Collected Works of St. John of the Cross,* p. 732.

9. *Conceptions of the Love of God,* p. 391, in *The Complete Works of St. Teresa of Jesus,* trans. E. Allison Peers (London: Sheed & Ward, 1946).

10. *Interior Castle,* p. 346, in *The Complete Works of St. Teresa of Jesus.*

11. Translated by Kieran Kavanaugh and Otilio Rodriguez. Reprinted from *The Collected Works of St. John of the Cross* with permission of the Institute of Carmelite Studies, 2131 Lincoln Road N. E., Washington, D. C.

12. Archimandrite Vasileios, "Dying and Behold We Live" in *Hymn of Entry,* p. 117-119.

13. Ibid., 120.

14. This and other stories of the Fathers can be found in Sister Benedicta Ward, trans., *Sayings of the Desert Fathers: The Alphabetical Collection.*

15. Vasileios, "Dying and Behold We Live," p. 127.

2

Buddha's Way

Buddha's teaching is everywhere. Today it is raining. This is
Buddha's teaching. People think their own way or their own
religious understanding is Buddha's way, without knowing
what they are hearing, or what they are doing, or where they
are. Religion is not any particular teaching. Religion is everywhere. We have to understand our teaching this way.[1]

SHUNRYU SUZUKI

BUDDHA

Courtesy of the Government Museum, Mathura, India

Path of Awareness

Joseph Goldstein

The passion and inspiration which are the essence of the spiritual path come from wanting to understand and realize what is true. Buddhism and Christianity are two containers. As we prepare to step onto the path it is as if we are thirsty, and we come across several different jars of water. We can either spend all our time looking at, comparing, and analyzing the containers, or we can drink the water.

How do we set out in search of what is true? When we listen to different teachers and read various books, we find that each has a particular idea of how to go about practice as well as certain concepts about what is true. We may feel confused, not knowing where or how to begin. There is a story that illustrates this dilemma, involving a fellow named Mulla Nasrudin, a well-known Sufi character who always plays the part of the wise fool. One day Nasrudin's friend came by and asked to borrow his donkey. Nasrudin said, "I'm sorry, I don't have it." Just at that moment the donkey brayed outside the window. The friend became infuriated. "How can you say that you don't have your donkey? I just heard it." Nasrudin turned to him and said, "Well, who are you going to believe—me or the donkey?"

Who are you going to believe? In one discourse, the Buddha replied to that question by saying: "Don't believe anyone. Don't believe me. Don't believe the teachers. Don't believe books or traditions. Rather, look to your own experience. In that way we become our own refuge, not dependent upon any external authority or system."[2] The very important question is then, how do we look to our own experience? For the most part, we are so caught up and identified with various neurotic habit patterns of mind—thoughts, emotions, bodily tensions—that it is difficult to really look. We see life through the colored glasses of our biases and preconceptions. So we need a discipline that allows us to examine and investigate what is taking place in a nonjudgmental way. In the tradition of Theravada Buddhism we practice vipassana meditation, which cultivates an awareness that is free of view.[3] It is a simple settling-back into the moment. By being with whatever is happening, we cultivate a non-interfering, choiceless awareness.

If we really want to find out what is true in our experience, we need to pay attention to the present moment, because the only place any experience can ever be is now. If it is in some imaginary future, we will never reach it. An image that I have found helpful in my own practice is that of riding on a train. Normally we sit looking ahead out the train window, in anticipation of what is coming up. We look out, ahead of ourselves. But just think of what it is like to sit on the train facing backwards. What is the experience of looking out the window then? The last moment is always just falling away. There is no anticipation, because we can't see what is coming. We can only be right there, in the moment. There is more of a sense of backing into the experience, rather than of trying to go forward into it. The key point is that we can only look forward to what we know. As long as we're anticipating the next sights and sounds, the next feelings and sensations, we are caught in the known. It's only when we are facing backwards, in the sense of allowing ourselves to come right back into the moment, that we are able to drop into the *un*known, into what Krishnamurti calls "freedom from the known."

Anyone who has practiced a spiritual discipline, whether prayer or sitting meditation, is familiar with mind's tendency to get lost in fantasies of the past and future. So much of one's life is spent in recollection and anticipation. Take a simple task, such as attending to the breath. How difficult it is to be fully with each breath! Our minds have not been trained to be present. The practice and discipline of being in the moment has an amazingly powerful capacity to cut through confusion. Listen. (Rings gong). There is just the hearing, just the sound. There is no gong, no ear, no body, no me. (Rings gong again). Can we simply hear? If we are able to settle back into the moment, there is no confusion. There is no difficulty. There is just what is happening. In Zen, this quality of experience is often referred to as the "suchness" of the moment.

When people first begin to practice mindfulness, they tend to become grim: "I'm going to be mindful if it kills me!" People tighten, because they are trying to hold on to the moment. But mindfulness is not grimness or tightness. It is an extremely gentle and delicate quality of mind. Another tendency is to create concepts and ideals of what it is like to be aware. Perhaps we have a memory of someone who seems very "present," and we try to imitate that person. Or we may have read a description of enlightenment, and we try to imitate that. There is a wonderful story about this, involving the Korean Zen master San Sunim, who lives at his center in Providence, Rhode Island. One morning he came down to the diningroom and was sitting at breakfast, reading a newspaper. His students also came down, and when they saw him eating and reading, they were aghast. They had read instructions on mindfulness: "Pay attention to what you are doing. If you are eating, eat. If you are reading, read." They confronted him, asking how he could be eating his food and reading a newspaper at the same time. San Sunim, without hesitating, told them, "When you eat and read, just eat and read!"

Awareness is universal. There is no experience, no relationship, no situation, no object, nothing which falls outside the field of awareness. Although certain conditions are conducive to the practice and cultivation of this awareness, it is a pitfall to set up a boundary or limitation, thinking that awareness can only be practiced in certain situations. Reality, or dharma, is the totality of experience; there is no part of our lives outside it. When we understand that truth and are able to connect with it deeply, we begin to develop a real sense of appreciation for every aspect of our lives, whether we're sitting in the meditation hall, washing the dishes, going to the bathroom, or walking down the street. A few years ago a popular song came out which ended with this wonderful line: "Some people say that life is strange, but what I'd like to know is, compared to what?" Life is a totality: it is not divided into spiritual and mundane, or holy and not-holy. It is all equal. We are the totality of our experience. The path of awareness brings attentiveness and investigation to the whole range of who we are.

The Buddha once told a story about an old hermit who practiced in the jungles of India. One day he heard the loud roar of a Bengal tiger close to his hut. The hermit was frightened and started to run through the jungle, with the tiger chasing him. He ran and ran, and after awhile he arrived at the edge of a cliff. He jumped over the edge and caught onto the end of a vine. He looked up. There was the tiger, growling down at him. He looked down. There was a second tiger at the bottom of the cliff. Near his head, two little mice started to gnaw away at the vine. Please place yourself in his situation. There you are, hanging onto the vine, tiger above and tiger below. The vine is being gradually eaten away. How would you feel? How would you be? Well, the story goes on. The old man turned and saw two strawberries growing out of the side of the cliff. He reached over, plucked and ate them, exclaiming, "How delicious!"

Our situation is no different. We are hanging between birth and death. The mice are eating the vine. That *is* what is happening. That is our situation. Are we able to respond to the gift of each moment? Can we say "How delicious!" to the strawberry? Can we say "Ouch!" to the thorn? Can we *be* there in a full way for whatever is offered in each moment's experience? That is the path of awareness. We learn to develop an appreciation for the entire range of our experience: the ten thousand joys and the ten thousand sorrows.

As our awareness of the moment becomes increasingly precise and refined, we begin to develop insight and wisdom into the whole process of our lives. We also see the patterns of our thoughts and emotions, and we begin to have glimpses of who we are on the level of personality. There is another Nasrudin story I could relate here. One day Mulla Nasrudin went into a bank to cash a check. The teller asked him for some identification. Nasrudin looked and looked, but he didn't have any. The teller said, "I'm sorry, I can't cash this check." Nasrudin thought for another moment. Then he reached into his coat pocket, took out a mirror, and looking into it said, "Yeah, that's me alright!"

That is the beginning stage of practice. We become quiet enough to take a look into the mirror: "That's me, alright!" We see both the good qualities and the unwholesome ones, honestly and without judgement. We begin to understand deeply that everything is continually changing. There is nothing static. Whether we look at the sub-atomic level, the cellular level, the personality level, the level of our interpersonal relationships, or whether we look around us at the mountains, cities, the earth, the galaxy, the universe . . . it's all in a process of change. There is not a single thing which stays steady. Of course, this may seem obvious. If you ask anyone on the street, "Do things change?" they will say, "Sure!" But somehow we don't live our lives in accordance with that truth. We know it intellectually, but we don't really know it. As we practice the path of awareness, we experience deeply the momentariness of experience. Everything is in constant transformation: there is nothing to hold on to.

All of practice can be summed up by one instruction, which as quoted in the great Mahayana text, *The Diamond Sutra*, is: "Develop a mind which clings to nought." Don't cling to anything. Because if we are attached, if we grasp at what is changing and deny the flow of experience, inherent in that grasping is suffering.

What is it that seduces us into attachment? The most powerful objects of attachment are sense desires: pleasant sights and sounds, pleasant sensations in the body, and stimulating ideas. But please don't misunderstand this point. There is nothing inherently wrong with pleasure itself. It can be a harmless joy to experience beautiful sights and sounds or inspiring thoughts. The problem arises when we become attached. It is the clinging, the addiction, which is the problem.

Our society has conditioned us, particularly in the West, to believe that happiness lies in the gratification of desire. I once saw a cigarette commercial which summed up this message. A handsome young man stands in front of a Hawaiian waterfall, with a beautiful woman next to him and paradise all around. He holds a cigarette in one hand, which completes the picture! The caption reads, "I don't let anything stand in the way of my pleasure!" That message, which we hear frequently in our society, creates the "if-only" syndrome: If only I had a better job, then I'd be happy. If only I had the right relationship— I know there's someone out there who could make me happy. If only I could go to Hawaii. If only I'd brought the right cushion to this place! Then my legs wouldn't hurt, and I would become enlightened, and *then* I'd be happy! If only . . . if only . . . if only . . . And of course, inherent in each of those statements is dissatisfaction. We've all had a thousand "if-only's." We've achieved and enjoyed some of them, but always the situation has changed, and then we've had to find a new "if-only." Sooner or later we learn that happiness or completion is not to be found in gratification of the senses.

One night Mulla Nasrudin was scrounging around under a lamp-post, looking for the key to his house. After some time his friends came along and started to look on the ground with him. None of them could find the key. Finally one said to Nasrudin, "Where exactly did you lose it?" He replied, "Oh, inside." They asked in amazement, "Well, why are you looking out here?" Nasrudin answered them matter-of-factly, "Because there's more light out here!"

It's going to be a long look. If we keep searching for a sense of wholeness outside of ourselves, and outside of the present moment, we are doomed to what is known as the wheel of *samsara:* we will go on looking, around and around, forever.

Another attachment which causes suffering in our lives is the attachment we have to opinions. We all have so many ideas about politics, economics, education, relationships, and spirituality. One famous saying from the third Zen patriarch is, "Do not seek truth; only cease to cherish opinions." Again, this doesn't mean that you must cease having opinions. We have each had our own unique set of experiences, which has given us our particular window onto the world. Could we possibly honor our own viewpoint, while at the same time having a deep respect for everyone else's? Obviously the dharma is not limited to one little porthole. Can we open ourselves to that sense of respect and appreciation for all viewpoints?

A third kind of attachment, which is particularly appropriate to discuss in this context, is what Trungpa Rinpoche aptly coined "spiritual materialism." The spiritual path can be used to strengthen ego. For example, we could be holding onto the expectation that someone else is going to enlighten us. We might be waiting for someone to come along and give us a zap on the forehead—great cosmic awakening! Or we may become attached to our particular technique or path, thinking that ours is the highest way, the best way, the quickest way, the ultimate way. Wei Wu Wei said, "Disciples and devotees, what are most of them doing? Worshipping the teapot instead of drinking the tea." Of course we don't want to throw away the teapot; it is an important part of what we are doing. It gives us the ability to drink the tea. Can we feel tremendous respect for the teapot—without attachment?

Having looked at attachment to sense desires, to opinions, and to spirituality, we are ready to examine the most subtle and the most deeply conditioned attachment, which is attachment to the idea of self or ego. The basic delusion we suffer comes from referring every experience back to the concept of self: it is my emotion, my thought, my pain, my body, my wife, my husband, my country, my earth. . . . This process creates the basic field of duality within which we live our lives. And once there is a self, there is automatically an other-than-self. Then we have to defend this self and protect and gratify it. We build barriers and walls between self and other. Subtlety and depth in practice only come when we are able to let go of the reference point of self and simply be with things as they are.

In Asia people have devised a clever trap which they use to catch monkeys. They hollow out a coconut and put some kind of sweet in it.

Then they make a little slit in the bottom of the coconut which is just big enough for the monkey to slip its open hand into, but not big enough for it to withdraw its clenched hand through. They attach the coconut to a tree or stake. The monkey comes along, smells the sweet, puts its hand in, grabs the food . . . and is trapped. When the hunters approach, the monkey becomes frantic and terrified, but it can't get away. Who is keeping the monkey trapped? There is no force, other than its own clinging. Theoretically all it has to do is open its hand, slip it out, and be free. But it's a pretty unusual monkey that can do that!

People often ask, "How do I let go? I know I'm holding on, but how do I let go?" I would reply, "If you were holding a hot burning coal in your hand, would you be asking how to let go?" You would drop it because you would be aware of the suffering involved. As we pay attention to our experience in a precise and accurate way, we see and experience the suffering of attachment. By being attached to what is changing, we create our own suffering. Having that awareness, letting go takes place naturally.

Through vipassana meditation we gradually begin to let go of our attachment to the particular constellation of experience we call "self." As we pay careful attention to the process of mind and body, we begin to experience that what we are *is* the unfolding of momentary experience— moments of seeing, hearing, tasting, smelling, touching, thinking, mind states. . . . We *are* this changing process. It doesn't refer *back* to anyone. There is no one *behind* it to *whom* it is happening. That experiential understanding is called "purification of view." We begin to get a glimpse of the inherent selflessness or egolessness of the process. In each moment there is *just* what there is.

It is like letting go of the Big Dipper. When we look up into the sky at night, we naturally orient ourselves to the Big Dipper. But what is the Big Dipper, really? There are several stars in a certain relationship to each other, which create a pattern in the sky. Would it be possible for us to look up at those stars and not see the Big Dipper? It would be difficult because we have been so conditioned to see the stars in a particular way. When we let go of our attachment to the idea of Big Dipper, we see that there is no intrinsic division between that constellation of stars and all the other stars in the sky. We have created the separation through our own concepts, and we have done the same thing with ourselves. Each of us has created a constellation and given it a name: "Joseph." When we let go of the attachment to the pattern, we see there is no fundamental separation; there is simply seeing, hearing, smelling, tasting, touching, thinking, feeling . . . there are simply all the stars in the sky. Can we experience just what there is in each moment, free from attachment to ideas and concepts, but still be able to use these ideas and concepts when it is appropriate? Can we move freely between different levels of mind? Through continuing the practice of awareness and letting go of attachment, we come to a level of insight called "vipassana happiness." We begin to experience, in a clear and concentrated way, the rising and passing away of all phenomena: internal, external, subjective, and objective. The mind becomes steady, and a tremendous luminosity arises. Attention and mindfulness are effortless, and we experience rapture and bliss. One's consciousness could be compared to a piece of crystal that is polished and sparkling. There is a pervasive feeling of having finally come home, of "This is what it's about!" You could sit for hours on end: there is no pain in the body. You could just sit, with great equanimity. It is a wonderful time. You might rush to your teacher: "I've experienced this wonderful state! I'm experiencing concentration, mindfulness, and rapture. . . . " He or she will probably say something like this: "Now pay careful attention to those states, because they are just corruptions of insight." Of course they are also factors of awakening, but because there is still a strong tendency to become attached to these states, we have to pay attention to their changing nature and go on.

As the path unfolds, it takes another turn. The next development is somewhat dramatic, because the mind begins to tune in more strongly to the dissolution aspect of experience. Everything is passing away: thoughts, feelings, sensations, the breath. Consciousness itself is dissolving. As we first taste this, tremendous fear arises. We have been so used to finding something stable to hold onto for security, but now one's whole being is in the process of momentary, instantaneous dissolving. We feel a sense of misery and disgust. Before we were able to practice for hours on end: at this point we can hardly sit for ten minutes. It is too uncomfortable. We call this stage of practice "rolling up the mat."

Anyone who has a real sense of spiritual practice knows that the path is not a particularly blissful journey. There may be times of bliss and times of rapture, but there are also times of profound connection with the inherent suffering of existence. It is only when we come to accept the totality of experience that we can open to ourselves and to others with compassion. So when we find ourselves in a state of fear and misery, we learn to settle into it, to soften and accept it. Out of that comes what is known as the "urge for deliverance." This is the urge to be free of this state of continual dissolution. It is not particularly a thought; it is an impulse in the mind. This then leads to the next stage of understanding, which is true equanimity. When the mind settles back in a totally balanced way, it becomes like open space. Everything is arising and passing: there is no movement toward holding on to what is pleasant, and no movement toward pushing away what is unpleasant. Everything becomes soft. We could stay in that equanimity for a long time. This is where all the factors of enlightenment are ripening and maturing.

Like a balance scale, the adjustments become finer and finer, until there is no longer any movement of mind. Everything is still happening— the world continually appears and disappears—but the mind is perfectly still. Out of that stillness comes an intuitive and spontaneous opening to the unconditioned, to that which is beyond this mind and body. The name for that experience could be one of many: nirvana, the absolute, godhead. It is the opening to the zero center.

Imagine that all of experience—sensations, thoughts, emotions, concepts, people, buildings, the stars, the galaxies, everything—is on the surface of a sphere. Usually we separate out one little corner of that sphere, one little collection of experiences, and say, "That's me." Everything else, all the other experience potential in the universe, is outside of "me," outside of self. When we learn to simply be with experience as it is, and we open to the totality of it, we discover the center of that sphere. What is the center? The center is a point, and a point has no dimensions: no width, no breadth, and no height. It is, but it doesn't exist. Zero center. The point defines the sphere and puts it into a true relationship, but it is not a thing of itself.

The intuitive, sudden, wordless opening to zero center radically transforms our understanding of who we are. We see that we are not the small little constellation of experience we thought we were. From the reference point of the absolute, we see that we are one with all experience.

In closing, I would like to share with you a teaching I heard from Kalu Rinpoche, who is one of the great Tibetan meditation masters:

We live in illusion and the appearance of things. There is a reality. We are that reality. When we understand this, we see that we are nothing. And being nothing, we are everything.

Liturgy

Traditionally, "taking refuge" in the Buddha, Dharma, and Sangha is equivalent to becoming, or re-affirming that one has become, Buddhist. It is both a gesture of renunciation and aspiration. One renounces beliefs and actions that perpetuate suffering and delusion, acknowledging the fundamental homelessness of the spiritual journey. At the same time, one reveres the Buddha as example and teacher, the Dharma as doctrinal and experiential truth, and the Sangha as the community of practitioners.

This particular version of the three refuges is a Theravada liturgy. It is usually chanted in Pali, the original canonical language of Buddhism and the language still used by most Theravada Buddhists in Southeast Asia. It may be recited at the start of monastic ceremonies, such as ordinations, or to begin long periods of intensive practice. Many monks and nuns also chant it alone each morning, at the beginning of their day of meditation.

See also Tai Situpa Rinpoche's commentary on the three refuges in the Tibetan Mahayana tradition later in this chapter.

The Three Refuges

I take refuge in the Buddha
I take refuge in the Dharma
I take refuge in the Sangha (recite three times)

I pay respect to the exalted one,
far from defilement, perfectly enlightened.

I pay respect to the Dharma,
well expounded by the enlightened one.

I pay respect to the Sangha,
disciples who have practiced well.

The exalted one is indeed to be respected,
far from defilements, perfectly enlightened,
fully possessed of wisdom and excellent conduct,
one who has proceeded by the good way, knower of the
    worlds,
excellent trainer of those who can be taught,
teacher of all beings, the awakened one,
all-skilled in teaching Dharma in the world.

Well expounded is the enlightened one's Dharma,
to be seen here and now, openly offered,
inviting one to come and see, leading inward to the
    truth,
to be seen by each wise person, to be seen for oneself.

All compound things are impermanent.
They have the nature to arise and pass away.
To be in harmony with truth brings true happiness.

There is no greater refuge.
The Buddha, Dharma, and Sangha are my refuge.
By the power of this understanding
May I be blessed throughout all time.

Twentieth-Century Buddha-Nature

Eido Tai Shimano Roshi

Most Zen stories take place in China, and they usually take place during the T'ang Dynasty. But it is important to realize that a Zen story is also a twentieth-century American story. There is no time difference or space difference. What I am going to tell you about is happening here in America.

Each one of you also has the opportunity to experience who you really are. That is the most essential point of human life, and naturally it is the most essential point of this meeting between Christianity and Buddhism.

There was a Zen Master who lived in China, and I want to say that I love him. I am saying I love him before I introduce his name, so that you know how much I love him. His name is Bunen, and he is usually known as Ummon. Literally, *Um* means "cloud," and *mon* means "gate." So he is Master Cloud Gate, or Master Ummon. When he was young, because of some mysterious reason which we cannot find any rational or logical explanation for, he was led to the path of the buddhadharma. He began to study in various schools of Buddhism, and he ended up with Zen. He sat zazen for many years, perhaps. The story doesn't say how many years. This is Chinese ambiguity. (Laughter.) So we can assume that he sat for one year to ten years, somewhere in that range.

One day Ummon was sitting, sitting, sitting, and he became a little impatient. Nothing was happening. He thought, "What am I doing? Am I not wasting my time? When will I see my own true nature?" This is a common doubt and a common human question. But he kept on. At one point, his dharma friend told him about a Zen hermit, Master Bokushu, who was sitting zazen in a hut, and so Ummon decided to go on a pilgrimage. He walked and walked, until finally he reached Bokushu's hut. Now, before I go on with this story, I would like to say that hermits are often misunderstood. Many people think a hermit lives the way he does because he is hiding from social life: he is too introverted, too shy, or too lazy. People think this way because hermits are so mysterious. But one of the things which I believe the most strongly is that meditation practice is not a passive activity at all. You use your body, and you use all your senses. And if you really sit, you sweat. And not only that, you radiate. You radiate your positive spirituality. It is as if you were broadcasting the DBS— which means Dharma Broadcasting System. (Laughter.) This is a very, very, important point about sitting.

Not having any students, the hermit Bokushu did not have any attendants. He just sat. He melted into the universe, and the universe melted into him. They intermingled. One day Ummon, the traveling monk, came to Bokushu's hut. He knocked on the door. (Roshi makes knocking sound.) Now, the way someone knocks tells everything about their state of mind. If they knock so . . . (knocks rapidly, impatiently) that says all. In the Rinzai Zen tradition, there is such a thing as dokasan, which roughly translated means "private interview." Before dokasan begins, each student strikes a small bell outside the interview room. The master is sitting inside the room and listening. So, before the student even enters the room, the interview is already finished. (Laughter.) But the student does not know that. So this is where practice and everyday life come to one point. If someone contemplates enough, and concentrates enough, then knocking on the door naturally becomes . . . (knocks slowly, definitely). This is Oriental mysticism. (Laughter.) By the way, don't be concerned if my talk goes this way, and then that way, and then this way. I shall not forget that everything is inside the broad way.[4]

Inside the hut, Bokushu heard the knock, and he thought, "It is worthy." So he said, "Who is it?"

"My name is Ummon."

Again, this is important to say well. Ummon passed this second examination. The master Bokushu thought, "He is worthy," and so he said, "Come in." Ummon came in, sliding the door to one side. As soon as he did, Master Bokushu stood up, grabbed the monk's robe at his chest, and said, "SAY!"

Ummon was dumbfounded. Then Bokushu pushed him out backwards and closed the door. That was the end of the interview.

Now, suppose you encounter such a direct, straightforward question: Say! What do you say? It's a not-so-easy question. Some of you may say, "Say what?" (Laughter.) Of course, Bokushu meant, say something about your true nature, itself. So Ummon was rejected. He was surprised and shocked, and went to a nearby temple and sat zazen. He s-a-a-a-t. This time he sat differently, desperately. He sat with all his cells. No thoughts. No pain. No time. He just sat. When we become desperate, zazen is so simple. But for some reason we are able to become desperate only once in a great while.

Years ago, when I was living on Manhattan Island in New York City, something happened that was unfortunate, and I was feeling discontent and very unhappy. One day I was walking down Riverside Drive when all of a sudden a wind came up from the Hudson River. Normally we don't think about the significance of the wind, but for some reason when we are in a bad state the wind can be so refreshing. I started to wonder, what is this wind? This movement of air is just ordinary and yet somehow it provides all this freshness, and it pervades everywhere. And then, without thinking, I put my palms together and became so grateful for the fact that I am alive. I am able to breathe in and out and I am able to appreciate this simple wind (makes wind-like sound with breath). Now when I think it is a very good day, I also think that perhaps I am missing a great opportunity to see something that I normally miss seeing, or hear something that I normally miss hearing. So sometimes to feel bad is good and to feel good is bad.

Back to our story. Ummon was sitting in the temple. A few days passed. Lucidity took place. Transparency took place. A sort of unification took place. Finally Ummon thought he was ready to pay another visit to ask for guidance. He walked to the hut, step by step, not looking around, very concentrated . . . step, step, step. He came to Bokushu's hut, and then knocked on the door. (Knocks slowly.)

"Who is it?"

"Ummon."

"Come in."

And then, "SAY!"

Ummon was thrown out again. He went back to his temple, and more than ever he concentrated on zazen. He went into such a condition that we say, even though he was not blind, he could not see. Even though he was not deaf, he could not hear. Even though he could smell, somehow he could not smell. All of the six senses became numb. Now he went to visit Bokushu. This time, when he walked into the hut, the universe came in with him, so to speak. Bokushu stood up, grabbed him, and—"SAY!"

Ummon couldn't say. Bokushu pushed him out the door, but as he threw the sliding door shut, Ummon's right leg was caught inside. At that moment, with this great stimulation and readiness of time, Ummon had an experience. Stimulation and readiness of time are the two indispensable elements for this kind of religious experience. In this case, the elements were strong, so for the rest of his life Ummon was crippled. At the expense of his right leg, he achieved realization.

Now, this may seem like an eccentric or strange story. But you should know that you also have the same opportunity to practice until the time has ripened for you. If you do, you will realize the essential question of who you really are. If I ask, "Who are you?" you may say, "Mary." But Mary is merely a name that was given to you. It could have been Nancy or Judy. So, who are you? "SAY!" Hmmm. . . .

When the time is not ready, we don't even want to sit. We don't even search. But when the time is ready, for some reason which is impossible to describe rationally, the thirst for searching comes. And then we naturally start to sit. And by the way, sitting is not the only method. Because I have a Zen background, I speak of sitting. Many people, for various reasons and with various stimulations, have realized this true nature.

We should be careful, talking about this topic. If we say "true nature" again and again, no matter how beautiful this name may be, it becomes a concept, and it loses its impact. My teacher often said it this way: "endless dimension, universal life." That is also good. But it is important for us to know that this something which we realize is unnameable. So sometimes I just call it "something," because after all, it is *quite* something!

The story of Ummon is a Chinese story from the T'ang Dynasty. Here we are in America, not China. This is the twentieth century, not the T'ang Dynasty. And yet who you are is the same if you are American or Chinese or Tibetan. Fundamentally there is no difference whatsoever. There is no East, no West, no man, no woman, no youth, no old age. Years ago many people would come from New Jersey to visit our center in New York. For some reason they dressed sloppily, and their zazen was not as straight as people's zazen in Manhattan. One day I was giving this talk: no East, no West, no youth, and so on. And then I said, " . . . except for the people in New Jersey; they have no buddha-nature." But that was a joke. (Laughter.)

What is most important in this lifetime is for each one of us to realize our real nature. When that happens, what we call fundamental reality is realized, and everything disappears. But then, the body comes back again. We still have this tangible body (hits chest). We have everyday life. The experience of one's true nature could be called fundamental or absolute reality, and this everyday life could be called existential reality. The relationship between these two is just like the relationship between the ocean and the waves. Ocean and waves are two different names, but everyone knows that they are inseparable. We can not have an ocean without waves, and vice versa.

Whether you are a layperson or not, and whether you are Buddhist or Christian or something else, do not think that it is impossible for you to have such an experience. As long as you are a human being, you can have such a fundamental, absolute experience. On my way to this conference I visited Reno, Nevada for a few days. It was not because I wanted to gamble, but because I have a friend who lives there who says he is "the only Buddhist in Nevada." He becomes lonely without dharma friends, and so sometimes I go to visit him. I met a young friend of his who had heard his teacher in school say, "God is simple; God is ordinary." Another teacher told him, "God is boundless; God is infinite." And for some mysterious reason, he took these statements seriously. God is ordinary. God is infinite. How could this be possible? This was his own koan, although he did not know anything about koans. Day and night he thought, "God is simple. God is boundless." He thought, thought, thought, thought. . . . This was his readiness of time. And then one day he was in the library, still repeating this mantra: "God is simple. God is boundless." And all of a sudden, he *saw* it. He realized the simplicity of God and the boundlessness of God, and these were no longer paradoxical to him. After that, his life changed. His viewpoint changed. He could have a universal breakfast. He could have a universal walk. He could have universal jealousy. His actions were no longer self-centered.

Only when you have had that kind of experience can you have what we call *anjin* in Japanese. *Anjin* is peace of mind, or rather, being without anxiety. You may still worry about this or that, but the fundamental anxiety disappears. No matter what happens, you are able to accept it. To taste this delicate and subtle boundlessness, timelessness, and fearlessness is the most essential thing for all of us. This is not religious talk, actually. This is the talk of fact. When you get this, and if your being is this, then whether you are sitting or you are doing just this, just this, just this, that will be a great contribution to the peace of the world and the creation of a better twentieth and twenty-first century.

Profound Motivation, Profound Action

H. E. the Tai Situpa Rinpoche

The most important principle of the Mahayana path is motivation. When one's motivation is profound, selfless, and pure, then one's actions will also be profound, selfless, and pure. Therefore, attitude is the essence of everything we do.

It is similar to protecting our eyes from the brightness of the snow. It is not necessary to cover the snow with dark paint. We can put on dark glasses, and that will be equally meaningful and beneficial. In the same way, when we act with pure motivation, everything we do and say becomes meaningful and appropriate. That is the basic principle of the bodhisattva path. For this reason, Buddha Shakyamuni taught that virtue and nonvirtue don't depend on how things appear: the intention or motivation determines what is positive and what is negative. The great bodhisattva Shantideva also said that the most evil being in the universe, at the first moment of developing selfless and limitless loving-kindness and compassion, will become a "son of the Buddha," the greatest of all beings.

What makes it possible to become a bodhisattva—a compassionate one? It is possible because our essence is ultimate bodhichitta or, in other terms, it is buddha-nature. The essential quality of one's mind is buddha-nature. Ultimate bodhichitta is ultimate loving-kindness and ultimate compassion. That is the connection each of us has to the bodhisattva path. It is the beginning, or ground. But even though buddha-nature is our true essence, if we don't develop it as our essence, it will not awaken. In the same way, if we have a precious seed but we don't plant it, the seed will not grow and will always remain a single seed. When we plant this seed and cultivate it properly, it will grow and develop, and eventually it will produce many more seeds. Where we began with one single grain, after some time we will produce food for all beings on the earth. So also, if we develop our precious essence, we will produce great benefit to others. Without developing it, there will be no benefit. This is the reason many beings continue to suffer in samsara, the reason Buddha achieved realization, and the reason great beings are able to benefit others.

The Mahayana path has three aspects: profound view, profound meditation, and profound everyday-life action. With these three, we can achieve the ultimate freedom, the ultimate peace, the ultimate realization of buddhahood. The profound view of buddha-dharma—not only of the Mahayana, but of all the Buddhist teachings—begins with taking the refuge vow. We take refuge in the *buddha, dharma, and sangha.*[5] There is an outer aspect and an inner aspect of this refuge. The outer meaning of taking refuge in the buddha refers to the inspiration and example of Shakyamuni Buddha, who was a historical person: In the one who realized the ultimate truth, the one who was able to find the true view, in the perfect Buddha, we take refuge. The dharma is the teaching of the Buddha, the path he discovered. It is the path that guides beings from ordinary levels of existence to the total realization achieved by the Buddha himself: In the profound and noble path, in the path that is safe and sure, in the vast and deep dharma, we take refuge. The sangha is the community that follows the dharma. It is made up of the practitioners who have already developed themselves as well as those who aspire to develop for the sake of others. We take refuge in the higher-level sangha for guidance and in the ordinary sangha for companionship. They are all our friends on the path, our good and wise companions, whose universal compassion is free from expectation: In the mighty sangha we take refuge. That is the first or outer aspect of taking refuge in the buddha, dharma, and sangha.

The inner aspect of refuge involves our original aim, which is to achieve the realization of our own essence, which is buddha-nature. Buddha isn't someone outside us who is coming from somewhere else to help us. Before his enlightenment, Shakyamuni Buddha was as we are. He followed the path of dharma, achieved the realization of the essence of everything, and became buddha, awake. We also are capable of achieving the same realization. That is our aim, that is our motivation, and that is the inner meaning of taking refuge in the buddha. When we take refuge in the dharma, or the teachings of the path, we understand that all appearances, all phenomena, and all experiences are manifestations of the ultimate truth. To be able to have such understanding and realization depends on having the right intention and the right action. Therefore, doing whatever is meaningful for oneself and others and avoiding whatever is meaningless for oneself and others is the inner refuge in the dharma. As for the sangha, when we see that nothing really belongs to us except our own body, speech, and mind, we have the freedom to devote ourselves to the right way of using this precious life: right action, right speech, and right intention. We are able to use our body, speech, and mind with profound motivation on this profound path. That is the aspiration for how to conduct ourselves in this world, and it is the inner meaning of refuge in the sangha.

Taking refuge is the first step on the path of buddha-dharma. In the Mahayana tradition, one also makes the commitment to be a bodhisattva. Therefore, we vow to develop *bodhichitta,* or loving-kindness and compassion. The object of our vow is endless and limitless. Our aspiration on the path is not only for ourselves, not only for mankind, but for all beings in the universe. In Buddhism, all beings are said to live in six different realms: the realm of the gods, the semi-gods, human beings, animals, spirits, and hell-realm beings. These are not only six different places, but each realm is also the result of one kind of neurosis. Therefore, as human beings, we have the nature of the whole six realms within us. For example, when we are strongly controlled by anger, we suffer as if we were in hell: it is hot, it is cold; when we are controlled by our stinginess, we suffer like an insatiable spirit; when we are overwhelmed by our ignorance, we suffer like an animal; when we are controlled by our desire, we are indeed human beings; when we are controlled by our jealousy, everything makes us envious, and we suffer like the semi-gods; and when we are overwhelmed by our pride, we suffer like the gods.

When we look at all the realms of existence, and even when we look within the human realm to each nation, each family, and each individual, we realize there are countless different ways of seeing and perceiving. Each of us has our own attitudes, our own way of looking at the world. But there are two things we all have in common: hope and fear. Always we hope to be happy and to find peace; always we are afraid to suffer. That is the common culture of all sentient beings. Round and round samsara's endless circle of hope and fear, from sorrow to sorrow, we spin. To help free all beings, so that they may find eternal joy which is permanent, invaluable, and unstained, we must use our body, speech, and mind to develop buddha essence, *our* essence. Vowing to use each moment fully and totally, not for our own pleasure, but for making human life meaningful for oneself and for others, we promise to achieve enlightenment. That is the purpose of bodhichitta.

In every situation, there is the possibility and opportunity to develop bodhichitta. But the most profound way to develop it is through the "four immeasurable thoughts." These are immeasurable loving-kindness, immeasurable compassion, immeasurable great joy, and immeasurable impartiality. Loving-kindness is similar to the feeling a kind mother has toward her own child. It is the desire that all beings will have their wishes fulfilled. All beings, including oneself, wish to be happy. That will only be possible to realize if the causes and conditions that produce happiness have been accumulated, even on a relative level. Therefore, one has the motivation to do whatever is helpful and meaningful for oneself and others. Therefore we say, "May all beings enjoy happiness and the causes of happiness."

Compassion is similar to loving-kindness, but it particularly refers to the suffering of beings. All beings, including oneself, fear suffering: we always want to avoid it. However, fighting to be free of suffering only causes more suffering. It is only when beings become free of the causes and conditions that produce suffering that they will be free from suffering itself. Therefore we say, "May all beings be free from suffering and causes of suffering."

Great joy is the joy one feels in knowing that others are able to be free from suffering. It is simply the opposite of jealousy and pride. In the bodhisattva vow, we say, "From now on I invite all beings to take part in the relative and ultimate aspects of happiness. My body, my speech, my mind, my accumulation of knowledge, and my accumulation of wisdom I dedicate for the benefit of all beings. May all beings equally enjoy this for their relative and ultimate peace." In this way, you are joyful about others' happiness. If you have this understanding, everyone's happiness is the cause of your happiness, basically. The fourth immeasurable thought, impartiality, means that you dedicate loving-kindness and compassion to everyone, equally.

The second aspect of the Mahayana path is meditation. In the practice of the bodhisattva path, the main body of the practice can vary, depending on the individual's particular quality and weakness. In general, the practice of the buddha-dharma is to clarify and develop one's weakness, so that the weakness itself then becomes the enlightened quality. Therefore, the practice is suited to the individual. However, at this time I will briefly describe a short meditation of the bodhisattva path. It is divided into two categories: relative bodhichitta and ultimate bodhichitta.

The practice includes sitting meditation, which is one example of relative bodhichitta practice. When we meditate, body posture is important. This is not only true for practitioners from Eastern cultures. Whether human beings are American or Tibetan doesn't matter: body is body, mind is mind. The correct way of sitting makes it possible to concentrate, because body and mind have a strong connection. Therefore, the straight back, the crossed leg, the hands together, the relaxed shoulders, and the position of the throat, tongue, and teeth are all very important. With the proper body posture, we do shamatha meditation, which pacifies the confused mind. It is the same if you are spinning around in a room: You won't be able to see what is on the walls or on the floor. But if you look around slowly, you will be able to see everything. When the body is well-grounded and pacified, you are able to communicate with the essence of mind more directly.

Having pacified the mind, we take refuge and arouse bodhichitta. Then we do bodhisattva practice, such as tonglen, which means "giving and taking." With the outbreath we breathe out all our goodness and wisdom, which we share with everyone. Then we breathe in negativity and neurosis, which we take away from others and into ourselves. This is done step by step. First we give and take using our mother as the object—someone who is very close to us and is a part of us. Then we take another step and do the same for our closest friend. When we are able to do so for that person, we move on to someone whom we don't feel very good about. And next we do it for our enemy. When we are able to do tonglen for our most hated enemy, then we are able to do it for all sentient beings. We practice this way until we are able to really mean it. At first we may just try to do it and try to mean it, but gradually we are able to really do it. So this is another relative bodhichitta practice. Ultimately, there is no one to give anything to, and there is nothing to take away. But relatively, there is indeed suffering and those who suffer. Therefore, this is relative practice.

Next we move on to ultimate bodhichitta practice. One looks into the outer world and sees the colors, the people, the elements, and so on and, experiencing them, one sees their reality, which is interdependence. There isn't any reality in anything, beyond its relative and interdependent existence. Having seen this, one looks back to one's own mind. Who sees? Who experiences the world? Who thinks that everything is only interdependent? Who is this? There is no one. One's mind has no color, it has no weight, it has no size, it has no shape. There isn't any solid existence in the mind. Seeing this to be so is to see the emptiness of the mind. Then there is one final step, which is to see that even this realization is empty. Even this is nothing. But still, there is clarity, which is the quality of wisdom. The ultimate is free of solid existence, is emptiness, and yet it isn't just like an empty pot: It has a clear quality.

Clarity and emptiness are inseparable. This union is the nature of mind. With this understanding, one meditates and tries to remain in this nature for as long as possible. When thoughts come, we let them come: good thoughts, bad thoughts, it doesn't matter. If we try to stop them, we create unnecessary effort and more thoughts. If we follow them, our thoughts will lead us forever. So we let them come, and we let them go. At the end of this meditation on ultimate bodhichitta, we dedicate the merit of our practice to the benefit of all beings.

Dedication is one of the most important aspects of bodhisattva practice. Practically, in one lifetime, with this physical body, physical speech, and confused mind, what one person can accomplish is so little—*so* little. But if we have pure intention and pure dedication, we can accomplish everything. When we dedicate the merit of our practice impartially to all sentient beings, without expectation of anything in return, the benefit will be limitless. So we have the preparation for practice, which is taking refuge and rousing bodhichitta; then we have the main practice, which is the practice of relative and ultimate bodhichitta; and finally there is the conclusion, which is the dedication of merit.

Meditation is the concentration and dedication of one's body, speech, and mind according to the view of refuge and bodhichitta. For that particular time we are not doing anything except what we are doing. That is meditation. But if our practice stops there, we will not experience the total benefit of meditation. We have to apply the view of meditation to action in everyday life. Profound action is the third aspect of the Mahayana path. All positive or "right" actions on the bodhisattva path are abbreviated into six aspects, known as the six paramitas. The first is generosity. In the Mahayana sense, generosity doesn't only mean that one should give away material wealth. There is also the generosity of protecting others from fear and of giving one's understanding and knowledge. To be a guide for others and to offer one's wisdom is profound generosity. Similarly, morality, the second paramita, is more than simply refraining from negative actions. One also does one's best to be useful and to accomplish meaningful things. The best and ultimate aspect of morality is that which benefits others. And when we practice the third paramita of patience, we are patient with negativity as well as with positive states of mind. If we are overwhelmed by our happiness, that is lack of patience. Fourthly we practice diligence not only in performing beneficial actions, but also in abandoning that which is meaningless. The best diligence is unchanging. Because we have complete understanding, our faith and trust are unchanging and our diligence is like armor. The fifth paramita, meditation, means that in every single action, in every moment, we always have the presence of our motivation and meditation. And finally there is wisdom, which is the wisdom of what actually is. It is the realization of the essence, which is the ultimate wisdom. In this way, all positive and meaningful actions are included in the six paramitas.

The paramitas are more than just a relative approach. We practice the patience paramita until we attain the realization of nonduality through that practice. First we learn to be patient with our parents, then with our friends, then with someone we don't care about, and finally with someone who is evil. We also develop patience in different kinds of situations. For example, sometimes we experience positive actions with positive motivation. Many people lose their patience when someone treats them well, because they feel overwhelmed by that person. But that is not being patient. Then we experience negative actions with positive motivation. For example, teachers and parents punish children when they do something wrong. The action seems negative, and it hurts, but the motivation is pure. Thirdly, there are positive actions with negative motivation. This hurts us the most. In Tibet, we have a saying: "He hides a sharp rock inside a snowball." When such a person throws a snowball, he is smiling, and it seems to be a friendly action, but really he is intending to hurt us. And so we must learn to have patience for that kind of very nasty experience. When we are able to do that, we develop patience for negative actions with negative motivation. Then we are able to have patience with all sentient beings. Having practiced in that way, we are now ready to overcome the final obstacle, which is duality. One stops seeing oneself as a person who is being patient and others as the object of patience. One also becomes free from the action of patience itself. At that level, one achieves the paramita of patience.

This has been a brief explanation of how the view, meditation, and action of the bodhisattva path work together. In this way we are able to develop ultimate bodhichitta through the methods and practice of relative bodhichitta.

Ego's Unmasking

Loppön Lodrö Dorje

Vajrayana Buddhism originally developed in India. After Shakyamuni Buddha presented the basic teachings in the sixth century B.C., the early sangha, or community, gradually shaped these teachings into a

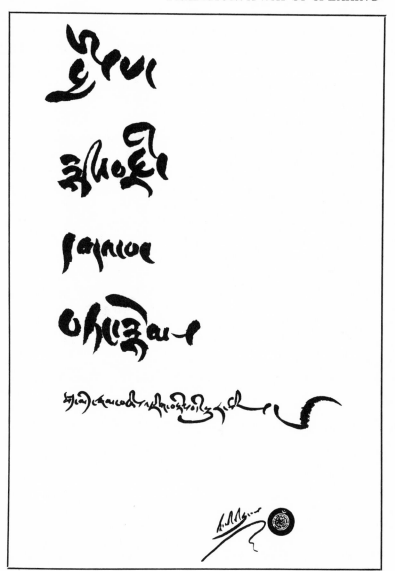

THE FOUR IMMEASURABLE THOUGHTS

This Tibetan calligraphy by His Eminence the Tai Situpa Rinpoche reads:
Loving-Kindness, Compassion, Joy, Impartiality: May these four bring peace
to the world.
Below, on the right, is the signature and personal seal of Tai Situpa.

monastic training. By the second century A.D., the Mahayana school had shifted the emphasis of that training from self-liberation to the principle of compassion and the need to relate more actively to the lay population. Parallel to the evolution of Christian monasteries in tenth-century Western Europe, the Mahayana monasteries became elaborate monastic universities, combining spiritual training with secular culture. Meanwhile, outside the monasteries, a tradition of practicing yogins and siddhas was being maintained through oral transmission from teacher to disciple. In the last period of Indian Buddhism, before it was destroyed by the Muslims in the twelfth century, a style of meditative training known as tantra, or Vajrayana, was being transmitted through lineages which existed both inside and outside the monasteries. Through various guru-disciple relationships, Mahayana and Vajrayana Buddhist teachings were taken to Tibet, where they were preserved until the Chinese takeover of Tibet in 1959. Recently, these teachings have been brought to the West by Tibetan masters. For example, His Eminence Tai Situ Rinpoche and the Venerable Chögyam Trungpa Rinpoche are both lineage holders of the Kagyu school of Tibetan Buddhism.

What kinds of personal motivation bring us to a path of contemplative practice? Why are we interested in spirituality at all? From A Buddhist perspective, the motivation comes from an awareness of dukkha, or suffering. The open, self-existing background of our existence—the background out of which our thoughts and self-identity arise—is energetic, free from ignorance, and free from clinging of any kind. In other words, it has no reference point. Because it is without a handhold, the first moment of self-consciousness or duality is accompanied by panic. Bewilderment immediately follows panic, and this leads to confusion and pain. Suffering begins with a vague sense of "I" and "other," and with the question "Who am I?" Try saying "I" to yourself. There is an echo of definiteness and importance. Mind then freezes its projection of the world into "other": into a tangible form or emotion that will hold still. Therefore we can say, "I am." "I am embarrassed." We don't just say "embarrassed." Or if I say, "I am happy, I won the race," there may be a temporary modesty when someone congratulates me, but I know who won. *I* won, because *I* trained so hard, and because *I* am such a disciplined athlete. Or if someone says, "I hate Tom," that "I" is dense and full of pride; it stands on a mountain of justification. Tom is "over there," and Tom is definitely unpleasant, unworkable, and irritating: "I can't even stand to see him again." "I" is solidified, "Tom" is solidified, and the double-freeze process of ego is thus complete. In Buddhist language, this entire process of creation is called "ego." Ego is two-fold frozenness. There is the frozenness of "this," which we refer to as "I" or "me" or "Tom Jones," and there is the frozenness of "that," which is other-than-me, or the object of experience.

If we ever look closely, it is completely questionable as to who created what in the first place. It is difficult to discover who "I" is, who "other" is, and who is talking to whom. We know that "I" has a name, such as Joe, Fred, Mary, or Tom, and there may temporarily be a definite feeling-tone associated with "I," such as depression or elation. There is a story-line about where and when "I" was born, where and how "I" grew up, and so on. Similarly, the "other" may have a tendency to be always lovable and wonderful, or always threatening, depending on one's habitual tendencies of projection. Nevertheless, both "I" and "other" are somewhat dubious. What is more, we are generally so involved in projection that it is difficult even to have ordinary, decent relationships. This process of ego also obscures any sense of intrinsic sacredness and synchronicity with the world. Instead, ego manifests as confusion, alienation, and blindedness.

According to the meditative tradition of Tibetan Buddhism, there are three stages of training for overcoming the obstacles of ego. Each of these stages embodies a general principle of how human beings can train in a spiritual discipline. The first is the narrow way of self-liberation, sometimes called the Hinayana; the second is the open way of working with all sentient beings, or Mahayana; and the third is the way of devotion and appreciating sacredness, or Vajrayana. These three are sequential, so that in order to reach the last discipline, which is the most free of form and technique and also the most demanding, the practitioner must first establish the preparatory ground.

The narrow way of self-liberation is not exactly narrow in the sense of narrow- or closed-minded; it is narrow in the sense of getting down to business, without any sidetracks. The fundamental outlook is that it is necessary to relate with oneself before looking any further. At this level, the spiritual teacher has the role of elder or preceptor. He is the father figure who helps us by giving us good, practical advice. Even if we believe that the teacher or spiritual lineage could confer blessings which would help us in our spiritual quest, we still need to begin by examining the state of mind of the potential recipient of such blessings. Who is open enough to receive the blessings of the lineage? Who is able to contain that? If there is no individual training, trying to avail oneself of sacredness is like putting a baby in the middle of a mansion. There might be automatic television sets and automatic food service available, but the baby doesn't even know how to move his arms and legs yet. So there is a need to begin by understanding ourselves through the mindfulness-awareness training of shamatha-vipashyana meditation. This leads, on the one hand, to an understanding of one's karmic problems and confusions: emotional up- heavals, discursive thoughts, and all varieties of alienation. We discover how we are not friends with ourselves, and how we are not friends with others. We discover the whole cemetery ground of our lives, including all our hidden corpses and skeletons. On the other hand, we also discover our inherent strengths.

In shamatha-vipashyana meditation, particularly as it is practiced in the Kagyu school, the emphasis is on letting the mind settle to its natural state of wakefulness. The practitioner sits upright and relaxed, which naturally brings a feeling of being dignified and alert, as when you are well-seated on a horse. The legs are loosely folded, the hands are on the knees, and the eyes are open. The breathing is also natural and relaxed. One places one's attention on the outbreath. As thoughts arise they are simply acknowledged, and then the attention returns to the outbreath. The psychological attitude is one of attentiveness combined with open- ness or outwardness. The shamatha, or mindfulness, aspect of the prac- tice is the moment-to-moment acknowledgement of one's experience. Every time you realize you are caught up in a fantasy, you mentally label your thoughts "thinking" and then return to the breath. This process cul- tivates a sense of familiarity and relationship with one's discursive thoughts and emotions. In time, this bare attention to thoughts naturally begins to expand and to include vipashyana, or awareness, both in terms of the sensory and psychological environments. A breeze is coming through the window. A car passes by. Sunlight fills the room. You also begin to see all of your emotional cycles, thought patterns, and the flux of changing qualities of mind.

The action connected with this stage of training is renunciation. In this case, renunciation does not involve an aggressive rejection of the world; it means that you are willing to be simple in your life. There is a willingness to be content with little and a willingness to be alone. When we practice meditation, there is no one there to have a conversation with; nor do we avoid the feeling of psychological aloneness by opening a book or turning on the television. In Buddhist training we don't even have recourse to sharing our thoughts with God. We are simply alone. When we renounce the echo of self-confirmation, we are brought into immediate contact with our experience. Beyond formal meditation, renunciation means that we don't create pollution: we don't put our demands onto other people and our environment, and when our expectations are not met, we don't respond with resentment.

As a result of this first stage of training, we develop familiarity with our particular habitual patterns. Out of that comes acceptance and friendship toward our hangups, so that the ongoing struggle with oneself lightens up and begins to dissolve. The question of "Who am I?" becomes more relaxed. It is an open question. We begin to have trust in simply being, and we have a sense of uncertainty at the same time. The "I" of "I am" has begun to soften, and this then allows the "am" or "other" to unfreeze as well. We could just sit and appreciate the breeze and the brocades, the sound of birds, and the smell of rain.

The next stage is the Mahayana, the way of great vision and great action. Because of the openness and relaxation that has already developed, we experience that other people are full of goodness and genuine motivation, and we also see their suffering. Everywhere we look, in ourselves and in others, we see a potential openness and we also see the pervasive struggle to hold on to a tunnel-like vision of the world. We see people trying to love each other, or trying to hate each other, and we see that neither of those ever turns out to be quite satisfactory. The tenderness that arises from simultaneously appreciating people's good intentions and the pain of their suffering is technically known as karuna in Sanskrit, which we translate as "compassion." It is also described as a glimpse of universal buddha-nature. In this case, the buddha-nature that exists in oneself exists in the whole environment. We can no longer completely separate ourselves from others. The teacher's role at this stage becomes much more interactive and communicative. He is more inquisitive about you as a human being, beyond your religious concerns. You may ask him a spiritual question and receive the response, "How did you like the fish we had for breakfast?" He presents a mirror which reflects your neurosis, and he also leaves enormous space for your buddha instinct to emerge. He is interested in having a personal relationship with you.

Meditation training at this stage involves mindfulness and awareness, as before. However, there is now an added element. During the previous stage we may have developed a tendency to settle into the peaceful and harmonious aspect of meditation practice. Having relaxed our initial struggle, we began to feel good. But now, stepping out into the world, we discover that the streets are loud and grimy. A bus roars past and leaves a trail of diesel fumes. We watch people walk down the street, and we vividly see the pain and aggression on their faces and in the way they walk. It is all somewhat shocking and unappealing, perhaps even frightening. Opening up one's awareness brings about paranoia, along with compassion. It brings about a sense of contrast. The practice that specifically works with that contrast is *tonglen,* or "exchanging oneself for others." Any unpleasant experience that others present to us is deliberately accepted and shared. We allow anything that might potentially freak us out to come to us. Someone may say "I love you" or "I hate you." In either case, paranoia tends to arise. Nevertheless, whatever it is, we accept it, and then we make the psychological gesture of giving back our strength, generosity, and sanity.

At this stage, the path is a process of overcoming paranoia and communicating with others. In practical terms, this includes taking a commitment to work with people. We develop what is known as "skillful means": the intuitive ability to encourage other people's sanity and the means to accomplish whatever needs to be accomplished. In life situations, we learn to let go of the tendency to accept and reject, so that we view our home life, our work environment, and our leisure activities as viable practice situations. Nothing is unworkable. We could practice in any environment, because the essence of practice is to acknowledge and accept the confusion and chaos that is present, and to then offer wakefulness to others. Through our training we break down territorial boundaries between "I" and "other," pleasant and unpleasant, sacred and profane.

The third stage, the Vajrayana, proclaims that buddha-nature or wakefulness is powerful, and that it is more fundamental than confusion. Potential enlightenment is an immediate reality. A glimpse of enlightened mind can be experienced, and practice can then proceed on that basis. The practitioner's view associated with this style of training is called "sacred outlook." Things as they are, without ego, are recognized as vivid and full of energy, and the sense perceptions are bright. The phenomenal world itself is brilliant and impressive. Realizing this, a natural attitude of respect toward the ordinary world grows into a pervasive experience of sacredness. We still practice mindfulness and awareness, basically speaking. However, one's awareness begins to include a lot of energy, compassion, brilliance, and devotion. These qualities arise out of the emptiness or egolessness developed in the previous stages. Devotion in this case is the ability to tune in to the mind of the guru and the mind of the lineage. The guru is immersed in sacredness, and he is therefore one's link to that awareness. Because of the preliminary training of mindfulness and awareness, and because of the personal experience of the trustworthiness of the path, a natural surrendering and devotion take place. It is not that we think we are going to be saved, but we realize that, through devotion, ego is constantly unmasked and exposed, so that we are able to communicate with the world and further realize things as they are. So devotion to the guru is not exactly a personal, chummy issue. At the same time, it *is* important that it is based on a human rather than abstract relationship. For us as students, this makes the relationship earthbound, literal, and ordinary: we are not floating in the stratosphere of our imagination. The teacher, on the other hand, knows all of our tricks and can do whatever is necessary to awaken us—which at different times may involve confirming, devastating, or ignoring us.

On the basis of the intimacy of the relationship, the guru empowers the student to do particular meditation practices. These can be of two kinds: those without form and those with form. Shamatha-vipashyana meditation is a practice without form. Practices with form, which are still based on the same perspective of the emptiness of self and other, include mantra recitation, liturgical chanting, and visualizations of various kinds. Visualization of a particular deity, such as Avalokiteshvara (the deity of compassion) or Manjushri (the deity of wisdom), cultivates an understanding of how to identify with a particular aspect of enlightened mind. At the end of each practice session, the visualization is dissolved and the practitioner concludes with formless awareness practice.

Warriorship and celebration are two metaphors used to describe the Vajrayana path. When awareness and sanity become strong and diamond-like, there is a confidence that confusion and chaos could be overcome with warrior-like daring and a fearless willingness to communicate. Celebration, on the other hand, comes from an immense appreciation of the sacredness of the world: appreciation of the wetness of the rain, the taste of food, and the vastness of the blue sky. One appreciates one's fellow human beings, and one's teacher in particular. There is even appreciation of seeming negativities and confused emotions. Previously there may have been a tendency to feel that one's depression and resentment were not sacred, but at this stage we are able to include those as part of the celebration as well. The path becomes a continual unmasking process—an ongoing celebration into nakedness.

Poem

The following stanzas are from a song, or doha, composed by a lineage holder of the Kagyu school of Tibetan Vajrayana Buddhism. A doha is a traditional form of expressing spontaneous realization and/or devotion, and it is a vehicle for transmitting the Vajrayana teachings from guru to disciple. A collection of such songs, called The Rain of Wisdom, *is recited as a group liturgical practice on special occasions.*

In this doha, Khakhyap Dorje (1871-1922) is supplicating his guru, Lodro Thaye. He is also expressing his own insight into the futility of samsara (a life based on clinging, hope and fear) and admonishing himself to practice the guru's instructions wholeheartedly. The second to last stanza contains the pith instruction on the nature of the liberated state, where the vivid, experiential world of relative reality ("appearance") and the transcendent world of absolute reality ("emptiness") are recognized as inseparable.

The Song of Devotion and Longing

Kye la!
Jetsun, you are the refuge, the embodiment of all the
    buddhas.
Although you attained enlightenment innumerable
    lives ago,

In order to guide those wandering below in samsara
You have been kind enough to return in human form.
Father guru, great treasure of kindness, please think of
  me.
Grant your blessings so that my being may be mixed
  with the dharma.

In this lowest of the low times, when the five
  corruptions are rampant:
Life is brief like a flash of lightning in the sky.
Wealth is impermanent like dew on the grass.
A friend who loves you in the morning hates you by
  the evening.
All these are like last night's dream.
In general, everything is impermanent, moving and
  changing.
Now, cast away all desires of fixation on permanence.
Father guru, please think of me and look upon me with
  kindness.

. . . .

When the enemy greatly famed as the Lord of Death
  approaches,
It will be too late for regrets.
From the bed of this dharma person will come an
  ordinary corpse.
All men, high and low, will be disgusted and deride
  me.
The time will come when I will wander aimlessly in
  samsara.
Think of this and sharpen your intelligence.
See all phenomenal appearance as the play of the guru.
Dissolve this mind into the mind of the lord.
Supplicate from within this inseparability.
May the clear sounds of this song of devotion and
  longing
Encourage the kindness of this infallible refuge.
It is time to cultivate the essence of this mind.

Overwhelmed, I supplicate from my heart.
Father, please look on me with kindness and grant
  your blessings.

. . . .

In general, without pursuing the illusion of whatever
  arises,
Rest within the union of appearance and emptiness.
See the essence which is groundless and rootless.
The seer and the seen are both empty.
In the midst of their nondual union
Lies the great spectacle of the primordial natural state.
The face of the guru of my mind is seen
And I am certain to hold the royal seat of great bliss.
Therefore, you faithless one with a hard heart,
Supplicate continually without distraction,
And cast away unnecessary activities.
Father, please know me; knower of the three times,
  know me.
Trusting that you know best whatever you do,
With a song of longing through the six periods of day
  and night,
Your son supplicates with one-pointed longing.
Father, please look on me with kindness and grant
  your blessings.

Unfabricated devotion blazes.
Please raise the wisdom of the simultaneity of liberation
  and realization.
May auspicious coincidence come together for the
  spontaneous benefit of beings.
Lord, please make me inseparable from you.[6]

                    KHAKHYAP DORJE, THE XVTH KARMAPA

Chapter 2: Notes
1. Epigraph: *Zen Mind, Beginner's Mind,* p. 127.
2. "Do not be led by reports, or tradition, or hearsay. Be not led by the authority of religious

texts, nor by mere logic or inference, nor by considering appearances, nor by the delight in speculative opinions, nor by seeming possibilities, nor by the idea: 'this is our teacher.' But, O Kalamas, when you know for yourselves that certain things are unwholesome and wrong, and bad, then give them up. . . . And when you know for yourselves that certain things are wholesome and good, then accept them and follow them." (from the *Anguttara-nikaya*, ed. Devamitta Thera. Quoted in Walpola Rahula, *What the Buddha Taught*, p. 3.)

3. *Vipassana* ("insight meditation") is Pali, the language most commonly used by the Theravada school of Buddhism. The Mahayana and Vajrayana schools generally use Sanskrit (as well as native) terminology. The Sanskrit counterpart of *vipassana* is *vipashyana*.

4. "Broad way" or "great way" is a literal translation of *Mahayana*, the name of the school of Buddhism which includes Zen.

5. An example of the refuge vow liturgy was shown earlier in this chapter under the title "The Three Refuges."

6. Translated by the Nalanda Translation Committee under the direction of the Venerable Chögyam Trungpa, Rinpoche. (c) Chögyam Trungpa. Reprinted from *The Rain of Wisdom* by arrangement with Shambhala Publications, Inc., 314 Dartmouth Street, Boston, Massachusetts 02116.

3

Renewal, Transmission, and Change

We do not speak today of the *reform* of religious life but rather of its *renewal*. Renewal is something deeper, more living and more total than reform. Reform was proper to the needs of the Church at the time of the Council of Trent, when the whole structure of religious life had collapsed, even though there was still a great deal of vitality among religious. Today the structure and the organization are firm and intact: what is lacking is a deep and fruitful understanding of the real meaning of religious life.[1]

THOMAS MERTON

Interpreting Zen in an American setting was a lot easier than I had expected. Briefly, it boiled down to not *trying* to change anything whatsoever; when changes occurred, they did so very gradually of their own accord and were only in the *outside* forms.[2]

JIYU KENNETT

98

Birthright

Judith Lief

This meeting of Christianity and Buddhism is taking place in the context of a highly secularized world, in which the qualities of sacredness and human dignity have generally become submerged. In our present society there doesn't seem to be a common inspiration running through people's bloodstreams, the way there has been at certain times and in certain places on this earth. This is a period of upheaval, of widespread weakening of traditional values, of cynicism and despair.

Within such a cultural atmosphere, it seems crucial that those people who share a concern for the transcendent element of life band together in order to reignite the spark of sacredness. That spark is what will burn the solidity and angularity of aggressiveness in this world and allow people to express the full humanity which is their birthright.

Doctrine Versus Experience

Thomas Keating O.C.S.O.
Joseph Goldstein
Eido Tai Shimano Roshi
Thomas Hopko
Reginald Ray

FATHER KEATING: It is my understanding that doctrine is extremely important for cultivating spiritual experience, and experience is extremely important for vivifying doctrine. These two are a married couple that should never be divorced. For when doctrine is shunned, spirituality either becomes confused with magic or a crutch which is leaned on too heavily. On the other hand, without experience doctrine becomes as dry as dust: it is no more than a series of rational concepts. So there must be an ongoing, living interaction between spiritual practice and its conceptual background.

Until recently, mysticism was looked down upon in the Western world, and many people who experienced touches of the Absolute simply avoided telling anyone, out of fear that their friends would think them crazy. That was probably not an idle fear. We could probably even find in some psychiatric hospitals people who were thought to have had psychotic episodes, which were actually powerful mystical experiences that were incomprehensible to them. Because they could not conceptualize and express their experiences to themselves, they believed they were going mad. Some years ago, a young man arrived at Saint Joseph's Abbey in a state of great agitation. He had had a strong experience of the transcendent, but he had no conceptual apparatus to understand this experience. It contradicted everything he was prepared to understand about his relationship to God. He came looking for someone who could tell him whether or not he was losing his mind. All that was wrong with him was that he didn't know how to express his transcendent experience to himself. Spiritual practice must have an adequate conceptual background to support it, whether that support comes from a master, suitable literature, or a community of people who have some familiarity with the mountains and valleys along the way.

JOSEPH GOLDSTEIN: I would agree, Father Keating, that both doctrine and experience are necessary, but I think that the heart of wisdom is always one's practice, while doctrine always comes to us as second-hand knowledge. Spiritual discipline is what actually effects the transformation of mind and allows the opening to the absolute to take place. At the same time, without study and without scripture, we could become narrow in our practice. One of the most inspiring aspects of dharma, or truth, is the incredible richness of its manifestations, and if we limit ourselves to practice alone we can easily become attached to our particular method or lineage. But unless doctrine is studied skillfully, it can mislead us into thinking we know something, and that is a deadly state of mind. There is a story that illustrates this, which comes from Eastern Europe. It is about an old Hassid rabbi who would cross the village square every morning on his way to the temple to pray. One morning, a large Cossack soldier, who happened to be in a vile mood, accosted him, saying, "Hey Rebby, where are you going?"

And the rabbi said, "I don't know."

This infuriated the Cossack. "What do you mean, you don't know? Every morning for twenty-five years you've crossed the village square and gone to the temple to pray. Don't fool with me. Who are you, telling me you don't know?"

He grabbed the old rabbi by the coat and dragged him off to jail. Just as he was about to push him into the cell, the rabbi turned to him, saying, "You see, I didn't know." (Laughter.) We really don't know. But if we practice in a deep and transforming way we can study while still keeping the mind open, and having what is known in the Zen tradition as "don't-know mind."

This realization came home to me forcibly one summer when I was teaching at Naropa Institute. I had just returned from India, where I had been intensively involved in my practice and study of Theravada Buddhism. This tradition has an extremely consistent and complex set of scriptures involving the psychological analysis of mind, all of which had always seemed absolutely valid to me in terms of my experience. After I had been in Boulder for a few weeks, I saw a poster announcing a talk by one of the great teachers of the Nyingma sect of Tibetan Buddhism, Dudjom Rinpoche. The poster described him as the incarnation of Shariputra, who was one of the chief disciples of the Buddha. From the point of view of the Theravada teachings, when a being becomes fully enlightened there is no longer rebirth, so that would make this claim impossible, because Shariputra had achieved enlightenment. At the same time, Dudjom Rinpoche is also a great enlightened master; he wouldn't lie. (Laughter.) And so I experienced my own framework of understanding, which was so fresh and strong in my mind, coming into contact with this totally contradictory assertion. It was a wonderful lesson, because in the end I realized that I didn't have a clue whether Dudjom

Rinpoche was the incarnation of Shariputra or not.

When it is rightly understood, doctrine itself is practice. During the time of the Buddha, there were people who became enlightened simply by listening to his teachings. Words are pointers to the truth—they are like fingers pointing to the moon. If we get too involved in a study of the fingers, we are missing the point. But if we can listen with a totally open and receptive mind, it is possible, even in hearing a single word, to open in the deepest way. As you sit now, listening to these words, try to listen without thinking about what is being said: try actually doing what is being said. Just let the words enter the mind. Then doctrine becomes practice. You will find that they are not separate.

EIDO ROSHI: I am interested in this question of doctrine and experience. Which comes first? For those of us who are practicing the buddha-dharma in twentieth-century America, there is already a Buddhist doctrine for us to follow. But if we think about Shakyamuni Buddha's case, before his great enlightenment there was no Buddhism as such. Through his spiritual experiences he formed or spelled out the Buddhist doctrine for his students to follow. It was their task to believe, to understand, to practice, to realize, and to integrate what was given to them by the Buddha. These five steps are also the way for us in America to follow the buddha-dharma. Therefore I would like to say a few words about them. Some of you may say that this approach is too well-organized, but this is not my invention; I was taught this way.

First of all, there is a difference between compulsory belief and optional belief. Perhaps this is the same difference that exists between dogma and doctrine. In Buddhism, belief is always optional. Perhaps we can't believe that we could be a Buddha, that we have buddha-nature—or rather, that we are buddha-nature itself. So when we hear the statement that everyone has buddha-nature, this leads us to ask, "What does it mean? What is all this business?" When we question like this, in time we begin to understand. Then we can start to practice. Without practice we have nothing. I must say this, no matter how often people say I am stubborn for giving practice so much emphasis. When there is practice, then realization will take place.

I was recently at Rocky Mountain Dharma Center, and one evening I was asked to give an extemporaneous talk. I hadn't prepared anything, but when I went into the shrine room, where a number of dharma students had been doing intensive meditation practice, I sensed a wonderful, lucid atmosphere. So the atmosphere talked through my tongue as follows: You are here because of at least two expectations. The first is that you will be free from anxieties, and the second is that, when you achieve that, you will be able to stay in that state of mind forever. The first expectation is possible to achieve, but the second is not. If you know that, then you can expedite your first expectation. When we see a river we normally think that it is a river as such, and the water moves within it. But that is not true. It is because the water moves that we call it "river." Practice is like a river. It is really nothing, of itself.

The final step is integration, which I don't have to tell you much about. In the Zen tradition it is said that if you utter the word "buddha," wash your mouth; if you utter the word "enlightenment," wipe your lips. And if you speak about doctrine, you are not a good Zen teacher. There was a Zen master in China who was aware that it is impossible to convey the collected doctrine in a verbal way, so he always kept a stick with him. Whenever a student came and asked a question such as, "Master, tell me what buddha-dharma is," he just struck the student. One student thought that if he hid the stick, he might receive an answer. So he did this, and then he came to the master and said, "What is the essence of the buddha-dharma?" The master replied, "AH!" (Laughter.) But in my opinion, even to say "Ah" is too much. To give a talk or to participate in a discussion at a conference is even worse. (More laughter. . . .)

FATHER HOPKO: I recently went to a meeting of the Orthodox Theological Society in Athens, Greece, and the first four speakers all said that in Orthodoxy theologia is ultimately the silence of the union . . . but then we all kept on talking.

(Laughter.)

There is a famous saying in the Eastern tradition—probably coming from Evagrius, but usually attributed to Saint Nilus because Evagrius was considered a heretic—that says, "He who truly prays is a theologian, and a theologian is he who truly prays." It is also said that he who cannot be silent should not speak. In the Eastern Church, the words coming out of the silence are traditionally called "anointed words" or "words proper to God." According to Gregory the Theologian of the fourth century, the task of theology is to find words adequate to the mystery. And so I think it would be correct to say that doctrine which is true and right, and which arises out of experience, itself becomes the means for leading people back into the experience.

REGGIE RAY: In the history of Buddhism, many different schools and traditions have arisen out of certain people's conviction that the current teaching was stuck: the doctrine was being overemphasized or had become too far removed from personal experience. For example, the emergence of Mahayana Buddhism in India, around 100 B.C., seems to have been a reaction to the dogmatism and exclusiveness of certain Hinayana schools. Historically, whenever people have started to make the literal word into something real, a movement of divergence or reformation has soon followed. On a smaller scale, I think that every Buddhist teacher also struggles with this as a potential problem in working with his students. Perhaps that is why Eido Roshi continually emphasizes the importance of practice. He and other teachers tend to acknowledge that if we lose the reference point of direct experience, then there is no hope; whereas, if that reference point is constantly being reaffirmed, then we have a basis for correcting the natural tendency to solidify or somehow twist the teachings.

QUESTION (from audience): In the history of Buddhism, have there been practices or teachers that have misguided students and led them into deluded experience? And if so, how is this deviation checked? Is there any safeguard built into the tradition?

JOSEPH GOLDSTEIN: I think the final reference point is summarized by the Buddha's instruction to look to our own minds. If we find that what we are doing is conducive to the growth of love and wisdom, it is skillful and should be cultivated; if it is conducive to the growth of hatred and delusion, it is unskillful and should be abandoned.

FATHER HOPKO: And yet, one of the main reasons that Christians practice obedience to a spiritual director is that we cannot always trust what we think we are doing. I may think I am being kind, when in fact I am being greedy. And Christians often find that they are in disagreement among themselves. For example, there was a propensity among certain people of Jeremiah's time to say, "Thus says the Lord," when it had nothing to do with the Lord. Jeremiah warned, "Do not listen to the words of the prophets who prophesy to you, filling you with vain hopes; they speak visions of their own minds, not from the mouth of the Lord" (Jer. 23:16-17). But in my experience the Buddhists don't encounter the same kind of challenges. From what I have seen here, they always tend to agree, basically speaking. All the Buddhists seem comfortable with each other, whereas, at least in the bigger picture, Christians are not always comfortable with other Christians.

REGGIE RAY: Well, to begin with I think it is important to appreciate the context of this dialogue. It is taking place in the United States, where Christianity is the established, prevalent religious tradition. American Buddhism, on the other hand, is still fresh and young, and in general people who are practicing it are devoted and inspired. They have chosen it out of their own free will. Buddhism in America has its own unique set of problems, which correspond to its present cultural situation, but dogmatism and divisiveness do not tend to be among these. If we were in Southeast Asia, in ancient India, or in Japan, I'm

sure we would find the same kinds of internal conflicts that
Christianity is experiencing in this country.

QUESTION: I suspect that the essential difference between the
Buddhist and Christian attitudes toward reform is this: every
Buddhist is ultimately free to open a new school; so far as I
know, to do so is not in itself heresy. If experience bears out a
new teaching it is recognized as valid. In Christianity, however—
at least in the Roman Catholic Church—the matter is somewhat
more complicated, because of the question of orthodoxy, of
which the magisterium[3] is the criterion and the judge.

QUESTION: I'm an Episcopalian priest, and I sit zazen. I have
encountered times over the past decade or so when I felt that a
certain scripture didn't speak to me at all. But now, some years
later, some new lights have shone on me from different
teachers and from different parts of scripture, and I feel
grateful that I had enough faith in the teachings that I wasn't
able to understand. I would keep coming back to it and fretting
over it, until after a while—and I believe this came partly out of
my sitting—it was illuminated for me. So it seems to me that
faith plays an important role when it comes to doctrines that
one doesn't understand.

JOSEPH GOLDSTEIN: I agree totally. Just to clarify, don't-know
mind doesn't mean you throw something out: don't-know mind
means *open*-minded.

QUESTION: I recently heard a Christian theologian praising the
practice of memorizing a scripture, becoming one with it so
that all one's personal interpretations could be bypassed. In
terms of my Buddhist practice, which includes chanting, this
made sense to me, and I'm wondering if any of the faculty
would like to comment on the value of knowing a text by heart,
as a way of bringing practice and doctrine together.

EIDO ROSHI: When I chant various sutras, either in Chinese or
Japanese, I do not think about the meaning. However, because

of having memorized it, and because of uttering it as single-mindedly as I can in each circumstance, I feel that I am talking to an unknown or unnameable something. During the chanting period, it is as if there is a dialogue going on. For this reason, to memorize, and then to chant the sutra single-mindedly, has more significance than understanding all of its intellectual meanings.

FATHER HOPKO: Yes, I think that this as also an important issue for Christians. Memorization of scripture allows the words to become part of one's own system. As Saint Paul says, "Let the word of Christ dwell in you richly" (Col. 3:16). But one great problem for us is that the scriptures are now translated into so many different versions, especially in the United States. This is a real problem in my church. When people have the same translation all the time, and they memorize it, then they are really able to go beyond the words. But when they have fourteen different translations they end up discussing, interpreting, and deciphering the text, rather than going deeper into the meaning. Particularly in the liturgy, when the Psalms are worded differently every time you hear them, it is almost impossible to let the words become part of your life.

QUESTION (cont.): Do you find the same difference that Eido Roshi mentioned—between the times when you are reciting scripture and the times when you are reflecting on it?

FATHER HOPKO: There is definitely a difference in the Christian tradition between thinking about a text and letting it work its way into your system. One of my teachers said that when we try to meditate on the scripture, most of us do the wrong thing. We ask, "What does this scripture mean for me in my life?" But he said that the real task is just to let the word enter into you, and then when you need it, it will come. Perhaps Father Keating would like to say something on this topic.

FATHER KEATING: The practice of lectio divina, "divine reading," is the very heart of the Cistercian path. One begins by reading a passage from the scriptures, maybe only a few sentences. Then one expresses one's response, either in words or by reflection. This takes place in an atmosphere of silence and solitude, which intensifies the power of the text. Little by little one comes to rest in a single thought or single aspiration suggested by the text. Finally one might rest in a single word. This is what the tradition of the early Christian church meant by "contemplative prayer." It is the loving attention to the Mystery, with a minimal amount of thinking. There is just enough activity to keep the fire of love burning. One rests in the warmth of the fire until it burns down, and then puts on another twig. Thus one gently nurses oneself, so to speak, into deeper and deeper interior silence, until one might move into an even deeper intuition. A door might open inside, and one falls into a moment or two—or longer—of no reflection. Then you come out again. The reading of scripture has always been a part of Christian practice. But what in recent times has been lacking, for various historical reasons, is precisely the most important element, which is the movement into interior silence. Contemplative prayer has been considered appropriate only for cloistered monks and nuns. This kind of misapprehension is what happens when the living tradition is lost.

QUESTION: Father Keating, it seems to me that doctrine in the Buddhist tradition always relates directly to practice, but in the Christian tradition this isn't always the case. As a Roman Catholic, I see the mystical path as only one way within the tradition. Very often doctrine is aligned with what Tessa once termed the "crippling institutionalism," which is also part of this tradition. I often see an unfortunate conflict between the institutionalized doctrine and the mystical path, and I was wondering if you would comment on that observation.

FATHER KEATING: There has been a split between institutional structures and mysticism at certain times in the history of the church. I think it must be said, in all honesty, that unless the contemplative dimension of the Christian life is being preached, the gospel is not being fully proclaimed. This has been a serious problem for Christians in recent centuries. The Protestant Reformation took place at a time when the contemplative tradition had been lost even in monastic circles. Hence the reformers did not have the contemplative tradition to take with them. It is fortunate for us as Christians that the East has preserved its mystical tradition and has even had a renewal of it during the last century. I personally feel that such a renewal is now necessary in the Christian churches.

Living Fire

David Steindl-Rast, O.S.B.
George Timko
Joseph Goldstein

BROTHER DAVID: My greatest concern in these discussions is that from the very beginning we all agree that it is experience that matters. Our discussions will only have meaning if they come out of experience and then return to experience. I am not saying that we should see tradition as something opposed to or totally separate from personal experience. In fact, it is my contention that religious awareness inevitably leads to religion, even if it is one's own private religion. This is because the human mind always responds to such an experience in these three ways: first, intellect inevitably interprets it, and that leads to doctrine. Secondly, the will draws consequences from such an experience, and that leads to morality. And thirdly, we spontaneously celebrate our religious awareness through ritual. Wherever we find religious tradition, we find these three elements: doctrine, morality, and ritual. An image I like to use is that of a volcano. Religious experience is like an eruption of living fire. The lava flows down the side of the mountain until it cools, developing a hard rock-like crust. This is also what happens when experience is replaced with a commentary on the experience. As the crust becomes thicker, you have not only commentaries on the experience, but commentaries on the commentaries, and finally, commentaries on the commentaries of the commentaries. Everything becomes hardened. Doctrine becomes dogmatism; morality becomes legalism; and ritual becomes conditioned action which is empty of meaning. Our great challenge and responsibility is to continually break through this hard crust of religion. Again and again, we need to let the lava, the living fire, flow out.

FATHER TIMKO: I would like to question what we mean by "religious" experience here. Not every experience is valid for establishing a religion. There are individuals who claim to have heard God telling them to perform immoral acts, or to kill people. Certainly these are not examples of "religious" experience. There are fanatic religious groups which have based their philosophy on some kind of alleged communion with God, but which is really no more than emotional experience. The Fathers of the Eastern Orthodox Church say that we must be wary of all empirical experiences of the senses and emotions, because the divine can never be known through such experiences, and because they can lead us to delusion. They can lead us astray and trap us, so that we will never be able to truly transcend ourselves and be touched by the Mystery beyond ourselves. How do we avoid that trap? Very simply, the Fathers say we must begin with self-knowledge, which enables us to mentally perceive the Deity as the Wholly Other. We must watch ourselves and know ourselves so that we may discern between what is of ourselves and what is of God. Otherwise, based on what we believe to be genuine religious experience, we could become self-stylized gurus leading others to our deluded version of the truth.

BROTHER DAVID: I would of course also make a distinction between genuine religious experience, to which I was previously referring, and fake religious experience. Under peer pressure, it is particularly easy to get into faking a religious experience. Naturally you would feel left out if everyone else had it and you didn't. But if that is what we are talking about, then we are already on the wrong ground, and this whole discussion can have no basis. I would just like to say that I would tend to give the benefit of the doubt to those people who have the kind of pentecostal experience to which I think you were referring. I do not see any reason why we should not accept such experiences themselves as genuine. But what often happens is that the interpretation of the experience follows too quickly and is therefore too limited. The experience has been set up in such a way that it is immediately channeled into a very specific conceptual framework.

JOSEPH GOLDSTEIN: I would say that in general what is important is not so much what the experience is, but how we are relating to it. The entire path of meditative practice is one of learning a proper relationship to experience. Focusing or fixating on any particular experience could actually be an obstacle on one's path. In fact, one of the great values of following a genuine tradition is that it will steer us away from this potential trap.

Accumulated Wisdom

Thomas Keating O.C.S.O.

The world religions claim to lead to the source of all that is, which is called such various names as God, Allah, Brahman, the Absolute, and the Great Spirit. Now, in the eyes of many, the religions of the West are failing to provide a way to that source. In addition, the Western value system has brought the superpowers to the point where they are threatening to destroy the entire human race. Rightly or wrongly, many people, both in the West and in the East, look upon the Christian religion as being responsible for this dilemma—a conclusion that creates reservations in the minds of persons who otherwise might have sought the Ultimate Mystery through the Christian faith. At the same time, many Westerners find it difficult to identify with the Eastern religions, simply because of the cultural distance.

Those seekers who end up abandoning all traditional religions are left with a serious question: Is it possible to find unity with the Ultimate Mystery without drawing on the accumulated wisdom of one of the world religions? Without the experience and encouragement of a community rooted in a long tradition of spiritual discipline, how can one avoid needless mistakes and resist the back-sliding of human weakness? It is my hope that a renewal of the world religions and a restatement of their spiritual traditions might enable disillusioned seekers to return to the religion of their youth, so that we could then join together in order to rediscover and cultivate the spiritual practices which will revitalize our respective religions.

Tensions of Change

John Yungblut
Judith Lief
Reginald Ray
Loppön Lodrö Dorje

Thomas Hopko
David Steindl-Rast O.S.B.
Eido Tai Shimano Roshi

JOHN YUNGBLUT: I say this with fear and trembling, because I don't wish to appear out of harmony with my sisters and brothers here, but I do feel it is important to express my concern that the idol in our midst that seems to be crying out to be slain is unchallenged tradition.

One's religion is the last idol, in some sense. I represent the youngest tradition here, in that Quakerism is only 350 years old and is still in its adolescence. But at the time of its founding, George Fox said that we must slay two idols: the Anglican liturgy and the Puritan theology, with its emphasis on depravity. The Quaker tradition has no liturgy except for the handclasp and the silence. Paradoxically, Fox felt that by moving away from the church of his time, he was picking up the original, true tradition of the early church. There really wasn't much of a liturgy in the primitive church. Friends are now divided in some respects, between those who want to keep the practice as it was in seventeenth-century Quakerism, and those who feel that the more relevant tradition is to follow Fox's inclination to be open to the spirit wherever it leads.

From an evolutionary point of view, there is always a certain danger in holding fast to a tradition. The law of evolution is "assimilate or perish," and it seems to me that ideas and doctrines are like living creatures. If they do not adapt creatively to the changing environment, they become extinct. So I think we must recognize the need for traditions to evolve and change as well as to remain constant. I could quote here some pertinent lines from the hymn "Once to Every Man and Nation Comes the Moment to Decide," by James Russell Lowell:

New occasions teach new duties.
Time makes ancient good uncouth.
They must upward then and onward,
Who would keep abreast of truth.

It is not merely ancient *custom* that time erodes, but ancient *good*. What was helpful and good at one time may need revision at a later time, when seen in new perspectives.

JUDY LIEF: John, I think what you say speaks to the difference between living tradition and dead tradition. There is tradition that awakens, and there is tradition that has no real purpose beyond self-perpetuation. Obviously, the question is, what determines the difference?

JOHN YUNGBLUT: From time to time all traditions fail or seem inadequate. These are the times, to borrow a phrase from Bernstein's Mass, "When my spirit falters on decaying altars, And my illusions fail." A new leader then emerges in order to reawaken the living quality of the original spirit and to charismatically convey that to others. A period of trial and error and an adjustment, according to the new revelation, then follows.

BROTHER DAVID: I'm wondering what change a Quaker might initiate that would require you to say to him, "Well, this may be your own personal view of the needs of the future, but it has nothing to do with the heritage and development of the Society of Friends." In any impulse toward reform, what would have to be retained so that you would still feel that continuity with the past had been maintained? Is that even a relevant question for you?

JOHN YUNGBLUT: I think there are two central elements of Quakerism that must remain constant in order to protect the tradition's wellsprings of vitality. These are the Meeting for Worship, that is, some form of waiting upon the Lord in silence with the gathered company, on the one hand, and the testimonies that express concern for world peace on the other hand.

In general, I feel the secret is to remain rooted and grounded in the past, with a clear sense of continuity, while being open to the future and ready to evolve. For many Christians, the Biblical injunctions, as they have been traditionally interpreted, no longer speak with authority. From my own perspective, what does speak with authority are values that are now coming out of the process of evolution itself. As Thomas Berry, a student of Teilhard de Chardin, points out, humanity is "rooted in the spirituality of the earth." Because of this, a new ethic can be worked out as long as there is a willingness to be open to guidance. For example, many passages in the Bible condemn homosexuality. Do we really want to stay with that judgement or are we prepared to re-examine the tradition in the light of new understandings gained through the evolution of depth psychology?

BROTHER DAVID: If I understand you correctly, what you are proposing is not really so different from what we all could agree with, except perhaps for your particular stress on openness toward the future. It certainly seems that we share the feeling that it is important to be rooted in tradition, which, I would add, is very different from being *stuck* in tradition.

When spring comes, you can always tell the difference between a branch that has been stuck in the ground and one that is actually rooted. Only the rooted branch will bring forth new leaves. These will be similar to last year's leaves, but they will also be new.

JOHN YUNGBLUT: Yes. In terms of doctrine, there is one Quaker dogma, and only one, and that is the conviction that God is in everyone. To me, this assertion calls for radical re-visioning, re-imaging, and re-imagining of the entire myth of Christ. I believe there should be an opening toward this new perspective, which will also require certain changes and a readiness within the entire Christian tradition to grow and develop.

REGGIE RAY: John, I am intrigued by the term "ethical mysticism," which I understood from your earlier presentation to be an expression of the most central aspects of your tradition. I gather that the ethical aspect of ethical mysticism would involve relating to the rest of the world, and the mystical aspect would be the silence. Interestingly, in Tibetan Mahayana Buddhism there is a similar two-sided doctrine: it is said that the practitioner must join upaya and prajna. Upaya is skillful and helpful action in the world, and prajna is the wisdom inherent in unconditioned silence. Both are necessary, and in fact one implies the other. Perhaps we could even generalize by saying that these two must be upheld in some form by any tradition; otherwise the tradition has lost its foundation. Certainly this would be true of Buddhism.

JOHN YUNGBLUT: I think that is a very good way of expressing what I see to be the deepest bond between Buddhism and Quakerism. From what I have studied, Buddhism is also a life-affirming, ethical mysticism, and I accept what you are saying as an accurate comparison.

FATHER HOPKO: I have noticed that, when discussing doctrinal issues, Buddhists sometimes refer to the words of the Buddha as being authoritative. Would the Buddhists say that the Buddha is an important factor in ensuring continuity in Buddhism?

LODRÖ DORJE: There are different interpretations of the Buddha. It seems to me that there are three avenues through which any tradition is carried on. One is the formal aspect, such as the scriptures, the liturgy, the ethical code, and so on; second is the lineage of teachers, such as the gurus of the various Buddhist lineages; and third is the spiritual experience itself. All three could be important reference points for discussing continuity. When we emphasize the scriptural tradition, Shakyamuni Buddha is primarily revered as the one who taught the basic doctrine, which was later written down in the form of sutras. From the point of view of the personal relationship with a teacher, the lineage transmission is traced from one's own guru back through a succession of gurus and disciples to Shakyamuni Buddha himself. In that case it is acknowledged that the mind of the teacher *is* the mind of a buddha, and the role of the historical Buddha isn't as central. And from the point of view of personal realization, the notion of universal buddha-nature plays an important role. In that case, the buddha is a reminder or symbol of each person's potential enlightenment.

REGGIE RAY: It is interesting that in the early Buddhist tradition, the primary concern was the scriptural transmission of the Buddha's words. Around 100 B.C., certain people began to express the feeling that the rigidity of continuing to hold to the literal word would hurt the tradition. Some of these people claimed to have experienced the mind of buddha, and they began to reassert that the Buddha was an embodiment of enlightenment as well as a historical human being. Enlightenment itself has no history; it has no time or place. These people began to write the Mahayana sutras, which were based on their own direct experience of enlightenment. The Vajrayana tradition then evolved out of the Mahayana through a similar process. So there has been an interesting play, historically, between direct personal experience and the textual tradition as it is traced back to Shakyamuni Buddha. Perhaps I should just emphasize, though, that each new contribution or direction has been initiated by someone already thoroughly trained in the existing tradition. There is the sense that each new school includes the previous teachings and then goes further in a particular direction.

JOHN YUNGBLUT: What I'm hearing from the Buddhists, and what I think also exists in the Catholic tradition, is an unnecessary preoccupation with comprehensiveness, with not wanting to lose anything. The Reformation traditions, on the other hand, are concerned with getting down to the essentials. Because the emphasis is on returning to original Christianity, it is not possible to embrace large quantities of accretion. This makes it possible to cut through concerns with apostolic succession, canonical issues, and the various interpretations of texts. The Quaker tradition states that the mystical experience in silence and the social commitment to persons provide a sufficient balance for ensuring continuity with the mind of Christ. Ministry arises through the spirit and the community, by consensus. From what I understand you to say, Reggie, everyone who has made a great and evolving contribution in the Buddhist tradition did so on the basis of many years of study in the handed-on tradition. However, the Reformation traditions were willing to cut away from the existing structure. So I personally see that as a significant distinction.

REGGIE RAY: Wasn't George Fox a trained Christian?

JOHN YUNGBLUT: He studied the Bible, but he didn't have a formal theological education. I should mention one other point here. Much has been said at this conference about the importance of the teacher. In the Quaker tradition, Christ is the teacher, and Christ is really synonymous with the inner light that one is attentive to. So the Friends' Meeting for Worship in silence is to hear Christ the teacher. He is the only true teacher in this sense.

REGGIE RAY: Did Fox have disciples?

JOHN YUNGBLUT: He wouldn't have called them "disciples," because he strongly believed in the total equality of all Friends, both men and women. He would have just called them "Friends," a term that came from John's gospel: "No longer do I call you servants, for the servant does not know what his master is doing; but I have called you Friends" (John 15:15). The name "Quakers" arose in derision, to some extent, because the Friends would quake at meetings. Fox had a fantastic confidence that the community would somehow take care of itself, so that he didn't have to set up a hierarchy. Isn't that analogous to the community the Buddha left behind?

REGGIE RAY: Yes, except that in the early Buddhist community there were certain disciples who were given specific transmissions, or who were taught in one particular area or another, and these disciples then became focal points for the community. However, there wasn't any one person in charge, so in that sense it is a true comparison. I can't help wondering, though, whether some spontaneous hierarchy doesn't tend to evolve among the Friends, in the form of spiritual guidance of some kind.

JOHN YUNGBLUT: At our monthly meetings for business, we always reach for consensus. However, you are quite right that there are what we call "weighty" Friends who act as spiritual guides. But it all develops somewhat informally. They aren't appointed or even acknowledged necessarily. Friends find their teachers, though they don't have to bear that title.

BROTHER DAVID: I know that Eido Roshi, through his involvement with the transplanting of Zen Buddhism from Japan to America, has been confronted with the important question of how to balance change and continuity, and I would like to ask him to say something about his experiences.

EIDO ROSHI: Unlike Christianity, Buddhism is just now moving into this country. Zen Buddhism has its historical roots in both

China and Japan. If we were so stubborn as to just introduce traditional Japanese Zen Buddhism into an environment where the language is different and the culture is different, it wouldn't work. At the same time, if we become too quickly Americanized, we will lose the original taste of the tradition. How much we should Americanize and how much we should stick to the original tradition is a very big question. I am a stubborn person. That is my personal way. I don't know the Western culture very well, but I am willing to speak English. I am willing to shake hands, and I am willing to do something with the American people. But with regards to Zen practice, I feel, at least during my generation and maybe for one more generation as well, it is very important to have a deep respect for the original tradition. When we import the seed of an eggplant from Japan, that seed is very small. But when it is planted in this country, the eggplant becomes large, like this (demonstrates size). In my generation we need to cultivate the ground and to bring the original seed from East to West. Then the dharma will take care of itself. This is the way I feel.

BROTHER DAVID: In your experience, what are some of the difficulties that American students, in comparison with Japanese students, encounter in Zen practice?

EIDO ROSHI: In the Zen tradition, sitting is the most important thing. At least up until ten years ago, most Americans have been used to sitting on a couch or a chair. But sitting on a chair and sitting on a meditation cushion are two completely different things. In this case, even though it was difficult, the tradition had to be brought in as it was, without compromising and without Americanizing. But so many people are now sitting beautifully, comfortably on meditation cushions. Another difficulty has been chanting. If we chant the original Chinese or Japanese, of course the students ask me what everything means. But when we chant, whether it makes sense or not is a secondary matter, because it is mystical sound. The chanting *is* the meaning, though not intellectual meaning. That is difficult for most people, because they want to know the meaning.

REGGIE RAY: Brother David, where is the dimension of innovation and growth in the Benedictine tradition, and where has it been important to faithfully retain the traditional forms?

BROTHER DAVID: The Benedictine tradition is now 1500 years old. It was originally founded as a reform of the monasticism that had by then become decadent. In the history of the Benedictine tradition there have been repeated alternations between periods of decline and renewal. Each reform has always been characterized by a return to the Rule of Saint Benedict. That is the only element which ties all the different branches of Benedictines together. The Rule itself clearly states that all newcomers should be shown this book in a ceremonial way before they are admitted, and they should be told: "Behold the law under which you want to live; if you can observe it, enter; if not, freely depart." Three times the entire Rule is read to the candidate, and three times the ceremony is repeated. Therefore I would also say that in the future anything is possible as long as it is compatible with the Rule of Saint Benedict. Anything that clearly departs from the Rule could be a good development, but it would not be within the Benedictine tradition, strictly speaking.

FATHER HOPKO: For us this whole question presents a terrible problem, because we consider the Orthodox Church to be primarily a church of tradition. We also say, however, that the tradition is not contained in any one book or set of books. It is contained in the spiritual life. And as my teachers always said, the Christian church, just as life itself, must be constantly changing in order to remain the same. But how we come to know what the essence is, what we live and fight for, is the very meaning of prayer, meditation, reading, and everything we do in the spiritual life.

We claim that every member of the church—not just the bishops, not just the priests, and not just the religious, but everyone—is responsible for the church. If anyone sees something that they consider not to be in the spirit of the tradition, they must say so. Then it has to be fought out. The

whole history of our church is a history of fighting out
controversy. It has gone from controversy to controversy. That
is a sign of its life. The church is always in controversy,
struggling to clarify and struggling to bear witness. It is not a
struggle based on what *I* want or *I* don't want. We don't change
something just to change it. We live within the forms we have
received. But then, when it is necessary to defend the faith, or
the truth, we must be like a lion. So we say: in defense of the
faith, a lion; in defense of the self, a lamb. When the time
comes, the battle can be bloody—spiritually bloody as well as
literally bloody. As one example, Maximus the Confessor
fought over the controversy of who Jesus Christ is. He fought
for the truth that Jesus Christ, as incarnate God, has real
humanity: he has human freedom, human passions, and
human emotions. His adversaries claimed that Christ was
without true human freedom, energy, and will. They threw
Maximus in prison, cut off his tongue so he couldn't speak, and
cut off his hands so he couldn't write. He languished there with
a certain Martin of Rome until they both died. Twenty years
later a consensus of the faith decreed that Maximus was right,
and so now he is called Saint Maximus the Confessor. On the
other hand, both Honorius, the Pope of Rome, and Sergius,
the patriarch of Constantinople, were posthumously
anathematized for having borne witness to a false teaching that
was not in accord with the experience of Christ. And so, life
goes on. The important point is that we each bear responsibility
for the tradition. Maximus didn't say, "I'll leave with Martin
and start my own church." He said, "I will bear witness to the
truth even if you kill me."

LODRÖ DORJE: I suppose tradition is primarily a question of how the
essence of the teachings could be most successfully contained.
In general, I think the degree of flexibility a spiritual
community can manifest while still remaining true to the
essence of the tradition depends on the style of the teacher or
spiritual director. It might be interesting to say a little about the
continuity of tradition in the case of Vajradhatu, which is the
Buddhist sangha under the direction of the Venerable

Chögyam Trungpa Rinpoche. In the beginning of its evolution as a community, the primary question was how to bring the Vajrayana teachings from Tibet into Western technological society, with its completely different cultural heritage and worldview. The transplanting process presented a number of problems: in particular people's fascinations and preconceptions around Eastern culture, asceticism, possible spiritual experiences, and so on. In response to this situation, Rinpoche began by taking a big cultural leap himself. He decided to surrender his personal Tibetan monastic culture and to enter into the Western mentality. His teaching then began with an introduction to the basic background of the teachings, which is to say, with the practice of meditation itself. Beyond that, there was little prescribed form. Rinpoche seemed to be trusting the mandala principle, which is that within the space of reality, dharma, or teachings, spontaneously arise. It was an extremely roomy sort of containment, to the point that many people thought it was a free-style improvisation that had little or nothing to do with the formal tradition of Tibetan Buddhism.

Gradually a bridge has been made between the formlessness of the pure lineage transmission and the relative, social reality of the sangha, which in the beginning consisted of a group of primarily counterculture, spiritually-interested Westerners. Over the years Rinpoche has encouraged his students to become involved with business, families, and social enterprises, and at the same time he has also gradually introduced traditional Mahayana and Vajrayana liturgies, practices, and teachings. Most recently, elements of the monastic tradition, such as oryoki, a ritualized style of eating practiced in Chinese and Japanese Zen monasteries, and the traditional precepts or moral code, have been introduced in the context of certain intensive practice programs. Generally it could be said that Rinpoche has taken an evolutionary approach in bringing together the basic realization, or essence of the tradition, on the one hand, with the students' sociological and experiential background on the other. Each step of the way has been determined by the overall level of understanding present in the group mind. As practitioners develop a growing sense of meditative awareness, the meaning of the form can then be more easily transmitted to newcomers. In this way, because the community has an experiential understanding of what it is doing, new community members soon begin to get a feeling for what it is about. Our style is becoming more and more traditional, and the containment is becoming increasingly articulated. Interestingly, the container that has been evolving is not so much in the tradition of monasticism, as it was primarily in Tibet, but in the tradition of the Buddhist understanding of enlightened society. In other words, we are learning how we could exhibit nonaggression and compassion in our Western domestic and social environments, while also incorporating formal spiritual practice into our lives.

EIDO ROSHI: I can see we have examples here of two different ways of moving between the formality and the essence. The essence of the buddha-dharma already pervades everywhere, even prior to heaven and earth. What we need to transmit geographically, from East to West, are the Buddhist scriptures, as well as a certain formality. Through the transmission of formality, people are then able to realize the essence of the Buddha. I was quite interested, Lodrö, that you said your community is getting more and more traditional. When I visited Boulder five years ago, I was shocked by the sloppiness of the Vajradhatu students' sitting posture. When I spoke about this with Trungpa Rinpoche he said to me, "You Zen people are so strict. You start with such strict formality at the beginning. But we, on the other hand, start by taking it easy, and then gradually, gradually we introduce the tradition." Now, five years later, I realize that this was true. I see a great change. So this is one way. It is how the transmission of Tibetan Buddhism is taking place. You began in a casual American way, and gradually more and more tradition was introduced. Another way is what I am doing. I started with a stubborn Japanese tradition, and now gradually I am Americanizing.

Liturgy as Continuity

Judith Lief
Thomas Hopko
David Steindl-Rast O.S.B.

JUDY LIEF: In Vajrayana Buddhism, every initiation into a new ritual
or meditation practice is accompanied by the oral transmission
of an accomplished teacher. The teacher communicates the
essence of the form, and that human connection transforms
the text, gesture, or activity into a sacred empowerment. So,
personal transmission is what gives life to the traditional forms.
In fact, the continuity of that personal transmission from
teacher to disciple is the key factor in determining whether a
lineage of teachings is unbroken and therefore continues to be
vital. I am wondering whether other traditions also place such
importance on the role of oral transmission.

FATHER HOPKO: There is certainly a similar element in the Eastern
Orthodox Church. We experience a transmission called "the
mind of Christ," which can also be identified as "the mind of
the Church" or even "the mind of the Fathers." How does one
have access to this transmission in a living way? Through the
lex orandi, the corporate liturgy of the church, one can go
beyond personal meditation and prayer to experience the
meditation and prayer of the community. In a sense, liturgical
prayer is the prayer of Christ to the Father in the Holy Spirit.
We believe that when we enter into the liturgy of the church,
by singing with the community, contemplating the mystery,
and so on, we enter into the relationship of Christ, the Father,
and the Holy Spirit: we enter into the interpersonal
communion of the Godhead. Even during the practice of
personal meditation, there is this living situation within which
we pray. This context is made concrete through the daily and
seasonal rhythms of liturgy. There are morning, noon, and
evening periods when the entire church prays, and there is also
a common liturgical calendar. For example, on the sixth of
August every Orthodox church in the world is contemplating

the transfiguration of Christ. That creates a kind of continuity within which personal prayer takes place. When new liturgical elements are introduced into the church, they have to be in harmony with this context. So for us this is one means of ensuring a continuity of transmission.

BROTHER DAVID: I would add that in the Benedictine tradition, the atmosphere of the monastery, which includes the way time and space are arranged, plays an important role in the initiation and transmission process. In general, participation in the atmosphere of the liturgy is the vehicle by which the Catholic tradition is transmitted and contained. In fact, the liturgy is the teacher. The catechism is just a minor intellectual appendage. One must admit, however, that nowadays this is often not understood.

JUDY LIEF: Father Hopko, in your tradition do you have certain formal occasions, as we do in Vajrayana Buddhism, where the teacher or spiritual master elucidates on the meaning of the liturgy and helps you to tune into the important aspects of it, or perhaps confirms what you have experienced in relation to it?

FATHER HOPKO: Yes, but there is a sense in which when you explain the liturgy, it is not the liturgy anymore. To explain the liturgy is like trying to explain a poem: if the meaning the poem is carrying could be completely explained, the poem wouldn't have been written in the first place. The written liturgy, like a genuine poem, is a term of reference; the real experience is beyond words. So I would say that the words and the rituals aren't necessarily our teachers. They are the means of access to the teacher. The teacher is the lived experience. In that sense, the liturgy is ultimately silent.

It is interesting that, in the earliest days of the church, a person didn't learn the Lord's Prayer until relatively late in the process of his or her preparation for baptism and holy communion. For almost the first five hundred years of the Orthodox Church, a non-baptized person never saw the eucharist and never heard the Lord's Prayer, because only the initiate who had been sacramentally enlightened could call on the most high, all-holy, unconditioned, boundless God as "our Father" and enter into communion with him in the holy eucharist. This was also true of such teachings as the Holy Trinity and those concerning the Virgin Mary. Such "mysteries"—formally called the "dogmas"—were not discussed by neophytes and those just starting on the way. I think the process of initiation into the mysteries is one of the important things we can be reminded of by Buddhism, because to a large extent this has been lost in Christianity. You just can't tell someone everything all at once. Intellectually he can't understand it, and spiritually he can't bear it, because he hasn't yet had the illuminative experience that allows him to see.

One Voice

Thomas Keating O.C.S.O.

As we study and open ourselves to the wisdom of the world religions, we become more and more amazed to see a certain commonality and unity in the area of human values. I personally feel that this commonality has not been adequately grasped, and that if it could be, this would make an extraordinary difference in the world today. In the political arena, problems are still being resolved on the level of raw power, and there is no possibility of overcoming violence at that level. In fact, at this point, the political process has brought the human family to its maximum risk potential. The spiritual dimension, which is present in each of the world religions, is precisely what is needed so badly today. But historically the world religions have tended to oppose themselves to each other, with each being exclusivistic and claiming to be *the* path to the Ultimate Mystery. Out of a naive loyalty, people have fought for their respective religions to the point of blood. But through spiritual confrontation, we are discovering a deep commonality that is more profound than the divergences we also encounter in genuine dialogue.

My hope is that, if we could articulate the points of agreement among the world religions, a transcultural revelation of the basic values of human life which the world religions hold in common would emerge. We would identify the spiritual heritage of the entire human family, however diversely each religion and particular culture celebrates it. If this consensus could then be injected, with one voice, into the socio-political arena, the world religions would be contributing an all-important spiritual dimension to the decision-making process.

In the next generation the question may not be which religion one belongs to, but whether religion itself is of value. Those who have had some experience of transcendence must find some way to communicate the fact that the experience of the Ultimate Mystery is open to every human person who chooses to pursue the search for truth and embark on the spiritual journey—a journey which is literally without end.

Proposal

The following Guidelines have evolved from a set of eight "Proposed Points of Common Understanding Among the Religions of the World," drawn up by Father Thomas Keating in 1982. Since that time, the Points have been discussed and refined by a number of interreligious groups, including a sub-group of the First Assembly of World Religions which convened in McAffee, New Jersey in 1985 and the Snowmass Conference, which meets on a regular basis for the purpose of ongoing contemplative dialogue.

Guidelines for Interreligious Understanding

1) The world religions bear witness to the experience of the Ultimate Reality to which they give various names: Brahman, the Absolute, God, Allah, Great Spirit, the Transcendent.

2) The Ultimate Reality surpasses any name or concept that can be given to It.

3) The Ultimate Reality is the source (ground of being) of all existence.

4) Faith is opening, surrendering, and responding to the Ultimate Reality. This relationship precedes every belief system.

5) The potential for human wholeness—or in other frames of reference, liberation, self-transcendence, enlightenment, salvation, transforming union, moksha, nirvana, fana—is present in every human person.

6) The Ultimate Reality may be experienced not only through religious practices but also through nature, art, human relationships, and service to others.

7) The differences among belief systems should be presented as facts that distinguish them, not as points of superiority.

8) In the light of the globalization of life and culture now in process, the personal and social ethical principles proposed by the world religions in the past need to be re-thought and re-expressed. For example:
a) In view of the increasing danger of global destruction, the world religions should emphasize the corresponding moral obligation of nations and ethnic groups to make use of nonviolent methods for the resolution of conflicts.
b) The world religions should encourage civil governments to respect every religion without patronizing one in particular.
c) The world religious should work for the practical acceptance of the dignity of the human person; a more equitable distribution of material goods and of opportunities for human development; the cause of human rights, especially the right to choose and prac-

tice one's own religion or no religion; the solidarity
and harmony of the human family; the stewardship
of the earth and its resources; the renewal of their respective spiritual traditions; and interreligious understanding through dialogue.

THOMAS KEATING

Chapter 3: Notes

1. Epigraph: *Contemplation in a World of Action* (New York: Doubleday & Co., 1971), p. 118.
2. Epigraph: "The Goose at Rest" in *The Journal of Shasta Abbey,* Aug.-Oct. 1978, p. 4. Quoted by Rick Fields in *How the Swans Came to the Lake,* p. 369.
3. Magisterium is the official teaching of the hierarchy of the Roman Catholic Church on matters of doctrine and morality.

Part Two

Comparing Ways

We may come to Buddhist-Christian dialogue with a definite idea of belonging to one religion instead of the other: "I believe in. . . . " Or perhaps, "I don't believe in. . . . " Or we may come eager to hear that, behind linguistic differences, there is ultimately only one truth, one reality: all religions are saying the same thing. But a contemplative perspective warns us that easy, simplistic answers will deaden the possibility of real openness and communication. Differences and apparent contradictions should instead ignite our curiosity and invite us to question, look deeper.

If we are Christian, we believe that the ultimate goal of the spiritual path is union with God; the Buddhist aspires to realize shunyata, or emptiness, and thus achieve enlightenment. This appears to be a major doctrinal distinction: it defines Christianity to be a theistic religion, and Buddhism to be nontheistic. But what does this distinction actually mean? Chapter Four re-examines the concepts of God and emptiness through the lens of the contemplative experience. Chapter Five, "Views of Self and Ego," then looks at the person who travels on the spiritual path: Who is it that aspires toward union with God, or who aspires to realize shunyata? Is there a parallel to the notion of ego and egolessness in Christianity? In Chapter Six, "Sin, Suffering, and Virtue," the speakers describe the Christian and Buddhist views of the human condition or predicament and its relationship to the spiritual journey. Finally, Chapter Seven describes the "how" of the path: prayer and meditation are compared as the traditional methods for personal transformation in the two traditions.

4

God and Emptiness

When you go apart to be alone for prayer . . . see that nothing remains in your conscious mind save a naked intent stretching out toward God. Leave it stripped of every particular idea *about* God (what he is like in himself or in his works) and keep only the awareness *that he is as he is*. Let him be thus, I pray you, and force him not to be otherwise.[1]

ANONYMOUS

Like the center of a cloudless sky,
The self-luminous mind is impossible to express.
It is wisdom of nonthought beyond analogy,
Naked ordinary mind.
Not keeping to dogmatism or arrogance,
It is clearly seen as dharmakaya.
The appearance of the six sense objects, like the moon in water,
Shines in the state of wisdom.[2]

LODRÖ THAYE, JAMGÖN KONGTRÜL I

Heresy

Thomas Keating O.C.S.O.

The idea that God is an object outside of oneself to which one relates through prayer is totally unscriptural. It is heresy, and it should well be forgotten. It is an idea which is the result of a cultural conditioning originating in the world of philosophy and especially Descartes. The world-view that affirms the subject-object dichotomy has produced the fruit of modern technology, but it has also cramped the intuitive faculties of the Western mind and left education totally bereft of its spiritual dimension.

As Christians, the way we should look upon God is to see that we are in him and that he is in us. He is all around us and within us, so we can never escape from him, even if we should want to. We are distinct from God but never totally apart from him. God and the true self are the same thing. We are not God in the absolute sense of being eternal and infinite, but we are God in the sense that his life is in us and we participate in his divine life. If we are seeking God through prayer and mysticism, the way to do so is to go through our innermost beings to the source, where God is dwelling. As John of the Cross said of the Christian who has reached the transforming union, "One feels as if one *were* God."

Shunyata & Linguistics I

Judith Lief

"Emptiness" could definitely be a problematic word. It often carries the nihilistic implication of clamping down on or denying experience. A more accurate translation of shunyata would be "unbounded openness." Meditation that leads to an experience of shunyata involves letting go of mental supports and letting in fresh air. Shunyata is an opening of the mind which allows us to feel fully and to shed the protective survival mentality of "this" and "that," "I" and "other." It is an experience of bursting into an openness which is rich, rather than a sense of throwing everything out until all that is left is a blank kind of nothing. So shunyata includes rather than excludes. It is an opening to vastness rather than a withdrawal from reality.

When You Meet the Buddha, Kill the Buddha

David Steindl-Rast O.S.B.
Reginald Ray
Eido Tai Shimano Roshi
Thomas Hopko
H. E. the Tai Situpa Rinpoche

BROTHER DAVID: Recently Father Keating said that for too long religions have disagreed about nothing. I would now add that the nothing about which religions have disagreed is God. (Laughter and applause.) In the strictest sense of the word, God is nothing. The only possible alternative would be that God is *some*thing and certainly that is not the case: God is nothing. We live in a world of things and no-things. These are the two exhaustive possibilities, and I would like to suggest that of these two, the one that is by far the more important to every one of us—and I am now appealing to your experience—is nothing. (Laughter.) We can do without this thing or that thing, but as human beings we cannot do without *meaning*. We live in a world which is made up of things and meaning, and meaning is nothing. I would feel much more comfortable if I didn't have to use this word "God" at all, because it is a word that is so easily misunderstood today. But if I do have to use it, I would say that God is the direction in which we go in our quest for meaning.

All philosophical abstractions and scholarly definitions of the meaning of life are simply elaborations on the experience of belonging. Those peak moments of one's life break down the illusion of duality, the illusion of isolation. Even though we don't often allow ourselves to remember those times of communion with ultimate reality because they are so shattering to our little egos, still, we have all had them. So meaning is not somewhere "out there," toward which we move; it is more an experience of something reaching out to us. Actually, nothing is reaching out to us. Nothing is happening to us, you see. (Laughter.)

As Mother Tessa was saying earlier, the spiritual experience begins not with us, but with God. God loves us first. In that moment in which we are overwhelmed by reality, we know that ultimate reality comes toward us, reaches out to us, and speaks to us. The Biblical tradition says that everything in the spiritual life hinges on the reality that God *speaks* to us. In Buddhism, the emphasis seems to be much more on the silence. In Christianity and Judaism the emphasis is on the word which comes out of the silence and which leads us back into the silence, or back into what we could call the "emptiness of God." "Word" and "silence" are the terms Christians use to speak of the polarity within God. And specifically as Christians, we know that ultimate reality is reaching out to us because of Christ, who reached out to us in such an unprecedented way. Those who first encountered Jesus the Christ discovered, in a unique way, what God is like, and the world is still reverberating from their experiences. And so the Christian path is to come to know God, who is the silence and who cannot be seen, except through his icon. We can listen to the silence of God through his word and we can find that word crystallized in Christ. Where does this path lead us? According to Dionysius the Areopagite, in the end of all our knowing we shall come to know God as the unknown. Now this is totally different from saying that no matter how much we know, we shall never know God. We shall know God, but we shall know him as the unknown. It is the same in human terms: the more you come to know a person, the more you know that you don't know that person at all.

REGGIE RAY: Thank you, Brother David. Roshi, would you like to say something on this topic?

EIDO ROSHI: The moment the word "God" is uttered it becomes a concept, I'm afraid. And the moment we say "emptiness" it is no longer empty. And yet, if I don't say anything you may become confused. But if I do say something you could become equally confused. (Laughter.) This is the dilemma. At this point I think a Zen story could help us a lot. This story, like most Zen stories, takes place in China. It is about a verse which we chant almost every day, which goes something like this: *Buddha-nature pervades the whole universe, revealing right here now.* It is a beautiful concept. (Laughter.) Once, on a very hot summer day, the Chinese Zen master Mayoku was fanning himself like this . . . (Roshi sits back and fans himself). Watching this, his student thought, "We often say that buddha-nature pervades the whole universe, revealing right here now. We also say that buddha-nature is cool and lucid. Why, if that is the case, does my master need to use a fan?" So he thought that this was a good chance for a dharma argument. So he said, "Master, you often say that cool, lucid buddha-nature pervades the whole universe, revealing right here right now. Why then do you have to use your fan to cool yourself?" The master Mayoku smiled and said, "You understand the concept of buddha-nature, but you don't understand the vital buddha-nature itself." He continued to fan himself. The student watched his master and repeated to himself what he had been told. All of a sudden, for some reason, this young Chinese monk understood what his master meant.

　Although it is true, from an enlightened vista, that buddha-nature pervades the whole universe, revealing right here and now unless something is done—in this case . . . (fans air across the microphone) . . . buddha-nature or God or emptiness remain as concepts. For this reason we do meditation. For this reason we do bowing practices, we do chanting, and we do many other things. Doing something is so important. I have more to say, especially to Father Hopko, but

I will give him a chance to talk first. Later we can discuss "when you meet the Buddha, kill the Buddha." (Laughter.)

FATHER HOPKO: I think by a miracle I can be brief. (Laughter.) According to the tradition of Eastern Christianity, God is inconceivable and any concept, word, or idea is inadequate to the reality of God. Every time we gather to worship God in the eucharistic liturgy of the Eastern church, we pray with these words, attributed to Saint John Chrysostom:

> Holy art Thou and all-holy, Thou and Thine only-begotten Son and Thy holy Spirit. . . . for Thou, O God, are ineffable, inconceivable, in-visible, incomprehensible, ever-existing, and eternally the same.

If you equate God with a concept, you have an idol and not God. The scriptures say that there are many gods and many lords. But there is also the one God of all gods. He is the true God, the living God, the holy God. According to the Bible, the real problem is not *no God;* the problem is the *false god.* And I think you could say that, in fact, everyone has gods. There is no such thing, using modern language, as a true atheist. Whatever one adores, loves, lives by, and considers to be essential in life is one's god or idol. According to the tradition, physical and carnal idols are relatively harmless— much more treacherous are those we create in the realm of the spirit, when we try to create our own God. But that which falsely claims ultimacy, reality, is not God; it is the enemy of God.

When you encounter the true God, you encounter an absolute that is other than anything you know. You are dumb and cannot speak. All of your concepts are smashed as so many idols. In the Hebrew scriptures of the Old Testament, Moses, Elijah, Isaiah, and Job all bore witness, in the mystical contemplation of their experiences, that God cannot be seen. If we do have to speak about God, I think we could even go beyond saying that God is ineffable, inconceivable, invisible, and incomprehensible. The sixth-century work called *Mystical Theology*, attributed to Dionysius the Aeropagite, begins with a prayer addressing God: "O Thou who art beyond being supra-substantial, supra-essential! O Thou art beyond goodness! O Thou art beyond God!" Divinity comes from the one who is even beyond divinity. The supra-unknowable has made his supra-unknowableness known through supra-unknowing. These are words of Saint Maximus. In other words, God has shown himself. Relative to emptiness, this means that there is something. The Ultimate Reality, the God who is even "beyond divinity," radiates and shines forth with what is known in our tradition as the "divine energies": divine activities, divine words, divine expressions, divine epiphanies, and divine manifestations. Therefore we have access to him; we know the supra-unknowable God. In the fourteenth century, Gregory Palamas had a theological dispute with the Western Christians about this. Western theology claimed that God has no real relationship with the world and cannot be experienced beyond our ideas and concepts about him, which are always limited and therefore ultimately false. But Gregory Palamas said that God not only *can* be experienced, he *must* be known, because that is what our life is all about.

In the Eastern tradition we describe the ineffable experience of God as "luminous darkness," "sober inebriation," "drunken sobriety," "wise foolishness," "foolish wisdom"—and probably we should now coin two new phrases: "full emptiness" and "empty fullness." For example, God told Moses on top of the mountain, "You can only see my glory." Moses had to hide in the cleft of the rock and cover his face as the splendor of the Lord passed by. Gregory of Nyssa, in his mystical treatise *The Life of Moses*, interprets this story to mean that we can come into communion with God in his manifesting actions toward us, but God as he is in himself is hidden from us. He is always eternally hidden from us and is not known by any creature—not because God has not revealed himself, but because God cannot be directly seen. Otherwise God would not be God.

In a sense, therefore, we can't really talk about knowing or not-knowing; our experience is even beyond not not-knowing.

We not only have to jettison our positive concepts; we must jettison our negative concepts as well. We just have to shut up in the end. (Laughter.)

If someone asks you, "Does God exist?" you can say, "Well, if you mean, 'Is there emptiness, or God, or ultimate reality?' the answer is 'Yes.' But if you mean, 'Does God exist like everything else exists?' he does not exist." And in fact, you had better say that he does not not-exist, and he does not even not not-not-exist . . . if you have to keep talking. So, it's better not to keep talking and to just enjoy—and endure—the encounter. Right? (Laughter and applause.)

REGGIE RAY: Thank you. I'd like to invite the speakers to engage each other on this topic. Does anyone have any comments or questions?

FATHER HOPKO: Roshi wants to talk about killing the Buddha. (Laughter.)

EIDO ROSHI: You have a fabulous memory. Until this afternoon I had almost completely forgotten about this subject, "when you meet the Buddha, kill the Buddha," which I talked about last year. So, this afternoon you gave me this answer: when you meet the Christ, let the Christ kill you. Now . . . (laughter) . . . actually it is impossible for you to meet Jesus Christ. You may meet various people on the street, all kinds of people, especially in Boulder, (laughter) but one of the people who it is absolutely impossible for you to meet is Jesus Christ. Right?

FATHER HOPKO: No. (Laughter.) No, it's not true.

EIDO ROSHI: Well, anyway, you can explain later. Let me say what I had in my mind. (Laughter.) In the same way, strictly speaking, it is impossible to meet the Buddha—if we mean Shakyamuni Buddha—on the street in Boulder. It is impossible. There is only one person who you can always meet, wherever you go, and who in fact you cannot separate yourself from, and that is you, yourself. You are the one who constantly carries concepts.

And so when you meet the Buddha—when you meet your concept of the Buddha—crush that concept. When you carry the concept of Christ or God, or the concept of shunyata, then kill those concepts. But it is impossible for Jesus Christ to kill you. Right?

FATHER HOPKO: Well . . . (Eido Roshi laughs) . . . if we meet the concept of God or the concept of Christ, it must be killed. I would agree with that, absolutely. But something bothers me about "when you meet the Buddha, kill the Buddha." In my understanding, I am not the only one with whom I can have a relationship. In fact, the hardest relationship to have is with one's own self, because we don't seem to really have a self, except the mask in the mirror. So when we are in a relationship with ourselves, we're usually in big trouble. But the other who comes to me is the Christ. The one whom I meet mystically in the church, in the eucharist, and in my heart is the same one whose face is the face of everyone I meet. The only true image of God is the human person. That is why, according to the Orthodox tradition, there are no icons until the incarnation of God's son and word as Jesus Christ, and it is also why there have to be icons after the incarnation. Paul said that Jesus is the *eikon tou aoratou Theou*, "the icon of the invisible God" (Col. 1:15), and Irineus said, "The only glory of God we encounter is man full-grown." God has revealed himself.

I'll just end with a story about Saint Pachomius, who is considered to be the founder of the first Christian monastic community. One day a man came to the cenobium and said, "I'd like to join this community." When Pachomius asked him why, the fellow said, "I'd like to see God."

"You're coming here because you want to see God?"

"Yes. What do I have to do? How many prostrations, how many Psalms, how many prayers, how much fasting . . . ?"

Pachomius answered, "Listen, if you want to see God, you don't have to pray and fast. You don't even have to join the community. Just come along with me, and I will show you God." Pachomius took him inside and, indicating the meanest, lowliest, dirtiest, most demented of the brethren, said to him,

"Look. There is God."

The visitor said indignantly, "You mean to tell me that's God?"

Pachomius answered, "If you don't come to see God in him, you will see God nowhere."

God is formless, imageless, and the only vision of God we have is in the one made in his icon and according to his likeness, by grace. That refers to each one of us. God's eternal icon has come in human form as Jesus Christ, the one through whom God is now definitively and fully revealed. No man has seen God, but the only begotten son who dwells in the loins of the Father has come and made him known (John 1:18). Christ is identified with everyone, and therefore, when I encounter anyone I must let that person slay the ego in me. And that is what I meant when I said "if I meet the Christ, may the Christ kill me," because that is the only way of coming alive. (Applause.)

BROTHER DAVID: The Eastern tradition of Christianity is well-known for its doctrine of icons, which is quite unfamiliar to us in the West. Tibetan Buddhism, however, also has a rich tradition of iconography, and since I've always been especially intrigued by the iconocraphy of Tibetan Buddhism, I would like to ask Situ Rinpoche if he would tell us a little bit about the meaning of deities depicted in statues and thangkas, particularly in the context of discussing representations of God or the divine reality.

SITU RINPOCHE: The purpose is to signify the essence of one's own physical body and the essence of one's own mind. The essence of each of us, as Roshi said, is buddha-nature. Buddha-nature isn't something separate from us, or something we have lost and have to get back by practicing meditation. No. It is already there, but we have to awaken it. I think the meaning of "kill the Buddha" or "may Christ kill you" comes in here because that which prevents you from realizing buddhahood, or which makes you different from Christ, is duality. It is a mistake to think that you are the subject and Christ or Buddha is the object. Duality makes you unable to communicate, unable to realize. So what you kill is duality. Then you are able to realize the ultimate essence of yourself as the ultimate essence of Buddha, or, in Christian terms, of God.

In the example of Vajradhara (indicates painting hanging above Buddhist shrine), his essence, which is the same as our essence, has three aspects: nirmanakaya, sambhogakaya, and dharmakaya. His outer appearance, or nirmanakaya, is like that of Buddha Shakyamuni: he has the eighty lesser marks and thirty-two greater marks of a buddha's physical body. These signify the ultimate nature of one's own physical body. Vajradhara's ornaments, such as his crown, earrings, and so on, represent the higher levels of realization and manifestation of the Buddha, as well as his activity in the world. This is the sambhogakaya aspect. Then, the blue color of Vajradhara's skin represents the Buddha's mind and the ultimate essence of our minds, which is the dharmakaya. Blue is the color of space and the color of emptiness. The nature of dharmakaya is limitless, endless, and beyond any concept of "I realize this or that." It is free from subtle duality. So Vajradhara not only signifies the ultimate nirmanakaya, sambhogakaya, and dharmakaya of Buddha Shakyamuni, and of all the buddhas of the past and the future: it is also the essential nature of each one of us.

REGGIE RAY: This evening we've been discussing God and emptiness in a relatively sophisticated way. I get the feeling that there is no fundamental incompatibility in our different perspectives. And yet, earlier today when I was participating in the Christian liturgy, I was going along and really enjoying the whole thing until at one point I suddenly realized that I felt as though I was praying to someone. And then my next thought was, well, who is that someone? Now was that a misunderstanding on my part? (Laughter.)

BROTHER DAVID: Many people feel uncomfortable with the idea of a personal God because of the widespread Christian misunderstanding of God as a person who sits somewhere "up

VAJRADHARA[3]

144

there." On the other hand, ultimate reality must include the perfection of personhood, so it can't be totally impersonal. We might as well think of the ultimate reality as a person to begin with; this is much better than thinking of it as some sort of a cosmic pudding, which would be our alternative. So we ought to remember that the ultimate reality has all the perfection of personhood, but none of its limitations. We can address ourselves to God as we slide into prayer, just as we did this afternoon. We can also experience compassion reaching out to us. But we must also go beyond this personal quality, whether we are Christians or Buddhists, or anything else.

EIDO ROSHI: The word "emptiness," generally speaking, creates misunderstandings. But at the same time, "emptiness" has the positive meaning of *emptying* our concepts—concepts of God, concepts of dharmakaya, sambhogakaya, nirmanakaya. Even the concept of emptiness can be emptied. That is an accidental benefit of saying "emptiness" instead of "shunyata." It prevents the over-personalization of God.

REGGIE RAY: Rinpoche, could you say something about why emptiness isn't a nihilistic notion? I think that is difficult for many people to understand.

SITU RINPOCHE: Yes. If we just say "emptiness," it seems to be only empty. That is why I explain emptiness as three levels: there is relative interdependence, or appearance; ultimate emptiness; and the union of interdependence and the ultimate. There is no contradiction among these three. The essence of all relative appearance *is* the ultimate, which is emptiness. I agree, Roshi, that "emptiness" can create misunderstanding. I have difficulty using the word "emptiness." I used to use the word "voidness," but my English is not very good. Maybe that is also not a correct translation.

EIDO ROSHI: Sometimes I use "as-it-isness." (Laughter.)

SITU RINPOCHE: Yes, that is a good term.

EIDO ROSHI: But it has a fatalistic implication.

SITU RINPOCHE: Yes, sometimes people have that misunderstanding.

EIDO ROSHI: After all, "shunyata" is the best.

SITU RINPOCHE: Yes. (Laughter.)

REGGIE RAY: Perhaps we could open up the discussion. Are there any questions?

QUESTION (from audience): For a long time I have had a sense of relationship to a *personal* God from whom I can learn, in the way Brother David speaks of the sign or word of God which is present in phenomenal reality. In the Buddhist sense, I understand the experience of shunyata as something like having the ground pulled out from under you, of suddenly being lost without anything to hold onto. Is there also an experience of shunyata that includes relationship?

EIDO ROSHI: Before I say something about the probability or capability or even the possibility of having a relationship with shunyata, let me say a little more about shunyata. You are shunyata. Do you understand this? I am shunyata. And relationship is also shunyata. (Pause.) Got it?

QUESTION (cont.): Right. (Laughter.)

FATHER KEATING: But could we not at least say that our experience of shunyata is one of incredible tenderness and compassion— that it is one of the most profound analogues of human love that could be articulated?

EIDO ROSHI: I accept that. But yet, may I add that even *that* is shunyata.

SITU RINPOCHE: I think we somehow have to relate with people's development. At the relative level, we have faith, devotion, and trust in the ultimate truth, so that we achieve realization of the ultimate gradually, step by step. Then we see that relative appearance and emptiness are not two.

QUESTION: We've been talking about an experience, and we've called it "shunyata" and also "God." When I listen to both the Buddhists and the Christians I hear that basically there is no difference; there is no conflict. But very little has been said about the actual path or process that allows us to have this experience. And it seems unclear to me how, as Christians, a dualistic relationship to God leads us to the experience of shunyata.

FATHER HOPKO: First of all, I personally would not try to say at this point where there are differences or no differences. I am just trying to hear what is being said. I do know that what Situ Rinpoche said about relative and ultimate rang a thousand bells in me. God is at one and the same time totally other, totally beyond, beyond even apophaticism;[4] and yet he is also related to me. And both are divine. For the record, many Western Christians think we Eastern Orthodox are heretics on that point. (Laughter.) Still, I think we should be very careful about coming to final conclusions about what is the same or not the same in Christianity and Buddhism.

    The other thing I want to say is that I'm frankly sick of the word "relationship." I forbid my students to use it. (Laughter.) People these days are so interested in relationships: their relationships to themselves, to their spouse, to God, and so on. They are so involved in these issues that they can never see the other clearly enough to really experience the fact that duality is a myth. It's very interesting that in Greek theology, the term persona, which means "person," was specifically and consciously not used. Persona was considered to be only a kind of mask or a way of acting. And when you go as far as *persona est relatio* (i.e. person is relation), then everyone becomes neurotic. (Laughter and applause.)

BROTHER DAVID: I would just like to add that in any tradition we are referring to the common experience of being human. We then interpret and live out that experience in vastly different ways. And in my mind there cannot be conceived two ways that are lived out more differently than Buddhism and Christianity, because one is the way of word and the other is the way of silence. What greater disparity can you imagine! But they come from the same experience and, by very different routes, lead to the same experience. The proof is that when you get masters of both spiritual traditions together, such as we have here, you see that they get along wonderfully, and they're so similar you can hardly tell them apart! (Much laughter.)

Not Just Empty

David Steindl-Rast O.S.B.
H. E. the Tai Situpa Rinpoche
Thomas Hopko
Thomas Keating O.C.S.O.

BROTHER DAVID: Rinpoche, one of the difficulties I've had in our previous discussions concerns the idea that, in order to attain ultimate wisdom, awareness as we know it must be overcome. To me, wisdom without awareness is unimaginable.

SITU RINPOCHE: Wisdom is the union of clarity and emptiness, or we could say, awareness and emptiness. The essence of both is nonduality; that is the ultimate aspect. If you only have the empty quality of wisdom, without clarity, that is nihilism. And if you only have clarity without the empty quality, that is eternalism. But the inseparable union of the two, that is the ultimate. And when we say "ultimate" we don't mean the opposite of relative. The real ultimate isn't the opposite of relative: there is the ultimate aspect of the ultimate, and there is the ultimate aspect of the relative. That is the real ultimate.

FATHER HOPKO: In the Eastern Christian tradition, this union would be called "Palamite awareness."

SITU RINPOCHE: I see, I see. Is this Latin?

FATHER HOPKO: No, it is named after Saint Gregory Palamas, who developed the conception that, in the ultimate reality, there is always an eternal and unchanging expression which can be called relative in some sense. The greatest mystery is the union of the ultimate reality and its expression. Without that expression God would just be a monadic nothing.

SITU RINPOCHE: I see.

FATHER KEATING: Rinpoche, I have a question, which is of extreme interest to me, concerning the Vajrayana tradition. I know little of this tradition, though I wish to learn more. I understand that Vajrayana teachings enable the practitioner to experience the qualities of emptiness that are not just empty. In other words, there is a certain richness or luminosity—or perhaps we could call it the quality of love—that starts to emerge in one's practice. I'm not quite sure if I have the correct understanding here. And although we, as Christians, appreciated your presentation of Tibetan Buddhism very much, from your description we were left with some feeling that your tradition is lacking in a certain warmth—a certain quality of relationship or love—which would add a little enthusiasm to the search, you might say. (Laughter.) But your actual presence, and also what you were just describing to us, gives me the growing conviction that this emptiness is not just empty. As you said, there is a relative quality that is expressing itself there. I have the feeling that this teaching is very, very rich, and yet I also get the feeling that you keep hiding it in your back pocket someplace. I think that we Christians would be much more at home in the Buddhist presentation if we had more of an inkling of what lies, experientially, within emptiness.

SITU RINPOCHE: I think you already said it. In Tibetan we say *tong tang nyingje sungjuk,* which means "the union of emptiness and compassion," or you could say, "the inseparability of emptiness and compassion."

FATHER HOPKO: We say "union without confusion."

SITU RINPOCHE: It isn't that we are bringing two separate things into union. Union is there already. We just awaken it.

FATHER HOPKO: In the fifth century, the Council of Chalcedon used four negative adverbs to describe the union of the human, or created, with the divine in the person of Christ: without division, without separation, without fusion, and without change. That is how we try to conceptualize the great problem of simultaneous union and distinction. If you don't hold both, then either I am annihilated or God is, or we end up with something we know nothing about—a freak of some sort.

BROTHER DAVID: Christians speak about an active reaching-out of God. Before I can be compassionate, I receive compassion. In that sense, Christians say that God loved us first. Rinpoche, I'm wondering how you would describe the process by which practitioners realize the ultimate, or shunyata.

SITU RINPOCHE: I don't think we could say it comes to us. Even when we say that we "achieve" realization or "reach" certain levels on the path, it doesn't mean that we are actually going anywhere or reaching anything. And something isn't coming toward us and shaking our hand. It is simply an awakening. In Tibetan, the word for "buddha" is *sanggye*. *Sang* means "awaken" and *gye* means "total flourishing" or "total blossoming."

FATHER KEATING: I think that is a good explanation of the way Christians could also understand the spiritual journey. Thank you for your explanation, Rinpoche.

The Terrible Good

William McNamara O.C.D.

The so-called object of our quest, which cannot be objectified, is the Terrible Good. It is not nice. It is not manageable, and it is not in any way utilitarian. One of the most unfortunate things that can happen to any one of us, or to any church, is that we end up trying to use God—which occurs frequently in this age. People try to use God. But God will not be used. God will not be had. God will not be possessed. That is why it is important to remember that every time you or I enters into prayer, we enter into the cave of a lion, and who knows if we are going to come out alive? God is not a tame God, and that is why we may never speak about him glibly or casually. Anytime we refer to him without awe and astonishment, without holy fear—not psychological fear, but holy fear—we take his name in vain, which is one of the greatest sins of humankind.

Shunyata and Linguistics II

Eido Tai Shimano Roshi

We could talk on the subject of emptiness for two or three hours and still there would be no solution. It is simply because this is not a matter of concept. It is a matter of reality. The English word "emptiness" unfortunately has negative implications, while the original Sanskrit word *shunyata* does not. When English-speaking people hear about emptiness, they often feel fear. So we might as well not use the English words "emptiness" or "voidness." We could just say "shunyata." And instead of trying to understand shunyata conceptually or intellectually, we *experience* shunyata. Then we have no problem.

Theism and Nontheism

Ven. Chögyam Trungpa Rinpoche

As far as I can see, there is no difference between theism and nontheism, basically speaking. Declaring an involvement with any kind of "ism" turns out to be a matter of self and other. In fact, the whole question of self and other can then become very important. But if you really pursue any spiritual path, you will discover, surprisingly, that self and other are one thing. Self is other, other is self.

Spirituality is simply a means of arousing one's spirit, of developing a kind of spiritedness. Through that you begin to have greater contact with reality. You are not afraid of discovering what reality is all about, and you are willing to explore your individual energy. You actually choose to work with the essence of your existence, which could be called genuineness. An interest in spirituality doesn't mean that you lack something, or that you have developed a black hole in your existence which you are trying to compensate for or cover over with some sort of religious patchwork. It simply means that you are capable of dealing with reality.

Whether you worship someone else or you worship yourself, it is the same thing. Both theism and nontheism can be problematic if you are not involving yourself personally and fully. You may think you are become spiritual, but instead you could just be trying to camouflage yourself behind a religious framework—and still you will be more visible than you think.

Usually we say that in theistic traditions you worship an external agent, and in nontheistic traditions you do not worship an external agent. Nonetheless, in either case you might just be looking for your version of a babysitter. Whether you hire a babysitter from the outside world or from within your own family doesn't really matter. In either case your state of being isn't being expressed properly, thoroughly, because you are trying to use some kind of substitute. We are not trying here to sort out which tradition, or which particular type of merchandise, is better. We are talking in terms of needing to develop a personal connection with one's body and one's mind. That is why the contemplative traditions of both East and West are very important.

Chapter 4: Notes

1. Epigraph: *The Cloud of Unknowing and The Book of Privy Counseling,* ed. William Johnston, p. 149.
2. Epigraph: in *The Rain of Wisdom,* trans. Nalanda Translation Committee, p. 86. Reprinted with permission.
3. Vajradhara is the trans-historical buddha who embodies and expounds the Vajrayana teachings. As Situ Rinpoche points out, he also embodies the essence of one's own nature. In his left hand he holds a bell, which represents the feminine principle of prajna: nondual awareness or wisdom. In his right hand he holds a vajra, the ritual scepter representing the masculine principle of upaya: skillful action which awakens beings and liberates them from suffering. These two are joined in his cross-armed mudra, signifying the inseparability of prajna and upaya, wisdom and compassion, emptiness and form. This seventeenth-century Tibetan statue is made of gilded copper. It is reproduced here courtesy The Newark Museum.
4. Apophatic (literally "negative") theology applies negative language to God, emphasizing his reality beyond the limits of human concept. Its complementary (though not necessarily contradictory) trend is cataphatic, or "affirmative," theology.

5

Views of Self and Ego

Dear, dear! How queer everything is today! And yesterday things went on just as usual. I wonder if I've been changed in the night? Let me think: *was* I the same when I got up this morning? I almost think I can remember feeling a little different. But if I'm not the same, the next question is, "Who in the world am I?" Ah, *that's* the great puzzle!

LEWIS CARROLL

I have been crucified with Christ; it is no longer I who lives, but Christ who lives in me.

PAUL THE APOSTLE

Experiences of Self

Loppon Lodrö Dorje
David Steindl-Rast O.S.B.
Joseph Goldstein
George Timko

LODRÖ DORJE: Ego is a central issue in the teachings of Buddhism.
Basically it is described as the process of needing confirmation
or security, which then manifests as the many different forms
of neurosis or delusion. The entity we habitually refer to as "I"
or "me" is ego. We have the notion that there is always a central
experiencer: someone thinks my thoughts, someone comes up
with my ideas, someone feels my pain and my pleasure. And
we identify that someone as being continuous: "I" refers
equally to who I am now and who I was when I was five years
old. Ego is that which feels enriched by material possessions
and experiences and which takes pride when it is
congratulated. It is also the entity that feels defensive when it is
accused or threatened. "I" am threatened when my family,
company, or country is attacked. Ego is the creator of territory;
it is that which tries to construct a personal kingdom. This
notion of entity or self is technically known as the "ego of
personality." What the Buddha taught, and what a lot of other
contemplative traditions teach as well, is that the personality is
actually a compositing process. The narrow version of self-
identity doesn't really exist. But the Buddha also said that the
higher self, or the spiritual, purified self, also doesn't exist, and
this was a revolutionary statement. For instance, the Vedantic
tradition in India at the time agreed that the empirical self is
obviously fictional: obviously you are not just your attachments,
your physical body, or the flow of your sense perceptions. But
what you really are, they concluded, is Brahman. The teaching
of Shakyamuni Buddha stated that Brahman is also a false
identity.

Self and what the self projects are interdependent. In

other words, self as experiencer and the world which the self experiences are mutually dependent creations which confirm each other, constantly. To the extent that we regard the world we project as a solid, independently-existing truth, that is also regarded as ego process and is technically known as the "ego of phenomena." Beyond recognizing ego of self and ego of phenomena as empty of inherent reality, there is a further perspective, associated with the Vajrayana tradition, which is that ego is a perversion of primordial intelligence. Ego is seen as a deliberate ignorance or hypocrisy, or as a perverse twist of the basic awareness which is naturally and continually taking place. In other words, ego is not just a naive mistake: it is an expression of stubbornness.

The ego process gives rise to confused emotions. In order to continually recreate a sense of personal territory, we grasp what we like and develop aggression toward what we dislike. Ego is also a distorting factor. It fundamentally obscures one's relationship with the world. We have deluded and imprecise relationships with people and phenomena, and we lose touch with the basic sacredness of reality. Whether we are appreciating mountain scenery, eating breakfast, or making love, there is a tendency to bring all sense perceptions back to a reference point of "me," the perceiver. There is also a tendency to constantly refer to oneself and one's particular territory. We have definite ideas about what is meaningful, what is not meaningful; what is good, what is bad; what is religious, what is secular; whether one should smoke or drink or not; what one should eat; and so on. Generally, all these thoughts and opinions are based on deeply-ingrained habitual reactions of all kinds, which we call karma. The Buddhist path is therefore primarily concerned with the question of how to see through ego, how to tame it, and how to let it go. And corollary with the idea of egolessness is the assertion that there is no external savior. The spiritual journey is a personal process of unravelling confusion. At the same time, we also place a lot of emphasis on the value of working with a group of people. And in the higher levels, there is emphasis on the need for devotion to a spiritual master. In fact in the Vajrayana tradition, the higher realization is only available by virtue of receiving the blessing of the spiritual lineage. This presupposes, however, that one has already gone through the process of surrendering ego.

BROTHER DAVID: It is a good idea to distinguish between our "individuality," which separates us from others, and our "personhood," which relates us to others. I am born as an individual, and I grow toward becoming a person. One becomes more and more personal by developing wider and deeper relationships. By becoming truly a person, we become truly ourselves, not in isolation from others, but in interrelatedness with others. This true self is not our little individual ego. When we are fully related to all, we have found our true self.

JOSEPH GOLDSTEIN: I'd like to ask about the Christian understanding of experience that is beyond the reference point of the individual. Would Christianity say that awareness itself is always conditioned by self? Or can there be an experience of God that completely transcends individual identity and the realm of conditioned reality?

FATHER TIMKO: If "I" am there, such an experience of transcendence will never happen. It would be a projection. I like to use the analogy of a sugar cube, which is an individualized and separate thing. When you put it into a cup of tea or coffee, the sugar dissolves, and yet it is still there. It is there in a completely different way, in a different dimension: it is no longer there as a cube. So, as Gregory of Nyssa would say, "We have to be dissolved and to be in Christ." You are no longer there as an "I," as an individualized center or self. There is no "you." You are dead, as Saint Paul experienced. You are dissolved in something else, and now there is a completely different reality.

BROTHER DAVID: Yes. However I appeal to your experience that when we most lose ourselves—when the cube is the most completely dissolved—we become more truly ourselves than we are at any other time. Because really being myself does not at all have the feeling of being dissolved and not being there. Now I am really there! I think we have to do justice to the actual experience.

FATHER TIMKO: But I think that too is a projection. We just simply don't want to completely let go of that self, so we say, my true self is there. There is no such thing as a true self or a false self. There is only the self or the no-self. And, as Saint John Chrysostom said, "He alone truly knows himself, who knows himself as nothing." Let us just be what we actually are— *nothing!*

BROTHER DAVID: No, no. You see, we experience degrees of letting go. We are not talking about the ultimate yet, and who knows what the ultimate is anyway. But we all experience degrees of letting go and we know that to the extent we lose ourselves, we are ourselves. And therefore we can extrapolate that when we completely lose ourselves, we will completely become it.

FATHER TIMKO: When you use terms such as "becoming" I am wary. The Fathers talk about these experiences in terms of coming to a state of being, just being. Saint Maximus the Confessor says, "Creatures endowed with mind and intelligence participate in God through their very being, through their capacity for well-being, which is the being of goodness and wisdom, and through the grace that gives them eternal being." These days everyone has an identity crisis: "I have to be me." Why? Why can't I just be?

JOSEPH GOLDSTEIN: In the dissolution of the sugar cube, is there something in the Christian teachings that describes the moment of the last grain dissolving?

FATHER TIMKO: Gregory of Nyssa talks about standing on the edge of a tremendous precipice. You have to go ahead and make that final step and fall into nothingness. It is like dreaming that you are falling through space. There is no identity. You are just floating and falling, without any relationship to anything. In that moment there is nothing around that you can recognize, nothing that you can anchor to or cling to. You have become totally detached into a different dimension of being.

JOSEPH GOLDSTEIN: In at least some of the Buddhist traditions, that experience of dissolution is outlined according to different levels and stages. One very important level is what you just described: letting go without any reference point at all. There is just the changing phenomena. Then there is the level of dissolution which goes into a moment of unconditioned non-being, or the unmanifest. That is a different level, although it is still in the same direction.

FATHER TIMKO: Yes. That would be the following stage. You are letting go of the conditioned right there. Some Fathers describe a movement into a state of non-being. They stay there for a period of time, and then they come out of it.

JOSEPH GOLDSTEIN: How is that transformation described? What takes place, having come back from that experience? What is the effect in one's life?

FATHER TIMKO: One sees the transience of everything. One's value system changes, and the awareness and perception of reality changes. There is a new mindfulness of oneness. There is one consciousness, one love, one goodness, one truth, one intelligence. It isn't my intelligence and my goodness, or yours. There is just one ultimate being and wholeness or God, in the true meaning of that word. And one sees the sanctity and beauty of everything—the sacredness and sensitivity. All categories break down: cultural conditioning, nationalism, male and female. The new quality of being transcends all of that. My guess is that that transformation is probably the same in the Buddhist tradition, or in any tradition which comes to that state of experiential being.

JOSEPH GOLDSTEIN: I think that within spiritual traditions there are two descriptions of coming to oneness, and the two seem quite different to me. The first is as a process of expanding one's sense of self to include everything, so experientially it is like becoming a very big self. And the other kind of oneness comes out of the experience of being zero. The path moves in exactly the opposite direction. Instead of expanding to include everything we let go of being anything. Out of the zero comes a oneness not referring to anyone, a totally impersonal oneness.

FATHER TIMKO: And that second one is the true way, the only way.

JOSEPH GOLDSTEIN: I think so.

FATHER TIMKO: The other is simply the inflation of ego—ego blowing itself up.

BROTHER DAVID: I would challenge your experience—not your intellectual categories, but your experience—by proposing that both occur at the same time. I could speak about the inflation of my ego until it pops, or I could speak about it being absolutely zero. And both would be faithful to the actual experience.

LODRÖ DORJE: Perhaps I could address this issue from the point of view of the Mahayana tradition. Mahayana methods and teachings are meant to stretch you out, in terms of expanding your concerns to include every sentient being in the universe, and at the same time the other thrust is to dissolve ego. So the path works on you from both ends of the stick, so to speak.

This brings up another topic, which is the relationship between relative and absolute perspectives of ego. The relative perspective is that, as individuals, we aren't just isolated, but we are interrelated with everyone and everything else. Therefore, by letting go of self-concern we discover a natural empathy and compassion for others. Then there is an absolute aspect to experience, which is that neither self nor other actually exists to begin with. This is fundamental egolessness, and it is an experience which is inexpressible.

BROTHER DAVID: Lodrö, what did you mean earlier when you described the "purified self" as an expression of ego?

LODRÖ DORJE: From the Buddhist point of view, there is a lot of concern about the potential for recreating the ego process through spiritual experience. The point isn't to just create a big, fantastic experience and then to live off that as continual security. Nor is it to create a purified or spiritual version of oneself. The spiritual journey obviously has to be more dynamic than that.

BROTHER DAVID: I am interested in Abraham Maslow's description of what he terms the "peak-experience." I think his perspective could be a useful reference point in our discussion here, because he universalizes this experience. There is a tremendous tendency in every religious tradition for elitism in this area. Maslow shows that there is a common human experience that cannot be fundamentally distinguished from the descriptions of the realization of the mystics. This puts religion and mysticism on a totally different level in our time. I would like to quote one passage here, where he describes perception during the peak experience:

> Perception in the peak-experiences can be rel-
> atively ego-transcending, self-forgetful, ego-
> less, unselfish. It can come closer to being
> unmotivated, impersonal, desireless, detached,
> not needing or wishing. Which is to say, that it
> becomes more object-centered than ego-cen-
> tered.[1]

FATHER TIMKO: I don't want to give the impression that I don't see anything of value there, but Maslow's whole thrust is the process of self-actualization, rather than being in line with the Christian thrust, which is self-denial. Actualizing the self in transcendence simply reinforces the self and creates a different quality of self. But self-negation crucifies the self. The self is put to death.

BROTHER DAVID: Yes, I hear you. But I'm not selling Maslow; I'm selling the peak experience. This passage comes from the results of his experimental research. He does one thing with those findings, and I do something else; many other people like to do yet something else. I personally never talk about self-realization. I would still say, though, that the idea that each one of us naturally has this peak-experience has important implications.

JOSEPH GOLDSTEIN: I think we all agree with that.

FATHER TIMKO: Yes. The spiritual Fathers also say that this experience of the unconditioned is universal, although it is usually partial and fleeting in our lives. Sometimes it comes to us at the moment of death. I have talked to many people who have had it. It is a very peaceful, renewing, transforming experience.

BROTHER DAVID: Father Timko, where have you found this understanding? I don't think this is something one tends to learn in the seminaries these days—though I think this is unfortunate.

FATHER TIMKO: It came out of my experience of meditation and prayer, of watchfulness and stillness. It was also nurtured by reading the spiritual Fathers of the *Philokalia*. But no one really gave it to me. It just sort of awakened through an insight that unfolded and evolved. I feel that this confirmation of spiritual experience in ordinary human life is the way of real religion. Sometimes people in my parish ask, "Can we understand and do these things, living and working in the world?" And I say, "Oh yes." And so we have ongoing spiritual renewal groups, and we read passages from *Unseen Warfare* and from the writings of the Fathers, and we discuss these ideas. Over the years people have had some experience, and they are affected by it. They become more aware of their interior life, and that awareness has brought them to a different state of spiritual being.

LODRÖ DORJE: I would like to address the peak experience issue, by way of saying something in support of the conditioned experience—which makes up most of our experience. In fact, many of the spiritual experiences we have along the path are conditioned experiences. These are the path. They are the means by which we can begin to realize the unconditioned. At the same time, the question remains: how is the relative world transcended? In the Vajrayana tradition, there are three steps, crudely speaking. First is the dissolution of personal pride and the letting go of the reference point of personal ego. Then there is the notion of letting go of any conditioned experience whatsoever. Finally there is the level where you reappreciate the relative experience; in other words, the relative world is re-entered or brought back. This last stage corresponds to the notion of living in sacredness, or of transforming relative experience. So there is a process of going in—to union or dissolution—and then there is a coming out. Beyond that there is also the idea that relative and absolute reality are together already, from the beginning.

JOSEPH GOLDSTEIN: To add to that, I could play the Zen role here a little bit, and ask whether it really is a question of dissolving anything, or whether it is just that in a moment we see that the self never was. I think we could speak from both perspectives. Really there is nothing to dissolve, because the self was never there in the first place.

FATHER TIMKO: Right. Ego is an imaginary projection.

BROTHER DAVID: But how so many Christians have been stuck in this imaginary projection! How they have clung tenaciously, thinking that the Christian way is based on promoting the ego from the level on which it is now, to some super-level in heaven!

JOSEPH GOLDSTEIN: Well, it is an appealing idea, Brother David! (Laughter.)

Be Yourself

William McNamara O.C.S.O.

Some people tend to think that once the final breakthrough takes place, it is finished. As soon as you think it's finished, it is finished. You are finished. But you never are. The journey goes on and on and on. If Saint Francis of Assisi had lived twenty-five years longer, he would have become that much more Franciscan. Saint Thomas Aquinas would have become that much more Thomistic. Each one of us has got to become more and more distinctively, authentically, exquisitely human. That is why it is always appropriate to say to another human being, "Be yourself." No one ever becomes sufficiently himself or herself.

I personally don't think that, for most of us, it's time yet to be talking about no-self. First we have to become real, authentic selves. First we have to become humanized, in touch and in tune with the totality of being, with all of reality: the reality we see and the reality we don't see, the words we hear and the words we cannot hear. The great challenge is, after all, to become more and more personal, more and more human, in order to let life shape us.

If someone were to ask me how to become a saint, I would say, let life do it. If you try to sanctify yourself, you're going to queer the whole process. You're going to become solipsistic, narcissistic, and a mess. No one can sanctify himself or herself. All the cleverness in the world won't do it. All the practices and projects in the world won't do it. Ultimately one is sanctified by life. And to live is to love, and to love is to give and to give and to give, until one's life is spent. In that process something unheard of, and something we know nothing about, happens: the emergence of that utterly mysterious kind of goddened existence, the god-manhood.

Proclamation of Egolessness

Ven. Chögyam Trungpa Rinpoche
Thomas Keating O.C.S.O.

TRUNGPA RINPOCHE: The Sanskrit word *dana,* which at its Indo-European root is related to "donation," is translated as "generosity." Generosity, or giving in, is very important in Buddhism. Dana is also connected with devotion and the appreciation of sacredness. Sacredness is not a religious concept alone, but it is an expression of general openness: how to be kind, how to kiss someone, how to express the emotion of giving. So real generosity comes from developing a general sense of kindness.

    We have to understand the real meaning of dana. You give yourself, not just a gift, and you are able to give without expecting anything in return. Usually when you give something you expect some reward. But in this case, you don't expect anything. This is expressed in the meditation posture. When you sit in meditation, you open your arms, your front. You just open. So you are not conducting your practice in a businesslike fashion. I think the attitude of dana has a lot to contribute to the Western world. Some people think that God should give them something because they did something good for God.

FATHER KEATING: Yes, that is unfortunate. But the disposition of devotion you just described is exactly what is meant by true charity in the Christian sense: it is not self-seeking, but self-giving. Isn't it also true in Buddhism that dedication is a quality that is almost as essential as devotion for keeping us on the path? Would you say that the habit of expressing one's dedication—the resolution to continue the meditation practice

SENGAI

He creeps along the log
in fear and trembling,
He does not know that
the bridge is flowing
and the water is not.[2]

SENGAI

This "painting-poem" is by the Zen master Sengai (1750-1837). The Japanese calligraphy, which has been translated into English by Nancy Wilson Ross, is from a longer
poem by Fudaishi (d. 569 A.D.) Reprinted from *The World of Zen* courtesy of Random
House © 1960 by Nancy Wilson Ross.

and to submit to one's growing pains and the direction of the guru—is equally important? It seems to me that dedication and devotion are like two banks of a river. They enable both the spiritual energy and the energy of the emerging psychological unconscious to flow through. Without these two banks we would be swept away. Devotion and dedication enable us to have stable or skillful means in order to direct those energies toward efforts that are constructive, such as to use them in service to others and to further the development of one's consciousness.

TRUNGPA RINPOCHE: Yes. Those are both connected with the idea of giving up one's ego, one's egomania.

FATHER KEATING: Could you define "ego"? I also like to use this term, but I know that it has a precise psychological meaning that is not the same as the one you or I might use in the context of meditation. For the psychologist, the ego is an entity. Self-consciousness is crystallized into a kind of identity or individuality, which separates us from other people. Egolessness is a very difficult concept; it is not really understood by modern psychology. Exactly how would you define ego, as it is discussed in the context of Buddhist meditation?

TRUNGPA RINPOCHE: I think it is basically that which produces aggression, passion, and ignorance. Ego is not regarded as the devil's work, particularly. Ego can be transformed into wakefulness—into compassion and gentleness. But ego is that which holds to itself unreasonably. In English we say "ego-centered," for instance, or "ego-maniac."

FATHER KEATING: Is there an ego that is un-centered?

TRUNGPA RINPOCHE: Yes.

FATHER KEATING: And what name would you give to that? Egolessness?

TRUNGPA RINPOCHE: Egolessness, yes, or shunyata.

FATHER KEATING: Let me ask a question, then. This may actually be coming from a confusion of terms, but when one has shed this ego-centeredness, with its aggression and selfish self-seeking, is there not still an identity left, which may actually be very good? This identity may be experienced as self-control, goodness toward others, or even as union with God. And yet, that which is in union with God is still a self, a self-conscious or personal self. So now, is egolessness a further stage of the spiritual journey, a stage in which even a good ego, a transformed ego, ceases to exist? And would this experience be what Zen Buddhists call "no-self"?

TRUNGPA RINPOCHE: Well, I think now we have reached the key point. Egolessness means that there is no ego—at all.

FATHER KEATING: That's what I thought it meant. So I'm glad to have that clarification. This is not at all understood in modern psychology.

TRUNGPA RINPOCHE: Union with God cannot take place when there is any form of ego. Any whatsoever. In order to be one with God, one has to become formless. Then you will see God.

FATHER KEATING: This is the point I was trying to make for Christians by quoting the agonizing words of Christ on the cross. He cried out, "My God, my God, why hast thou forsaken me?" (Mark 15:34) It seems that his sense of personal relationship with God, as God's son, had disappeared. Many interpreters say that this was only a temporary experience. But I am inclined to think, in light of the Buddhist description of no-self, that he was passing into a stage beyond the personal self, however holy and beautiful that self had been. That final stage would then also have to be defined as the primary Christian experience. Christ has called us Christians not just so that so that we will accept him as savior, but so that we will follow the same process that brought him to his final stage of consciousness.

TRUNGPA RINPOCHE: Well, it could be said that Christ is like sunshine, and God is like the sky, blue sky. In order to experience either one of them you have to be without the sun first. Then you begin to develop the dawn.

FATHER KEATING: Yes!

TRUNGPA RINPOCHE: And then you begin to experience sunshine. First you have to have nothingness, nonexistence. And then the sky becomes blue. It's like jumping out of an airplane. First you experience space, and then your parachute begins to open. You jump out of the airplane, which is gone by then.

FATHER KEATING: Yes. But then out of that nothingness there begins to emerge a new life, which is not one's own, but is without a self, and is united with everything else that is.

TRUNGPA RINPOCHE: That's right.

FATHER KEATING: So that's a similar experience in Buddhism. It is also our understanding of Christ in his glory: he is so at one with the ultimate reality that he has completely merged into it.

TRUNGPA RINPOCHE: In order to be ultimate you have to be a non.

FATHER KEATING: A nun?

TRUNGPA RINPOCHE: Non. Nonexistent.

FATHER KEATING: Well, that's the ultimate of the ultimate.

TRUNGPA RINPOCHE: Yes. (Laughter.)

FATHER KEATING: But, how would you articulate . . . Perhaps this can't be communicated except by spiritual communion or interior enlightenment of some kind, but are there any words that point to that ineffable experience where reality is the same in oneself as in everyone else, and where action emerges out of the present moment without reflection, where one sort of knows how one should relate spontaneously, without thinking, to every moment of life?

TRUNGPA RINPOCHE: That is called "ordinary mind." It is not glorious, particularly. It is so ordinary.

FATHER KEATING: Couldn't be more ordinary!

TRUNGPA RINPOCHE: Very ordinary.

FATHER KEATING: Like fanning yourself on a hot day . . . a very sacred, very profound kind of ordinary mind. Very ordinary.

TRUNGPA RINPOCHE: Almost nothing. Not almost, even. Just so ordinary.

FATHER KEATING: So what is it that changes to bring this about? Reality doesn't change. I suppose it is just that we cease to be a self, in the possessive sense? Self-consciousness ceases?

TRUNGPA RINPOCHE: Everything changes. When you see sunshine, it's a different kind of sunshine.

FATHER KEATING: Are you looking at yourself when you see the sunshine?

TRUNGPA RINPOCHE: The sunshine is coming to you.

FATHER KEATING: In other words, the sunshine is looking at itself.

TRUNGPA RINPOCHE: Yes. That is why it is called "ordinary mind" in Buddhism. And often it is known as "one taste."

FATHER KEATING: Is there not a terrible sense of loneliness or nothingness that one has to pass through in order to really taste no-self, and to then emerge into this higher unity with all that is? Isn't it as if all reality was manifesting itself in some mysterious way, in the most ordinary things of everyday life? In other words, there's no self to look at within. And since there's no self, there's no personal God, no relation to anybody else.

TRUNGPA RINPOCHE: I think so. I think you said it.

FATHER KEATING: How can you help someone in that state?

TRUNGPA RINPOCHE: Bring them into ordinary mind.

FATHER KEATING: I imagine that even one's relation to food and drink, beautiful music, and everything else would all of a sudden become the same in that sort of tunnel of experience.

TRUNGPA RINPOCHE: Absolutely.

FATHER KEATING: So how do you live without a self? What do you do before your life opens out into a new and higher life?

TRUNGPA RINPOCHE: You just do it. That is what is called "old dog" mentality.

FATHER KEATING: Oh! What a beautiful expression. (Laughs.)

TRUNGPA RINPOCHE: He just sleeps.

FATHER KEATING: Meaning, he just exists.

TRUNGPA RINPOCHE: Yes.

FATHER KEATING: A question that I've been contemplating myself lately is, in the state of ordinary mind, would a person suffer anything? Without a self, it seems there is no one to suffer.

TRUNGPA RINPOCHE: No suffering. Just lots of pleasure. Sometimes the pleasure might be suffering, but you aren't bothered.

FATHER KEATING: If someone who was in a state of ordinary mind went through an excruciating kind of suffering, what would their response to that experience be? How would one respond to one's persecutors or to the physical suffering that might be, humanly speaking, unbearable?

TRUNGPA RINPOCHE: One's reaction would be to see space. There is lots of room, lots of space. Suffering is usually claustrophobic. But in this case, there is no problem, because the person sees space.

FATHER KEATING: For the sake of the bodhisattva ideal, would one relinquish the experience of no-self and return to the experience and sufferings of people who are still in the egoic stage?

TRUNGPA RINPOCHE: One proclaims; one proclaims constantly. But you are not talking.

FATHER KEATING: There's no you.

TRUNGPA RINPOCHE: Yes. It's like an echo. It is often referred to as an illusion.

FATHER KEATING: One final question, Rinpoche. According to the Buddhist teaching, can this state be reached through the technology of Buddhist wisdom alone, or is there a certain point when the self has to be torn out of you by the absolute? In other words, is that tunnel I spoke of so terrible that one could never go through it of one's own volition, unless one was kind of dragged through it by a power greater than oneself?

TRUNGPA RINPOCHE: It could only come about through admiration for one's teacher. You have to become one with the teacher and mix your mind with the teacher's mind. Then you begin to dissolve.

FATHER KEATING: And that presupposes that the teacher must have achieved this level to begin with. . . .

TRUNGPA RINPOCHE: That is what we call "lineage."

FATHER KEATING: That's what lineage means in Buddhism! That's wonderful! Rinpoche, you have provided a lot of clarification, at least for me, personally. Thank you so much.

TRUNGPA RINPOCHE: Thank you.

Chapter 5: Notes

1. Abraham Maslow, *Religions, Values, and Peak-Experiences* (Columbus: Ohio State Univ. Press, 1964), p. 62.
2. This "painting-poem" is by the Zen master Sengai (1750–1837). The Japanese calligraphy, which has been translated into English by Nancy Wilson Ross, is from a longer poem by Fudaishi (d. 569 A.D.) Reprinted from *The World of Zen* courtesy of Random House. (c) 1960 by Nancy Wilson Ross.

6

Sin, Suffering, and Virtue

The Noble Truth of suffering (dukkha) is this: Birth is suffering; aging is suffering; sickness is suffering; death is suffering; sorrow and lamentation, pain, grief and despair are suffering; association with the unpleasant is suffering; dissociation from the pleasant is suffering—in brief, the five aggregates of attachment are suffering.[1]

SHAKYAMUNI BUDDHA

Know for certain that thou oughtest to lead a dying life. And the more any man dieth to himself, so much the more doth he begin to live unto God. No man is fit to comprehend heavenly things, unless he submit himself to the bearing of adversities for Christ's sake. Nothing is more acceptable to God, nothing more wholesome to thee in this world, than to suffer cheerfully for Christ.[2]

THOMAS À KEMPIS

Sin: The Alienated Self

George Timko

In this presentation I will be speaking out of the tradition of the Eastern Orthodox Church, and I will be drawing largely on the spiritual direction of the Eastern Fathers who lived from the fourth through the fifteenth centuries, and whose writings have been collected into a work known as the *Philokalia*. Therefore, some of what I am about to say on this topic may sound somewhat alien to the Western Christian affirmation.

Let us begin this investigation of the question of sin, self, and alienation by going to a Book in the Old Testament Apocrypha, the Second Book of Esdras: The author says that a grain of "evil seed" has been implanted within us, a grain of evil seed which has sprouted into an "evil heart." Therefore he asks, "Who among the living is there who has not sinned? For an evil heart has grown up within all of us; an evil heart which has alienated us from God, and has brought us into corruption and the ways of death, and has placed us on the paths of perdition and removed us far from life. This then is why all those who dwell upon the earth find themselves undergoing a tremendous torment: because though they have the capacity for understanding, they go on committing all kinds of iniquity; though they received the commandments, they do not keep them; and though they have the law, they are unfaithful" (chapter 7).

"Sin" is often an uncomfortable topic; it is unpopular and disturbing because it can move people to guilt. Sin is usually associated with an external, legalistic behavior pattern. For example, many people feel it is a sin to dance, drink a glass of wine, or go to a movie. But in the spiritual tradition of the Eastern Church, the essential meaning of sin is found in the Greek word *amartia*, which means "to miss the mark." The same word is used when an archer misses the bull's eye; or if when traveling down the road, you make a wrong turn. It is the same idea: you have sinned; you have missed the mark and gone off in the wrong direction. Sin implies a sense of disruption, disharmony, and deviation in our human nature and being. With the presence of sin, a discordant, divergent, and corrupted condition has entered human existence.

Sin is essentially a state of interior consciousness and being, which effects us in a very deep way, rather than any particular action. Nevertheless, sin doesn't have to be there; it is something that we can get rid of in our lives. Mark the Ascetic says that "to refrain from sin is a work within our own natural powers." And according to Maximus the Confessor, even though we are in a fallen condition, we are still free beings with the potential of sinlessness. We have the real possibility of not sinning if we really want to. For sin is not part of our nature. It comes into existence through the incorrect use of our nature. In his words, "Sin arises from the wrong use of the powers of our soul: the thinking power of mind, the appetitive power of desire, and the inciting power of action. So long as the heart is stimulated by passion, sin clearly reigns there. But when impassioned thoughts have been completely erased from our hearts, then sin has been let go."

Sin emerges from self-centeredness, which breaks us off from the Source and Wholeness of Reality. Such a condition leads us to experience ourselves as separate and individualized egos. Maximus the Confessor says that human nature is one unified whole, but by our self-centering and self-love we have fragmented ourselves. Through the energy of the mind we have created selfhood and broken ourselves into pieces. Therefore we no longer experience human nature and human consciousness as a unified whole. We don't realize that the center of our being is something that transcends the ego, of the "I-me" consciousness which is selfhood and self-love. The Christian scripture refers to that transcendent center as God, who is the ultimate, infinite Mystery of Being. This is the mark we miss. For an the Psalmist says, "Against Thee, Thee only have I sinned and done that which is evil in Thy sight." We are off-target because we have come to identify ourselves with the false, fictitious target of the "I."

The spiritual Fathers of the Eastern tradition say that we can only experience true being by participating in the ultimate totality of being, which is God. Only then will we experience that we all share one consciousness, one love, one intelligence, one being. But this can only come about when we move out of the self-center into another dimension. In other words, the self has to die; it has to be killed. Christ said that if we want to be where he is, we have "to deny the self." He said, "Unless a grain of seed falls into the earth and dies, it remains alone. Only if it dies, can it bear fruit." That is also the way of the self. As long as I am centered in my own ego and find my identity in *me*, I am isolated; I am like that grain of corn that sits on the table, separate and alone. But, just as that corn comes to manifest a different state when it ceases to exist as grain, so I also come to embody and manifest an unself-conscious state of being when the self dies.

As long as I am centered in my self, then everything outside of that self is alien to me, and I experience alienation. First of all, I am alienated from the Ultimate Reality; I cannot have any kind of communion or relationship with God. As the *Unseen Warfare* puts it, "Selfhood closes the mind off to Divine Grace, and God cannot enter the soul unless it is emptied of the self." Secondly, I am alienated from other humans. All I can do is bump against them, as if we were all billiard balls. Thirdly, I am alienated from all of nature: from animals, trees, water, the air, and the earth. When I am centered in my own little self, it doesn't matter that I pollute the water, because I don't realize that I am that water. Water appears as something outside my self, separated and isolated from me. Finally, I am alienated from my own true being.

The Fathers say that when we are fragmented and alienated, we are in a state of delusion and distortion, and reality is not experienced as it actually is. This disintegrated, self-beguiled deception is sin. The Greek word *plany*, which alludes to roaming thoughts and a mind which has strayed off-course, has great application here. It is as if we were an ocean-going ship that has lost its bearings and gone off-course. Without realizing it, we could spend a whole lifetime straying and roaming about in a state of illusion. The correct course can only be regained through self-knowledge. This does not mean simply gaining some information about oneself after the fact, but seeing what is actually going on, both inward and outward, in the present process and movement of life.

Self-knowledge is the understanding and awareness of one's inner reality and an insight into the content of one's consciousness. It comes about through the process of watching the movement and activity of the mind, from moment to moment. In that way, one is delivered from delusion, because one is seeing what actually is. We see that alienation results from the fragmentation of the mind, the breaking-up of one's consciousness into little pieces, which we then identify with through the process of thought and attachment and desire and pleasure. This fragmentation dissolves the vital wholeness and tremendous energy of life which should be in us. In this regard, Gregory of Nyssa says that the mind is like a river that flows with great force and vitality at its source. And then, as the water continues along, it begins to divide into smaller streams here and there, until finally at the end of its course, the river has become dissipated. It has been so fragmented that it has lost its wholeness and there is no vitality left. In the same way, the energy of our inner being becomes completely lost when we are existing in a state of fragmentation, delusion, and sin. To reverse this process, the mind has to be recollected and brought back into its state of wholeness. The mind then regains its original vitality and force, and becomes wholly integrated and mindful.

My parish is in a residential community in Buffalo, New York. Periodically, I watch a woman who lives nearby taking her dog for a walk. It is an enormous dog; he starts moving this way and that way as he pleases, while the woman follows along behind, hanging onto the leash. When the dog goes by a tree, he stops and sniffs, and the woman also has to stop. The dog just drags her around. She thinks she is walking the dog, but it's not true. The dog is actually walking her. This is the same condition we are in. As long as the mind is fragmented, it is subject to all forms of delusions, passions, and forces that move and control and dominate us. Anger, pride, rage, hatred, jealousy, greed: all those alien, evil forces take over in our lives and lead us about without our realizing what is happening.

Are we destined to be victimized and to just go on sinning and being alienated, as we live our self-centered existence? Is there a way for us to extricate ourselves? The scriptures and the Fathers say that the way is through Christ. It is not that he is an external savior who is going to manipulate us like puppets and just pick us up out of our delusion. As Saint Paul says, we have to work out our own salvation, even though God works within us. Notice, he works within us, not outside us. We must come to be in the state of being that Christ was in as a man, which the scriptures and the Fathers refer to as "having the mind of Christ." In that mind we find our liberation and our salvation, for that is the mind of God. When Maximus the Confessor talks about Christ and his relationship to us, he says that Christ is the Divine Logos, the essential character of God, the mind and world of God, the intelligence and wisdom of God which became incarnate and embodied in man, and that that same reality has to be born and incarnated and lived and fulfilled in every human being. Christ comes not only as a teacher and example, but as one who has embodied the likeness of God and who enables us also to do likewise, so that we many be what he is.

What do we have to do? First of all, we have to change our minds as Christ has directed us. The Orthodox liturgy says that God has "designated the change of mind as the way of salvation." There is no other way, because the mind is the instrument or vehicle of sin, and therefore it is also the way out of sin. Now Hesychius of Jerusalem has something to say about that which has been mind-blowing to me. It is so clear and simple. He says that sin begins as thought knocking at the door of the mind. If that thought is accepted by the mind, then one moves into a visible act of sin. However, if the mind is quiet and still, attentive and aware, that is, if the mind has been changed, then thought no longer governs the mind, and sin cannot enter. If sin cannot enter the mind as thought, then there is no way that it can come to fruition. The Fathers always stress that the chief delusion of man is that he thinks his body is making him sin. He blames his body all the time. If lust awakens in him, he says, "That is a God-given thing in my human nature." He thinks that lust originates with his sexual hormones and not with his mind. But the body is a neutral instrument, say the Fathers; don't blame it. If you want to discover the source of sin, you had better start looking at your mind. According to Mark the Ascetic, "Having sinned, blame your mind and not your body. For if the mind had not run on ahead into sin, the body would not have followed."

The Fathers, who spent their lives watching and understanding the mind, have formulated and set down a clear description of the process of sin. They say that, first of all, the mind undergoes a provocation, some kind of stimulus, a suggestion. If one is attentive and watchful, there will be enough space to observe the provocation taking place and to let it dissipate. If not, then next there is a disturbance of the mind, which means that there is a response of the mind, a desire or preoccupation beginning to awaken. The mind is being taken toward the stimulus. Thirdly, there is a coupling, or a union, in which the mind gives itself over to the suggestion and begins to dwell with it. Fourthly, there is captivity. The thought has taken the mind captive and begins carrying us along. We are now lost, because we have given ourselves over and surrendered to the thought, and a kind of enslavement is taking place. And then finally, there arrives the state of passion in which the whole process becomes an overpowering energy within us. We react impulsively, instinctively, me-chanically. It is as though some force or power has taken us over. This condition of passion alienates our true being and creates all the many dif-ferent kinds of suffering and leads us into all kinds of sin. Of course, all this happens rather quickly. We usually don't see the stages because we are not trained in watchfulness and there is not enough space in the mind. So suddenly we find ourselves in the midst of a tremendous up-heaval of anger, of jealousy, and we have lost all stability and control, wondering with bafflement how and why it all happened.

According to the Fathers, the evil thoughts divide themselves into eight categories, from which all other passions and sins are derived: glut-tony, unchastity or impurity, anger, avarice or greed, despondency or de-spair, listlessness or laziness, self-esteem, and pride. Self-esteem is especially important to consider these days, for we have come to the point where it is accepted as a virtue. But if you look at Christ, who was the son of God and who had every opportunity to esteem himself and make claims to authority and power, you see that he did not do so. He emptied himself of everything, so that he was nothing. Kenosis, which simply means to empty the mind of all self-esteem and identity, brings us to a state of dispassion, where the passions are no longer an operative and controlling force within us.

Through self-knowledge we see that there is no exterior force or agency causing us to sin. We can no longer say, "Oh, the devil made me do it." Nor can we blame other human beings for our sin. The Fathers always say that, no matter what the conditions, we must always assume responsibility for our own behavior. All sin and evil comes out of our inner being, and from nowhere else. As Christ said, "All evil things come from within. For out of the heart of man come evil thoughts, fornication, theft, murder, adultery, covetousness, wicked-ness, deceit, slander, envy, licentiousness, and pride." If there were no anger and hatred coming out of me, or you, or any of us, there would be none anywhere. It is that simple. Sin does not have any existence of its own. Sin and evil have no actual substance; they are simply the negation of the good. Maximus the Confessor says, there are people who say that there would be no evil in the world if there was not some external power or agency that is always dragging us into the ways of evil. But if we observe closely we see that the power is in fact the natural energy of our own minds, which we nurture by our own agency and neglect. We create the demons within ourselves, by energizing them with our minds. And he who nurtures the energy of the mind to goodness simply does not move in the way of sin and evil.

Gregory of Nyssa says that the soul, the inner being of man, is moved by the mind of man. The mind determines what you are going to do and what you are going to be. If the mind is preoccupied with the desire of pleasure, you will move to gratification. If anger arouses the mind, you become that anger. Therefore, you have to observe and understand and work with your mind. Hesychius of Jerusalem says that you can be free of sin by guarding the mind. It is just as if you have some treasure in your house and you stand guard at the door. And Nicephorous the Solitary says that guarding of the mind is the attention and watching of the mind, from moment to moment. Only by changing the essential condition of his mind can man realistically deal with the sin, the suffering, the fragmentation, the self-centeredness, the alienation of his life.

I have heard that the essence of Buddhism, according to the Buddha himself, is this: "Not to do any evil, to cultivate good, to purify one's mind: this is the teaching of the buddhas."[3] The spiritual Fathers of the Orthodox Church also say that these are the preconditions for salvation and communing with the Reality of God. Christ said, "Blessed are the pure in heart, for they shall see God." Purity is the unfolding of man's inner being into the state of the ultimate mystery of being. Watching and changing the mind is the work of renewal and transformation, which can bring man into a different state of being, where he is the embodiment and vehicle of goodness, love, holiness, beauty, truth, compassion, and light. This divine quality alone will dispel all the sin and evil that man has been forced to endure and suffer, and will enable him to live a full, fruitful, joyful life.

First Noble Truth

Joseph Goldstein

The first realization on the Buddhist path is that suffering is pervasive. Certainly we don't have to look very far to verify this truth. Any newspaper or news magazine we pick up turns out to be a catalogue of suffering. People are suffering and dying from starvation, terrorism, epidemics, natural disasters, and all the various incurable diseases in the world. And then, through ignorance, people inflict pain on one another in the form of economic or political oppression. Often we become so familiar with the many manifestations of suffering in the world that we lose our sensitivity to it. But I think it is important to let the reality of suffering touch us, rather than to simply read about it and then shrug our shoulders with a feeling of helplessness.

There is another tendency we must be careful of, which is, when we begin to open to the intensity of suffering that exists in Africa, Asia, and South America, we may focus all of our attention outside of ourselves. We may forget to look closer: within our own culture, our own city . . . within ourselves. The truth of suffering has to be realized in all its dimensions. There is also suffering in the midst of apparently comfortable lives, a suffering that is an inherent part of human experience. It is not necessarily a result of social or economic injustice, but it is simply one aspect of the experience of being alive, of having a body and a mind.

Imagine standing in front of a mirror and deciding, with the greatest sincerity and conviction, "I am not going to get sick; I am not going to get old; I am not going to die. I have decided that I really don't want to go through those experiences." It would not be a realistic resolution. Taking birth in a human body means that we are going to get older, and that we will inevitably get sick from time to time. Our bodies are going to wear out, and we are going to die. It is interesting to see how our culture somehow conceives of death as being some kind of mistake. Another kind of pain, which we tend to be more aware of in our everyday lives, is the suffering of the mind. There is a wide range of experiences that occur when the mind becomes contracted and closed: the pain of anger, sorrow, fear, alienation, paranoia, lusting, boredom, and depression. All these states periodically occur in our lives, and some of them never completely leave us.

According to the Buddhist teachings, compassion naturally arises out of an awareness of suffering, as the spontaneous and intuitive response to pain. We might well wonder why, then, if suffering is so pervasive, the world is not a more compassionate place. If pain and sorrow are the conditions for compassion to arise, why are we not more compassionate? I would say that we all have a personal responsibility to investigate this question for ourselves. If we do look carefully at our own experience, we will find that we don't like to feel pain. We resist it. And in that resistance we close our hearts and close down the compassionate response. One of the great benefits of cultivating a precise meditation practice is that it enables us to see our particular resistances clearly. To begin with, almost everyone resists physical pain. We avoid it at all costs and try to ignore it when it is there, hoping that it will go away. We also have resistance to certain emotions that we don't like. For example, the experience of loneliness is unbearable for some of us. We respond by closing ourselves to that feeling, resisting it, and pushing it down. Then our lives become conditioned by the avoidance of loneliness: we will do anything not to feel lonely. Other strong emotions that many people resist are unworthiness, self-hatred, anger, and depression. There is so much pain associated with these feelings that we are not willing to open to them and experience them, and so we push them away. Eventually our lives become fragmented because we are not willing to welcome and embrace our shadow side. There is no one among us whose mind feels only happiness and rapture. We all have another side of experience that is painful. Can we be compassionate toward those feelings? Can we really experience them? It is absolutely essential to do so if we want to come to an integrated wholeness.

When I was in India studying with my teacher, I lived for some time in a small brick and thatch hut. Instead of a door, only a piece of canvas hung over the entrance. Every day I sat inside, doing my meditation practice. One morning a cat came walking into my hut, hopped up onto my lap, and sat down. At the time I had a general aversion to cats; I didn't relate well to them. So when this cat came in, I immediately picked it up and threw it out the door. It came right back in, and sat down on my lap. I picked it up and threw it out again. Now, those of you who are familiar with cats probably know how persevering they can be. I must have been sitting there for two hours, tossing out the cat. And the whole time I was getting more and more angry at this cat for disturbing my meditation. Finally the cat forced me to surrender. There was nothing else to do. It came in, sat down on my lap, and I let it sit there. Fifteen seconds later, the cat got up and walked out the door. (Laughter.) That cat was the buddha, coming to visit.

The more we resist, the more we feed what we're resisting. It is like leaning two playing cards against each other. As soon as you take one away, the other falls down. The more we resist—whether it's a painful feeling in the body, a painful emotion, or a difficult situation—the more our resistance maintains our suffering. When we look very closely at this process, we discover that there is one kind of resistance that is the root of all the others: it is the deeply conditioned resistance to an existential level of being. Resistance of any kind first arises because we see, on a basic level of experience, that life is a totally momentary, transitory, ephemeral phenomenon.

Recently, while I was on a teaching trip in Africa, I went on a sight-seeing visit to Victoria Falls, which is twice as high as Niagara Falls. It is an amazing place. I sat there for some time, watching the Zambezi River fall in an absolutely continual movement: falling over, falling away, falling down. There was not a moment when the river took a rest. And I realized that that is exactly how our experience unfolds. Existence itself is so momentary, so transitory, and so constantly dissolving that there is nothing to hold onto. Until we can open fully to this quality, life frightens us, and we resist its flow. It is like floating down the river toward the falls and trying to grab onto branches along the way. We grasp after pleasure and push away pain—which are actually two expressions of the same action. Meditation involves learning to surrender to the truth of impermanence, the truth of change. Just imagine what it would be like to spend one's whole life resisting something that is pervasively present all the time. It would be like trying to ignore an elephant walking down the supermarket aisle. It would take a tremendous effort. And yet that is what we usually do in our lives. We don't acknowledge what is there, and so our energy becomes narrow and constricted.

For compassion to grow in us, it is imperative that we open to all the levels of pain and suffering that are part of the human experience. Then our energy is freed and we are able to relax our resistance and let go of our grasping. In fact, when we open to the entirety of experience we discover, surprisingly enough, a lot of joy. An observation I have made many times is that the people who are the most aware and the most open to suffering are also the most joyous. When you meet enlightened beings who radiate compassion, it becomes obvious that the awareness of pain is not a morbid or self-indulgent state of mind. The Buddha is known as "The Happy One" *because* of his deep realization of the truth of suffering.

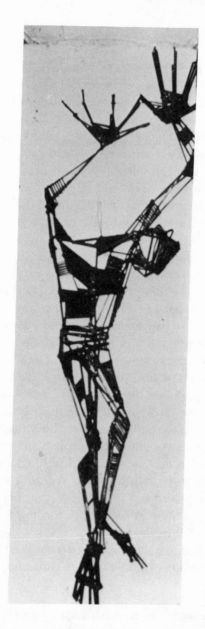

"Crucifixion 1968" by Brother Joseph McNally.
Courtesy of the artist.

Narrow is the Way

David Steindl-Rast O.S.B.

The people who wrote the gospels and letters of the New Testament saw that the glory they recognized in Jesus was not the opposite of suffering; it was the fruit of his suffering. We should realize the truth of this, because the way of the cross doesn't just belong to the life of Jesus. If we live the kind of life that Jesus lived—the contemplative life of keeping the eyes continuously on the vision and of then translating that vision into everyday action—we will inevitably end up on the cross. We may be reluctant to accept this, but in fact there is no bypass. This is just a basic law of life.

In an essay entitled "The Joy in the Thought that it is not the Way which is Narrow, but the Narrowness which is the Way,"[4] the nineteenth-century Christian existentialist Soren Kierkegaard argues that the spiritual journey is not separate from the way it is traveled. The way doesn't exist in the same sense that a road exists, regardless of whether anyone is traveling on it or not, but it is the "how" of the traveling that makes it the path. When we speak of life as a way, the real question is, how am I to walk on that way; how am I to live my life? Kierkegaard quotes Jesus: "For the gate is narrow and the way is hard, that leads to life . . . " (Matt. 7:14). Again, "narrow" is not an adjective describing the path; narrow *is* the path. The name of the path is narrow. Therefore, when life is narrow, we know it is the path. An alternative term frequently used in the Bible is "tribulation," which literally means "threshing the grain." The chaff flies away, and the grain falls through. We can't avoid tribulation; we can't avoid narrowness. It is a joy to know this, because then we know what we must do: we must suffer. And according to Kierkegaard, as we go along, we suffer more and more.

I would now like to quote a passage from the Prologue of *The Rule of Saint Benedict* which may at first seem to contradict Kierkegaard. Saint Benedict writes:

> Therefore we intend to establish a school for the Lord's service. In drawing up its regulations, we hope to set down nothing harsh, nothing burdensome. The good of all concerned, however, may prompt us to a little strictness in order to amend faults

and to safeguard love. Do not be daunted immediately by fear and run away from the road that leads to salvation. It is bound to be narrow at the outset. But as we progress in this way of life and in faith, we shall run on the path of God's commandments, our hearts overflowing with the inexpressible delight of love.[5]

Is the way only narrow at the entrance, or does it become increasingly more difficult, as Kierkegaard suggests? I believe this contradiction is a superficial one, because once we discover that narrowness is the way, we participate in the joy of understanding that it is so, which is also the "inexpressible delight" referred to by Saint Benedict. Life is a gift. We haven't bought it or earned it. Therefore we have a choice of two attitudes, both of which are painful: we can either feel anxiety because we don't trust that life is a good gift, or we can exchange that anxiety for a positive kind of suffering, which is a growing pain. This second choice is the suffering of compassion, which is the joyful suffering of going with the grain, of realizing that it is narrowness that leads to life.

When His Holiness the Dalai Lama visited the United States in 1981, someone asked him, in a small audience, how it was that Buddhists have developed such a wonderful path for overcoming suffering, while Christians have been wallowing in their suffering for almost 2,000 years. The Dalai Lama responded by saying, "It is not as easy as all that. Suffering is not overcome by leaving pain behind; suffering is overcome by bearing pain for others." And that is one of those answers that is as Christian as it is Buddhist. It is the basic statement that comes out of the fact that narrowness *is* the path.

The Essence of Ethics

Jack Engler
David Steindl-Rast O.S.B.

JACK ENGLER: In American society, many students bring to the contemplative life the peculiar idea that one's personal behavior, or ethical conduct, isn't all that important. Many feel it is enough to simply be mindful and do the sitting practice. It is as though we could come to the meditation hall, practice our contemplative disciplines, and then go back home and be angry with our spouse or cheat on our income tax. Perhaps we don't like to talk about morality because we are still rebelling against the Judeo-Christian moral code, which many of us have worked so hard to get away from. "Conscience" and "ethics" have become unsavory words which conjure up images of oppression and rigidity. It is true that without some kind of contemplative practice, ethics can be reduced to a set of legalistic do's and don'ts, rights and wrongs, and we may need to rediscover morality in a way that is different from how we learned it as children. Nevertheless, we must acknowledge that impeccability in our thoughts, our speech, and our actions is the very basis of our own growth and development. In traditional Buddhist cultures, moral training is considered to be the foundation of the spiritual path. There must be impeccable conduct—first, last, and always. Otherwise the contemplative practices will dry up, because there will be nothing to sustain them. They will just produce altered states of consciousness, without meaning.

In the Buddhist tradition, the instructions on morality start with five precepts. The practitioner vows to refrain from taking life, from taking what has not been given, from saying what is not true, from sexual misconduct, and from partaking of anything that causes mindlessness, such as alcohol and drugs. Each precept is a vow to abstain from a certain class of potentially harmful behaviors. For example, when taking the first precept, the practitioner asserts that he or she will refrain from taking life. It is not phrased "thou shalt not," but is simply stated as an intentionality. In fact, the expectation, at least in the beginning, is that one will not be able to completely live up to that intention. What does it mean, after all, to refrain from taking life? Does it simply mean to not kill other people or animals? Does it also mean that I ought to become a vegetarian? And when I'm walking down the street in the summertime, does it mean that I ought to take care not to trample willy-nilly on all the little creatures beneath my feet who also have a right to their space on this earth? That one precept can be practiced at many different levels. On face value, it may seem to be an obviously simple prescriptive rule, but by trying to follow it faithfully in all situations, it leads one into very deep waters. It begins to expose all of the root motives that usually push and pull us: the deeper greeds and aversions and the various concepts and fantasies that we unconsciously live by. A precept brings these hidden impulses to the surface, where they can be seen for what they are and worked with. It is not that if one doesn't live up to the precept in a particular situation, one has sinned. The precepts are presented as a challenge to be more mindful and more responsible for one's actions.

BROTHER DAVID: I would like to ask you to be more specific about sexual misconduct. For us in the Christian tradition, this is a highly problematic issue because there has been so much social influence on the religious tradition. Often we find a definition of sexual misconduct that has nothing to do with Christian morality, but has everything to do with the values of the society we live in. In this case, I'm wondering whether the Buddhist definition primarily speaks out of Japanese, Chinese, or Indian social values, or whether it is somewhat independent of social context.

JACK ENGLER: That is the same question, Brother David, that every student asks when they first hear about the precepts. Sexual misconduct is the one they most want to know about! I think you would find that different cultural traditions have each approached it a little differently. The root meaning of sexual misconduct refers to any exploitive sexual relations. In concrete terms, the precepts are situation-specific. They are deliberately phrased in an open-ended way because their application will vary according to differing circumstances. As we apply it in our sangha, refraining from sexual misconduct in a retreat environment means sexual abstinence. There won't be any sexual activity for the duration of the retreat. At other times, whenever one person takes advantage of another by using sexuality to gratify his or her own needs, without real care, attentiveness, concern, and respect for the other, then that is exploitive, and it is a violation of the precept. What that means in terms of specific conduct is left up to the individual to determine. That is the challenge of the precepts. If we were to translate them into an absolute, literal meaning that applied under all conditions, we would be treating them in a dead way.

BROTHER DAVID: Thank you very much. I think this is a really important contribution to the Buddhist-Christian dialogue, because this is also the root of the Christian idea of sexual misconduct. This is clear when we see the little which the Bible has to say about sexual sins as compared to the great number of warnings against exploiting others by taking advantage of them. Unfortunately, the popularized versions of Christian teachings have reversed this proportion. Exploitation is the real offense. But society has cast that meaning into particular laws, until the laws have become more important than the root meaning, and it ends up seeming that as long as you don't get into conflict with the laws, you can exploit others as much as you want. So I think there is a deep agreement between Christians and Buddhists on this level. But I wonder how well the Buddhists actually live that way. We haven't done so very well.

JACK ENGLER: I think we're probably batting about the same average!

Guilt

Rev. Sister Benedetta C.S.C.
Jack Engler

SISTER BENEDETTA: I think it is important that we learn to distinguish between two types of guilt. One is the genuine guilt which we're meant to feel and meant to use in a responsible way, and the other is neurotic guilt. For all of us there are times when our words or actions are such that we need to feel a sense of guilt, so that we can assume ownership for what we have done, and then express the necessary sorrow or regret and ask for forgiveness. That is always a difficult thing to do, but I think it is also essential. In that case, guilt arises out of conscience; it is real and needs to be deliberately faced. Neurotic guilt, on the other hand, is something we unnecessarily create for ourselves. It arises out of the superego: the voice that dictates to us what our behavior should be, based on the conditioning process that began in childhood. This voice comes from an external value system or authority figure that we met somewhere in our lives, and it can create unending feelings of inadequacy and guilt. So I would say that, to begin with, it is crucial that we learn to distinguish between true conscience and the superego.

JACK ENGLER: I would agree with you, Sister, that there is a healthy kind of guilt which allows us to acknowledge responsibility for our actions. The capacity to experience guilt is actually an extraordinary human development. If the patients I work with in my psychiatric clinic could experience real guilt, they probably wouldn't need to be in the clinic at all. As children, each of us had to develop the ability to experience that we could hurt the very people we loved. That is one of the most important attainments of early childhood. Out of that grows a sense of responsibility to one another.

I think that the Buddhist traditions tend to talk more about the neurotic kind of guilt—how to overcome the regret that binds us to the past with constant rumination. We go over the same things again and again, wishing that things had happened differently. Such fixations tether us to past events, so that we are never able to get beyond them, and we find ourselves constantly reliving the past. In Buddhist psychology, that kind of guilt is one of the "unskillful" or unwholesome qualities of mind, and it is part of the repetition and compulsion that makes up the realm of samsara, the realm of suffering.

SISTER BENEDETTA: Yes, neurotic guilt gets us stuck in the past, whereas I think if we're listening to the voice of conscience, it summons us outside and beyond ourselves and has more of a future orientation.

JACK ENGLER: I am reminded of old Father Bergen, an Irish priest from County Cork. After my parents, he was my first religious teacher. I grew up in an Irish Carmelite mission parish, and Father Bergen's brogue was so thick that I could hardly understand a word he said. But in those days, and in the Catholic parishes especially, all the children had to sit in front, with the parents behind them. Every Sunday, Father Bergen scared the daylights out of me by talking about hellfire and brimstone and my awful accountability before God. This generated enormous guilt in me. But the following Saturday, when I would go into the confessional, he would be totally different. I would confess what I thought were my horrible, evil deeds of the past week, and he would say, "Oh, that's not so bad. What was your intention in doing that?" And then maybe he'd give me just one Hail Mary to say. So he had these two ways of presenting the moral life I was supposed to be leading: one was a rigid code of ethics that inspired guilt, and the other was a gentle reflection back to the source of my actions, back to my intentions. But for many years the Sunday sermon was much louder in my mind than the quiet voice in the confessional, so that morality remained something external to me. It wasn't until I had been through various life experiences, including contemplative practices, that I could mitigate that duality a little and bring the voice of conscience back inside me, so that I could feel moral responsibility along with some kind of personal integrity.

QUESTION (from audience): It is my observation that we often feel guilty when we are not guilty, and we often are guilty when we don't feel that way. How does one go about making the distinction you both spoke of?

SISTER BENEDETTA: When I get to that state of confusion myself, first of all I try to identify where the guilt is coming from, and whether it is legitimate or just a trip I am laying on myself. Sometimes I may need to share my feelings with other people and let them help me to see more of what is actually going on. Personally, the way I have often gone is to work it out with a person who is highly-trained in therapeutic counseling. Also, one element I always need to come to terms with is the fact that right now, as I sit here, God sustains me in life—just as I am, with all my weaknesses and strengths, with all the parts that make up my being. If I can have some of that attitude toward myself, I can then handle some of my guilt better, whether it is guilt I need to experience or neurotic guilt.

JACK ENGLER: One other way of working with guilt from the Buddhist point of view is through meditation itself. In Buddhist contemplative practice, the issue is never really the mind-state itself. When we sit down with ourselves we realize that we experience many different mind-states in the course of a lifetime—or even in the course of a few minutes. These mind-states will always come and go; we can never stop them from occurring. Our freedom or our bondage comes from how we relate to them. So an important element in practice is not to worry about the mind-state itself—whether it is guilt or anything else—but to try and just be aware of our reactions to feelings and thoughts, so we can see clearly how we become entangled.

Some of you may remember the old Uncle Remis story of Br'ar Rabbit and Tar Baby. Br'ar Fox had set a trap to catch Br'ar Rabbit, because it is the nature of foxes to catch rabbits. He crafted a figure out of tar, with a carrot for a nose and buttons for eyes, and he set this down in the middle of a briar patch. He knew that Br'ar Rabbit was the kind of effervescent, histrionic, flamboyant personality that could not pass someone without wanting some form of acknowledgement. We are all like Br'ar Rabbit in that way: we need acknowledgement from our environment in order to have the sense that we exist.

Sure enough, when Br'ar Rabbit came down the road, he saw Tar Baby and cheerfully greeted him: "Good morning." No reply. You can see him hopping by for a few steps. And then he stops and does a double take, because his mind can't let go of his expectation. He turns around and again calls out, "Good morning!" Still no answer. "Didn't you hear me? I said good morning!!" He goes up to Tar Baby and says, "If you don't say good morning to me, I'm going to give you what-for!" Silence. He hits Tar Baby, and now he has one fist stuck in the tar. What does he do next? He does what the reactive mind always does: he expects that more of the same is going to liberate him. He hits him with the second fist. Now Br'ar Rabbit has two fists stuck, and he reckons that the only way to free himself is to push himself off, so he pushes in one foot . . . and then the other foot. Of course, by this time he is totally wrapped up in the tar. The story ends with Br'ar Fox coming out from behind a bush to collect his quarry.

When we experience the mind-state of neurotic guilt, we can either get stuck in it, or we can simply acknowledge it and let it go. It is not that we should repress our thoughts and feelings—that is an important distinction here. We don't deny what is taking place in our minds, but we are careful not to get hooked by our own reactivity.

QUESTION (from audience): Within the Catholic tradition, it seems that confession is the usual or prescribed way that guilt is dealt with, and yet confession has acquired a bad name and has alienated many people. Sister Benedetta, I'm wondering if you could say something about why this has happened.

SISTER BENEDETTA: I speak as an Anglican, but I think that, because we also have the sacrament of confession and have gone through many of the same stages as the Roman Catholic Church during the last twenty years, perhaps I can answer your question in fairly general terms. It seems to me that we used to think we would come to the practice of confession with guilt, and then by confessing particular actions, words, and even thoughts, we could suddenly be totally released into a state of forgiveness. I think we've learned that who we are as persons is an abiding state, from which there is a gradual growth and development. We don't suddenly and totally change. In my community, during the 1940's the practice of confession took place every other week. Then at some point confession was no longer built-in on a regular basis, and we were also given the freedom to choose the person we felt could best address our own particular spiritual problems. That led us to look at ourselves more, and to having a sense of the slowness of ongoing progress. We began to be able to live with ourselves as we were, and to realize that we need to live in a state of abiding penitence. Now I go to formal confession less frequently—perhaps three times a year or so. But when I do go, I am acting out of a sense of value within myself, and I am seeking forgiveness out of a real sense of guilt for my own sinfulness, rather than going from being totally caught up in guilt and feeling rotten, to feeling completely good, and so on, in cycles. I think you could say, too, that the recent exodus of religious from the orders has something to do with the general trend toward internalizing authority. Some people have realized that they were just being held by a structure of rules that was laid down, rather than being guided by real conscience.

QUESTION (cont.): How does Buddhism deal with guilt, since it doesn't, at least in its Western manifestation, have a formal practice of confession?

JACK ENGLER: I realize that this is perhaps an oversimplified response to a complex issue, but I would say that the important thing is always self-forgiveness. You may think God has forgiven you—or if you are a Buddhist that your teacher has forgiven you—but that doesn't resolve the issue of whether you have forgiven yourself. In meditation, the experience of allowing all the different states of mind to come and go in their own way leads you to the realization that all your thoughts and feelings are simply the warp and woof of human life. Before the end of an intensive practice session, you will have visited the states of bliss and ecstasy, happiness and well-being, envy and resentment, doubt and guilt . . . over and over again, until they lose their power over you. You gradually accept who you are, and who we all are, and come to recognize that we all suffer so much. From that naturally arises self-acceptance and a great compassion for all human beings.

The Illusion of Suffering

Tenshin Reb Anderson Roshih

On the way up the stairs to this shrineroom, there is a sign which says, "All dharmas should be regarded as dreams." In this case, dharmas means experiences, or things. Now, that may make the sign seem like a put-down of phenomenal existence. But I guess we, as Buddhists, could just tell the Christians that we love illusion; we love delusion.

When we say that suffering is illusion, that is a great compliment. All Buddhists ever work with is illusion; that's all we have. We don't work with enlightenment. So when a Buddhist calls something "illusion," he or she is really saying, this is our stuff. A buddha is someone who wakes up in the middle of delusion. Buddhas live in delusion; they don't live in enlightenment. Buddhas are enlightened in the midst of delusion. Deluded people are deluded in the midst of enlightenment. So if it is irritating to hear Buddhists call suffering or phenomenal existence "illusion," you could remember that we don't consider it to be an insult—although it is irritating to us, too.

Tenshin Zenki is my dharma name, given to me by my Zen master, Suzuki Roshi. Tenshin means "superficial, naive illusion." But the second part of my name, Zenki, means "total, dynamic functioning." So the whole name is "superficial illusion which is total, dynamic functioning"—which is a long-winded way to say "Just sit!"

Original Sin

Thomas Keating O.C.S.O.

Since we are comparing the Christian and Buddhist paths here, I feel it is important for us to first recognize where we agree. And in fact, in our time I would generally favor emphasizing what unites rather than what divides.

All the great religions are aware that the human family is in tough shape. There seems to be no disagreement about that. Why this is so is a question which causes a lot of agitation and which produces a variety of explanations. Down through the ages people have been wondering why we are the way we are. The term "original sin" is the Christian way of describing the human condition, and I would suggest it is perhaps equivalent to the Buddhist idea of avidya, or ignorance. In any case, original sin has nothing to do with personal sin. Perhaps it should not be called sin at all. It is simply the human condition: It is what we discover in ourselves when we evolve to full reflective self-consciousness. We find within ourselves all the self-serving habits which have been woven into our personality from the time we were conceived. This includes the emotional damage that may have come from our early environment and upbringing, at an age when we could not defend ourselves, as well as all the methods we have acquired, many of them now unconscious, for warding off pain. In order to grow, we have to break the pattern of ignorance, including the personal and cultural habits which stimulate, sustain, and reinforce that pattern. So the essential point, the point that everyone does agree with, is that, given our condition, for heaven's sake, let's *do* something about it!

Chapter 6: Notes
1. Epigraph: From the *Dhammacakkappavattana-sutta* (Setting in Motion the Wheel of Truth") in Walpola Rahula, *What the Buddha Taught*, p. 93.
2. Epigraph: "The Imitation of Christ" in *The Living Testament*, ed. Pennington, Jones, and Booth, p. 170.
3. The *Dhammapada*, verse 183, in Walpola Rahula, *What the Buddha Taught*, p. 131.

4. In *Edifying Discourses: A Selection*, trans. David F. and Marvin Swenson (New York: Harper & Brothers, 1958).
5. *The Rule of St. Benedict*, ed. Timothy Fry (Collegeville, Minn.: The Liturgical Press, 1981), p. 18-19.

7

Prayer and Meditation

(Roshi:) "Tell me, what about your Zen? What are you doing?"

(Johnston:) "I'm doing what you, I suppose, would call 'gedo' Zen."

"Very good! Very good! Many Christians do that. But what precisely do you mean by 'gedo Zen'?"

"I mean that I am sitting silently in the presence of God without words or thoughts or images or ideas."

"Your God is everywhere?"

"Yes."

"And you are wrapped around in God?"

"Yes."

"And you experience this?"

"Yes."

"Very good! Very good! Just continue this way. Just keep on. And eventually you will find that God will disappear and only Johnston San will remain."

This remark shocked me. . . . I said with a smile, "God will not disappear. But Johnston might well disappear and only God will be left."

"Yes, yes," he answered smilingly. "It's the same thing. That is what I mean."[1]

WILLIAM JOHNSTON

Natural Dharma

Ven. Chögyam Trungpa Rinpoche

To begin with, the main point of meditation is that we need to get to know ourselves: our minds, our behavior, our being. You see, we think we know ourselves, but actually we don't. There are all sorts of undiscovered areas of our thoughts and actions. What we find in ourselves might be quite astounding.

"Meditation" often means "to meditate on" something, but in this case I am referring to a state of meditation without any contents. In order to experience this state of being, it is necessary to practice what is known as "mindfulness." You simply pay attention to your breath, as you breathe in and out, and to every detail in your mind, whether it is a thought-pattern of aggression, passion, or ignorance, or just insignificant mental chatter. Mindfulness also means paying attention to the details of every action, for example, to the way you extend your hand to reach for a glass. You see yourself lifting it, touching it to your lips, and then drinking the water. (Rinpoche takes a sip from his glass.) So every detail is looked at precisely—which doesn't make you self-conscious, particularly, but it may give you quite a shock; it may be quite real. When mindfulness begins to grow and expand, you become more aware of the environment around you, of something more than just body and mind alone. And then, at some point, mindfulness and awareness are joined together, which becomes one open eye, one big precision. At that point, a person becomes much less crude. Because you have been paying attention to your thoughts and actions, you become more refined.

Out of that precision and refinement comes gentleness. You are not just paying attention, but you are also aware of your own pain and pleasure, and you develop sympathy and friendship for yourself. From that you are able to understand, or at least see, the pain and suffering of others, and you begin to develop a tremendous sense of sympathy for others. At the same time, such sympathy also helps the mindfulness-awareness process develop further. Basically, you become a gentle person. You begin to realize that you are good: totally good and totally wholesome. You have a sense of trust in yourself and in the world. There is something to grip onto, and the quality of path or journey emerges out of that. You feel you want to do something for others and something for yourself. There is a sense of universal kindness, goodness, and genuineness.

When you experience precision and gentleness, the phenomenal world is no longer seen as an obstacle—or as being particularly helpful, for that matter. It is seen and appreciated as it is. At this point, you are able to transmute the various defilements of passion, aggression, and ignorance into a state of wisdom. For example, when aggression occurs, you simply look at the aggression, rather than being carried away by it or acting it out. When you look at the aggression itself, it becomes a mirror reflecting back to your face. You realize that the aggression has no object; there is nothing to be aggressive toward. At that point, the aggression itself subsides, but its strength or energy is kept as a positive thing. It becomes wisdom. Here "wisdom" does not mean the usual notion of being wise. Wisdom is egolessness, or a state of being, simply being. The whole process requires a certain amount of mindfulness and awareness throughout, obviously. But you naturally develop a habit of seeing whatever defilement occurs just as it is, even if it is just for a glimpse. Then you begin to be freed from anxiety, and you begin to achieve a state of mind that need not be cultivated, and which cannot be lost. You experience a natural state of delight. It is not that you are always beaming and happy, or that you just stay in a state of mystical ecstasy. You feel other people's suffering. It has been said in the texts that the Buddha's sensitivity to others' pain and suffering, compared to the sensitivity of an ordinary person, is like the difference between having a hair on your eyeball and having a hair on the palm of your hand. So "delight" in this case means total joy, having a total sense of "is-ness." Then you are able to help others, you are able to help yourself, and you are able to influence the universe with an all-pervasive sense of is-ness which neither comes nor goes.

We follow these stages of meditation methodically, with tremendous diligence and the help of a teacher. When one reaches a state of no-question . . . (startled laughter erupts among the audience, as a loud thunder clap occurs nearby) . . . the natural dharma is proclaimed. (Rinpoche indicates environment with his fan.) Therefore one begins to feel, without egotism, that one is the king of the universe. Because you have achieved an understanding of impersonality, you can become a person. It takes a journey. First you have to become nothing, and then you can become somebody. One begins to develop tremendous conviction and doubtlessness, without pretense. This stage is called "enlightenment," or "wakefulness" in the ultimate sense. From the beginning, wakefulness has been cultivated through mindfulness, awareness, and sympathy toward oneself and others. Finally one reaches the state where there is no question whatsoever. One becomes part of the universe. (More loud thunder, accompanied by tumultuous rain.)

I think that is probably enough at this point. There are various details and technicalities regarding the types and stages of meditation, but since time is short, and also since it would be futile to talk about this and that too much, I would like to stop here. Thank you.

Corporate Mysticism

John Yungblut

From the beginning, Quakerism has emphasized the corporate element in religion. Alfred North Whitehead once defined religion as "what a man does with his solitariness," but Friends have deliberately chosen to experiment with the idea that togetherness affords a still deeper quickening of the spirit within. They have determined to explore the potential of group mysticism.

Now and again a form of corporate mystical experience emerges in what is called a "gathered meeting," in which there is a sense of unity with God and with one another. This is known as "waiting upon the Lord in silence." The underlying principle is that if each participant in the Meeting for Worship reaches for the interior center which is already one with God, they will all attain to the ground of being which is God, and at the same time they will experience communion with one another. There will emerge a corporate experience of presence, variously called "the spirit," "Christ the teacher," "God over all." Friends may recognize an authentic visitation with the customary phrase, "the Lord's power was over all." If, out of the silence, one is led by the spirit to minister to the assembled gathering, the words are understood to flow from the spirit or from Christ, the teacher, in the midst.

After the meeting, a participant might well whisper with appropriate awe to the one who ministered, "Thee was used." While waiting upon God is clearly understood to be motivated by a love for God, and not by a desire for any of his gifts, those who minister may arrive at a practical social concern, such as peace testimony. Such concerns are also prompted in one another following the Meeting. In this way, group mysticism is both an end in itself as well as frequently revealing itself as an ethical mysticism. The participants are challenged to translate the love of God into the action of testimonies before the world.

The leaders of early Friends recorded in journals considerable testimony concerning the promptings of the spirit, or the Christ within, experienced both in Meetings for Worship and in similar experiences that overtook them in solitude. However there was no formalized approach to meditation in solitude. It was simply assumed that every Friend would experiment with and faithfully practice prayer and meditation. And there was the expectation that every Friend would pursue his or her own effort to practice the presence from moment to moment in the affairs of daily life.

This lack of a corpus of instruction for the practice of meditation led, in the early nineteenth century, to the adoption of the philosophy and practice of three great contemplatives of the eighteenth-century Catholic Church: Archbishop Fenelon of Cambrai, Madame Jeanne de la Molle Guyon, and Miguel de Molinos. Their teachings were gathered and compiled by two Quakers, William Backhouse and James Janson, and printed in a little book entitled A Guide to True Peace. It is interesting that the counsel for which these three mystics were condemned and persecuted by their own church (that is, for the heresy known as "Quietism") took root and flourished in another branch of the church of Christ.

The central teaching of this little book is that we must look within for the meaning and purpose of life. In the depths of our being there is an inner sanctuary where true peace is to be found, a place where all grasping for power is overcome by unselfish love, a place where one can learn to be still and know God. The highest form of prayer is not that form of meditation in which discursive reasoning is still alive, but the direct perception of the divine presence in utter stillness and silence.

The Guide describes prayer as an intercourse of the soul with God. It is not a work of the head, but of the heart. The Guide laments, "Oh, how inexpressibly great is the loss sustained by mankind from the neglect of the interior!" It then concludes, "All our care and attention should therefore be to acquire inward silence."[2]

Training the Mind

H. H. Tenzin Gyatso, the XIVth Dalai Lama

Buddhist meditation can be divided into two types: analytic meditation and stabilizing meditation. When one cultivates penetrating insight, or vipashyana, that is analytic meditation. According to the system that is common to many traditions of Buddhism, insight is that which penetrates the meaning of the Four Noble Truths: the truth of suffering, the truth of the cause of suffering, the truth of the cessation of suffering, and the truth of the path that leads to liberation. In terms of the higher systems of buddha-dharma, insight also reveals the emptiness of all phenomena. Here, "emptiness" does not mean that phenomena are unable to perform functions. Emptiness refers to the absence of inherent existence. All phenomena depend on conditions; therefore it is clear that they do not exist under their own power. This realization, which is called the realization of emptiness, comes about through analytic meditation, which clears away false conceptions of reality.

I will now explain how one achieves a calm-abiding of the mind through specific forms of stabilizing meditation, or shamatha. In its ordinary state, the mind is scattered among so many objects of attention that it is powerless. Thoughts are like running water that has spread itself in every direction. However, just as one is able to channel running water in order to achieve a certain force, so it is that one can channel the mind in order to stabilize it. First of all, in terms of the general or common way, one stabilizes the mind by focusing it on a particular object. To begin with, one has to determine what that object is. The Buddha set forth many different types of objects according to people's various needs. For instance, someone who is mainly involved in desire might meditate on the ugliness of the human body. In this case ugliness means the actual physical nature of the body: one sees it as a composite of blood, flesh, bones, intestines, and so on. Usually we just see the outside of the body and think that it is beautiful and desirable: it has a good color and feels soft and pleasant. But if we were all wearing special glasses we would see that this room is full of skeletons. And here I am, a skeleton who is talking to you! (Laughter.) For someone who is mainly involved in hatred, that person would cultivate love and compassion. By meditating on those qualities, the mind is shaped into the entity of compassion itself. The person who is mainly involved in bewilderment would meditate on the twelve ni-danas, the twelve links of the dependent arising of cyclic existence.[3] The person who is dominated by many conceptions would meditate on the breath. There are many suggested objects of meditation. It is possible to meditate on flowers. One could also meditate on one's own mind. A Bud-dhist could take the Buddha's body as the object; a Christian could med-itate on Christ on the cross.

Having identified the object, how does one set one's mind on it? First of all, a good posture is important. Then, if the object of observation is external, one familiarizes oneself with it and gets used to what an internal reflection of that object would be like. One thinks about it again and again, ascertaining its form through thought. If one is meditating on the body of Buddha or the body of Christ, one identifies what that body looks like until it appears clearly as an internal image. Then one imagines it about four feet in front of oneself, at about eye level. One meditates on it as having the nature of bright light. This prevents laxity from arising. As much as one can, one reduces the size of the object. This helps to with-draw the mind and to channel its force. Once the object is set in terms of its appearance, size, and so forth, one holds the object with the power of mindfulness. One should stay with its exact form one-pointedly.

The two factors that may prevent calm-abiding are laxity and excite-ment. Laxity or lethargy prevents the mind from developing an intense clarity: the mind becomes too loose. Your feel a sort of heaviness of the mind and body, as if you had a big hat on top of your head. Thus, as an antidote, one should tighten the apprehension of the mind. However, ex-citement, which is a scattering of the mind to other objects of attention, could then increase. As an antidote to excitement, one should lower the level of apprehension and loosen the mind. This is how the mind is trained. One first holds the object by way of mindfulness and then looks with introspection to see whether the mind is becoming too lax or too excited. Then one applies the appropriate antidote.

In terms of the length of each session, for a beginner it is best to have many sessions of short length. Also, it is difficult to successfully cultivate this meditation while living in the city, in the midst of a lot of noise. Pe-riods of complete isolation and silence are therefore helpful. In this way, one can achieve ever-greater levels of meditative stabilization.

Calm-abiding can also be developed through the special techniques of tantra, such as the concentration called "abiding in fire" or "abiding in sound." In yoga tantra there is a technique which involves meditating on a very small symbol. For instance, one meditates on a crossed vajra[4] the size of a mustard seed, at the level of the eyebrows. Then one imagines that from one symbol two are produced, and from those two, four, and so forth, spreading out in all directions. In the highest yoga tantra, there are techniques for meditating on the inner energies. One meditates on drops of light or small letters in specific energy centers. Due to the power of meditating on these special objects which are placed in special points in the body, and due to having received initiation from a meditation master, these techniques serve as effective methods for forcefully stopping conceptuality. In this way one is able to transform the subtlest type of ordinary consciousness into wisdom consciousness.

The mind is made up of many levels of consciousness. When we die the gross levels naturally drop away, because the ability of the various elements of the body to support consciousness has decreased. Finally, at the time of death, one manifests the subtlest mind, the mind of clear light. Generally when this happens, however, one goes into a swoon, as if unconscious. But when one learns through meditation how to deliberately and forcefully withdraw the grosser levels of consciousness, the subtlest levels can be generated within great clarity and awareness. One then progresses over the path quickly. Finally, special insight, or vipashyana, and calm-abiding, or shamatha, are achieved simultaneously.

Long, Loving Look at the Real

Tessa Bielecki

I would like to talk about Christian prayer not so much in general terms, but as something intimately personal to me. It is difficult to be vulnerable enough to share what is at the heart of one's life: baring one's soul is not easy. But I would be most unhappy if I left here without having shared at least something of my Christian practice with you. Obviously prayer reaches a point where it becomes ineffable, so that it cannot be talked about, but I will just have to do the best I can, and go as far as I can with words.

One of the most simple definitions of Christian prayer I know comes from Saint John the Damascene, who said that prayer is "raising the mind and heart to God." Another wonderful definition comes from Teresa of Avila, who said that prayer is a "heart-to-heart conversation with God, whom we know loves us." The term "conversation" could be misleading here; we may think that prayer refers only to a lot of talk, which is not the case. Just as a human conversation involves periods of listening as well as speaking, so it is also in Carmelite prayer. I sometimes prefer to use the word "communion": communion with God, whom we know loves us.

Prayer is also sometimes described as "a cry of the heart." Of course, the heart can cry out in many different ways. In the Catholic tradition, prayer usually begins with a deliberate, verbal cry. This stage we call "meditation." We use some kind of exercise or method to quiet the mind and focus the personality. It is like setting up a scaffolding in preparation for building. Then we move on to contemplation, which is a more passive, receptive stage. Of course, I don't mean a limp kind of passivity, as if you were waiting to be run over by a steam roller. In my community we use the expression "wise passiveness." It is an alert, alive, and very awake state, like a cat ready to pounce or an army ready to strike. The contemplative moment which then unfolds is sometimes described as "a loving, experiential awareness of God." Or we could be more nontheistic and simply say, "a loving experiential awareness." In his poem, "The Dark Night," John of the Cross describes contemplative prayer this way:

> I abandoned and forgot myself,
> Laying my face on my Beloved;
> All things ceased; I went out from myself,
> Leaving my cares
> Forgotten among the lilies.[5]

Other descriptions include: "seeing everything against the background of eternity" and "an enlargement of the heart." I especially like this last one because when I hear Buddhists talk about their practice, they seem to have so much to say about mind, and I miss hearing about the heart. I know from the Buddhists I meet that the heart quality is there, but I don't hear it spoken about very much. My favorite definition of contemplation is "a long, loving look at the real." Because we are describing such an enormously full experience, each of those ideas—long, loving, look—is important. The contemplative moment is long in that it is not merely a fleeting moment, but includes a long-view interpretation; it is loving because it is a participation in the mystery of all things; and it is a look because it includes a perceptive appreciation of all that is real.

If we restricted our prayer entirely to meditation, at least in the Carmelite tradition, our prayer life would be considered terribly stunted. In fact, as we advance and grow more intimately into union with Christ, we may not need the preliminary step of meditation at all. John of the Cross teaches us in the *Ascent of Mount Carmel* how to discern whether it really is time to stop meditating and to move into contemplation, or whether we are simply lazy and don't want to bother meditating anymore. He also describes the necessity of letting go of meditation when it is time to do so. His instruction is, "If you find the orange peeled, eat it." You don't have to peel it again. It is unfortunate that Christianity has a reputation for being word- and activity-oriented, because contemplation is actually at the center of the tradition. Although the mystical tradition has tended to become obscured by many other elements, such as scholarship, social action, and discursive meditation, contemplation or nonverbal prayer is still very much at the heart of Catholicism.[6]

In my community there are two daily periods of common prayer. We get together every morning at six o'clock for Lauds, and then again at five in the evening for the prayer known as Vespers. Ideally, I prepare for periods of prayer with what we call "proximate preparation for prayer." You may be surprised to hear that my preparation is often physical activity. I go for a walk or a hard swim, a bike ride, or sometimes I turn over the compost. Other times I listen to music, or look at a work of art. Or I might go out into the garden and just sit and look, or even walk up and down between the rows. I do any focused, simple activity that will gather up the forces of my being into one concentrated act. But then there are also times when I just roll out of bed at a quarter of six and fall into the chapel. Or at a quarter of five in the evening, I may be madly dashing from some hectic activity or some exhausting personal encounter, and again, I just fall into the chapel. And that's alright, because that, too, is my practice. You see, my whole life is practice. But we all know that it is dangerous to say that, because it is also important to concentrate or focus our practice into definite periods of time, so that we don't become sloppy.

Besides the two periods of common prayer, we each have at least one hour of solitary prayer each day. On my best days I find two hours, but often it is difficult to fit the second hour in. Where do I pray when I pray alone? Anywhere. Sometimes I stay in bed. I may pray lying out in the sun or floating in the creek. Some of my best prayer is with our sheepdog, Zorba, or our cat, Tate. That cat has been with me longer than any other member of the community, and after eighteen years we have an extraordinary relationship. Looking into his eyes puts me right where I need to be—right at the center. But most often I pray in the chapel, because I feel that sacred space is important. One of the things that amazes me, coming to Boulder, is to see so many shrine rooms in the homes of Buddhist practitioners. It is unfortunate that you do not find such a special place of prayer in most Catholic homes. Of course, every space is sacred. But again, we have to concentrate that sacredness or we become sloppy; we forget. I can pray to God outdoors, but when I walk into a church, the sense of presence is different. It is focused. Within the chapel itself, the altar is a powerful focus, and inside the tabernacle is the consecrated host, the piece of bread that has been turned into the Body of Christ in the celebration of the Mass. There the quality of presence is palpable. Again, we can say that all bread is sacred, but the church that has the Blessed Sacrament has a presence that is different from the church without. When that Blessed Sacrament is outside of the tabernacle, we have presence at its most powerful. So, although God is everywhere, it is only natural that I am often drawn to the chapel to pray.

When I enter the chapel I take off my shoes, and I make a profound bow. For me, the quality of that bow predicts the quality of my prayer that day. In fact, that bow is my prayer. Once inside, I usually sit against the wall, on the floor. Unlike Buddhist practice, there is no strict posture for Christian prayer. I usually pray with my hands folded, which has always been a natural expression of reverence for me. Sometimes I pray flat out, prostrated. This I only do in private, because I try to be sensitive to other people who might be shocked by such a sight. An important dimension of Christian prayer is that there shouldn't be anything too unusual in terms of what anyone sees you doing.

Sometimes when I go to pray I find that I am distracted, so I have to begin by recollecting myself with a period of meditation. I may do a breathing exercise that I learned from Buddhism, or I may use what in Christianity is called an "aspiration." This involves the repetition of a single word that I have either deliberately, intellectually chosen, or that has somehow been given to me. The one I often use is, "Blessed be Jesus in the most holy sacrament of the altar," which comes from our ritual benediction. Another one that has come to me lately is a line from Francis Thompson's poem, "The Hound of Heaven": "Naked I await Thy love's uplifted stroke." I repeat these words over and over until they take over, until I am naked, awaiting love's uplifted stroke. Other meditations are not verbal, but involve a poetic image of Christ or a scriptural scene. One of my favorite images is of Christ cooking fish on the beach. Here is the resurrected Christ in his ultimate realization—which might lead us to expect some kind of miraculous spectacle. But what is the experience? Christ is sitting on the beach in the early morning, cooking fish. That image has always stayed with me, and has become more and more penetrating. Now even when I let go of the image, it never totally leaves me: it just becomes more transparent. I also find that reading scriptures can be a helpful recollecting exercise. First I read slowly and reflectively, ruminating on the words, and then I let go. From then on, there is no telling what will happen.

The Christian at prayer does not always sit in quiet serenity. Tranquility is, of course, an important dimension of prayer, but it is only one dimension. If this is the only kind of prayer we have known, we have missed out on a very rich realm of experience. For example, sometimes at prayer I worry and I weep with anxiety. This is not neurotic anxiety, but a genuine existential anxiety: it is an agonizing over the world. The entire world is with me there, explicitly and consciously. The man in El Salvador who is about to get his head shot off is in my prayer. I feel his fear. I suffer the pain of his wounds. I weep his tears. I weep the tears of his wife and children. I weep for the soldier who is about to shoot him. This is what we mean, in the Christian context, by "intercessory prayer." Unfortunately, this term has become so banalized over time that many people think it involves telling God what he should look out for, as if he didn't already know: "Please take care of my Aunt Sarah" or "Please watch out for South America." In our community, we say that intercessory prayer must be "saltatory before it can be hortatory." Before we can exhort God, we must first leap into the breach, into the situation. We must put our bodies on the line, where our mouths are; we cannot merely offer cheap petitions.

Sometimes at prayer, I laugh. And there are times, especially if I am out of sight, when I dance like David before the Ark of the Covenant. Sometimes I may be so full of joy that I can't contain myself, and I find myself squirming around. Or there might be another kind of restlessness, where I pace the floor, wring my hands, and bury my face in my hands. I might argue with God like Job, or struggle with him like Jacob. The Bible says that Jacob came out maimed; I have not yet come out maimed, but I have often come out exhausted. Christian prayer is not always relaxing and refreshing. It is sometimes a crucifixion, an agony.

Sometimes prayer can best be described as a slow, interior bleeding: an awed, stunned silence, with no words, no images. That silence can be a full, mysterious presence; at other times it can be a terrifying absence, the experience of abandonment. In the New Testament Jesus cries out on the cross, "My God, my God, why hast thou forsaken me?" (Mark 15:34). That, too, is Christian prayer.

It is important that we appreciate all these possible variations and dimensions, as we move in and out of the rhythms and seasons of our prayer life. As Nikos Kazantzakis said, "Blowing through heaven and earth, in our hearts, and the heart of every living thing, is a gigantic breath, a great Cry—which we call God." And the only way to respond to the great Cry which we call God is by the cry of the heart which we call prayer.

Letting Go of Thought

Joseph Goldstein
Loppön Lodrö Dorje
Judith Lief
Tessa Bielecki

George Timko
David Steindl-Rast O.S.B.
Reginald Ray

JOSEPH GOLDSTEIN: In the Buddhist traditions there are two main streams of meditation practice. One is the development of what could be called concentration, and the other is the development of insight. After listening to Mother Tessa's description of prayer, I would suggest that Buddhist concentration practices parallel what is called meditation in Catholicism, and insight practices parallel contemplation.

In Buddhism, concentration is achieved through focusing the mind on a particular object, such as a light, mantra, or visualization. Usually that concentration of mind is then applied to insight meditation. In Theravada vipassana meditation, for example, you sit with awareness of the process of mind as it unfolds, without trying to create or focus on anything and without leading the mind anywhere. It is a settling-back into the moment and allowing the dharma, or reality, to unfold. This practice brings about an ever-increasing refinement of perception, which penetrates the solidity of experience. Usually we tend to view ourselves as something solid and real. By settling back into the moment and observing the flow of phenomena, perception becomes so refined and so strong that it penetrates the apparent solidity of ego. As insight develops, there are stages of perspectives that one goes through. It is an ordered path, which finally leads to an opening to the unconditioned.

LODRÖ DORJE: In the Vajrayana Buddhist tradition, we find a similar description. I would just elaborate by saying that the element of exertion is important in distinguishing the two stages or types of practice. When concentrating or settling the mind, there is a definite sense of exertion. Then at a certain stage of the meditative process, you let go of any deliberate effort. By letting go, the quality of insight or awareness comes to you; it is not manufactured.

JOSEPH GOLDSTEIN: I'm sure it must also be true in the Christian tradition, or in any spiritual tradition for that matter, that an understanding of right effort is crucial. Effort is the foundation of practice, and yet it can so easily be transformed into a hindrance. The Buddha gave many teachings on the meaning and importance of right effort.

JUDY LIEF: It is interesting to me that letting go of effort doesn't necessarily correspond to a decrease in the formal or structured aspect of practice. For example, in our community the student first works with the simple, relatively formless meditation of attending to the breath. At this stage a great deal of deliberate effort is necessary. Working diligently with the thought process in that way allows the mind to settle. Then after some time, when greater relaxation is possible, he or she enters into liturgical practices and begins working with the imagery of visualization.

MOTHER TESSA: And how does someone decide when to move from one stage to the other and what imagery to use?

JUDY LIEF: First, the student requests the teacher to transmit the next practice. The teacher agrees to transmit the practice appropriate to the student when he or she is ready. Each practice has its own built-in form and structure.

MOTHER TESSA: It would never be that precise in Christianity. Prayer is much more spontaneous and fluid. You might not necessarily know in a given moment what you will do next. I may go to the chapel thinking I am going to meditate on a certain scripture, and I may never get to it. Or I may end up working with it for twice as long as I had expected. There is a tremendous open-endedness to it.

JUDY LIEF: Would it be correct to say that prayer begins in reference to an external God, as some sort of visualization or projection of one's mind, and then moves on beyond that initial dualism? Would that describe the movement from meditation to contemplation in Christianity?

FATHER TIMKO: The Christian begins with the perception of something other than oneself: something that transcends who we are according to our usual understanding. But even there we have to be careful. The transcendent reality is within the realm of our inner being. As Christ said, "The Kingdom of God does not come with observable signs; you can't say, 'Look, here it is!' or 'There it is!' For the Kingdom of God is within you" (Luke 17:20-21). Though the reality of God is Other, it is not an external thing.

BROTHER DAVID: And it isn't a *being*. I don't think there is one Christian denomination where you couldn't walk into church and hear someone speaking from the pulpit about God as a being. But that's totally unorthodox; it's just simply wrong. God is not *a* being. God is the Source of Being.

FATHER TIMKO: From a Christian point of view the understanding of God is crucial here. The Eastern Fathers see our relationship to God primarily in terms of God-likeness. Many of the Fathers say that if God appears to you in some external form or image or visible light, you can be sure it is an illusion and not God. Saint John of the Ladder says, "God appears to the mind in the heart, at first as a purifying fire and then as a light that illumines the mind and makes it God-like." He also says that when we speak of love we must be very careful in what we say because we are speaking of God. God is love. God is truth. God is good. God is holy. The person who abides in any of these qualities of God-likeness abides in God and God abides in him. In other words, if the quality of love is operating in you as a state of being, then that is the reality of God manifest. In most instances, the image of God refers to the actual manifestation of the divine quality of life and being within us. The inner appeal, the movement of the mind and heart in prayer, is not to some external agency. It is to that reality which is potentially present within us.

JOSEPH GOLDSTEIN: I would say, not even within us, but which *is* us.

FATHER TIMKO: Yes, all right; but only in the sense that it is actualized and manifest in us. In that sense Evagrius says that "a soul pure in God is God" and "a pure mind is the throne of God." Anyway, it is something within the realm of one's potential state of being; it is not something to be arrived at somewhere "out there." Sometimes I like to use the analogy of our electronic medium when I talk about this. When you turn on your TV you tune into certain signals out in the atmosphere. Where are they coming from? Evidently there is a source. They are not only "out there"; they are also "right here." All you need is a receiver that is functioning properly and you can tune into the transmission. You can't know the reality at the source. The reality, or picture, communicated is only actualized and known in the receiver where you are. In the same way, we can say that the reality of God cannot be perceived "up there" or "out there," or anywhere else in particular, but only here within me when my psyche is tuned in.

BROTHER DAVID: Much of our educational approach to teaching children how to pray has been misleading in that respect.

FATHER TIMKO: I think it has been horrendous. Some years ago my Church School teachers showed me an instructional book they had received, and in its centerfold was a picture of two telephones hooked up together. This was supposed to be an illustration of prayer. What does this communicate? Here you are at this end, and God is up there at the other end, waiting for your call? Just call him up! It's such a simplistic idea! It is a distorted view of prayer that deludes the youngest child as well as the oldest adult.

BROTHER DAVID: One thing I've noticed about descriptions of Buddhist practice is that the dissolution of the ego is much more directly in focus than it is in the Catholic tradition. I'm wondering, Father George, whether there is anything parallel to that in Orthodoxy.

FATHER TIMKO: Yes and no. By that I mean that there is not a direct focus so much as an indirect focus. In our tradition the term "meditation" isn't alluded to all that much, and when it is, it is used in the sense of pondering or reflecting on something. But there is a lot of emphasis on theoria, which is usually translated as "contemplation." Theoria is watching, observing, simply looking. It is an interior looking of the mind, of paying attention without any expectations. If you look with some intent you will see what you want to see. But the Fathers say you shouldn't look with some projected ideas. Just watch yourself, from moment to moment, and you will have enough to contend with. And they're right. When I recollect my mind, stop looking outside myself and just watch myself—my relationship to my wife, my children, my money, my possessions—there is a whole world of self-knowledge to be found there. And they say that you cannot actually commune with God until you know yourself, exactly as you are. Otherwise, you won't be able to distinguish what you are projecting and what your senses are bringing to you from what is spiritual. Therefore, the consciousness, the mind, has to let go of thought. That's the critical thing. Evagrius refers to prayer as "letting go of all thought." He says that "prayer is a movement of the mind to God. Prayer is the continual communion of the mind with God. Undistracted prayer is the highest activity of the mind. But if you wish to behold God and commune with Him who is beyond all sense perception and beyond all conception, you must free your mind from every impassioned thought. The mind that is a slave to passion cannot come to the realm of pure spiritual prayer. For such a mind is dragged about by passionate thoughts, and it cannot remain still and quiet. You cannot attain pure prayer while your mind is occupied with thoughts of material things and cares. For prayer means the letting-go of all thoughts and being with God."[7] Christianity became trapped at some point by thinking that prayer is verbalization and asking. That's a wrong understanding of prayer. The Greek word *prosevkomai* means to move into a condition or state of being in which there is no thought, no imaging, no desiring. It means to simply be still and silent and quiet in a mindful state of awareness. In such a state the self is dissolved. Only by being in that state can one truly commune with that Transcendent Reality. Nonverbalized prayer is central in the tradition of the Fathers, who say prayer is "directing the mind and heart."

JUDY LIEF: Is such contemplation practice part of the Orthodox service?

FATHER TIMKO: It is essentially a private practice. But even though the services verbalize, the liturgy has a contemplative aspect to it. The interior being is always called to being watchful and attentive to everything that is being said and done. Hesychius of Jerusalem says, "Attention is the silence of the mind, free of all thought." There are also places in the liturgy where you are called to lay aside all thoughts that pertain to this life. Saint John Chrysostom says that if your mind is wandering about in the marketplace, and you are thinking about business, then you aren't at the liturgy. There are moments of total silence. This happens at the beginning of the offertory, when the gifts are offered, and then in the communion. At those times there is no singing or verbalizing, but simply the inner awareness and focusing on communion. There are also times when we say, "Let us lift up our hearts." The heart is the inner being in which the mind should be centered and stilled; it is the interior nature of our consciousness. In the Orthodox tradition, we say that the mind should always be in the heart, which means that the intelligible, perceiving nature should be within the feeling, intuitive nature. When the mind is so recollected and stilled within the heart, it exists in a state of pure mindfulness.

JOSEPH GOLDSTEIN: In many Asian languages, there is one word which includes both heart and mind. And I think that's very much the Buddhist sense: those two are not separate.

LODRÖ DORJE: I wanted to say something about this idea of prayer as asking. In the Vajrayana tradition we have a liturgy form which we call supplication. It has the important element of transcending personal desire; in other words, one is not particularly supplicating for a Cadillac. We supplicate as a way of uplifting our state of being and increasing our sense of commitment and devotion. We might supplicate to have greater renunciation, or to develop unshakable faith in impermanence and karmic cause and effect, or to be able to connect with the realization of the lineage. So we say, for example, "Grant your blessings so that my mind may be one with the dharma," or "Let me mix my mind with the state of being of the realized ones." At the same time the foundation of mindfulness-awareness training is considered important. The practice of supplication usually isn't formally introduced to practitioners right at the beginning; it's considered to be an advanced practice. This is once again connected again with the principle of first training your awareness through applying some effort, in order to dissolve the heaviness of your projections. Then you could be available to what is beyond your projections. Also, liturgical practices are always alternated with some kind of formless meditation. You begin a session with a period of formless meditation, then there is a liturgical supplication and a visualization practice of some kind, and then you conclude the session by dissolving any constructed element of the meditation: you dissolve the form and just let your awareness open. So it's actually quite characteristic in our tradition to have a form aspect alternating with a formless or letting-go aspect during any one practice session.

FATHER TIMKO: We have to be able to let thought go, because thought is responsible for the self, for the ego. In that state of being or awareness in which thought is not operating, we can relate to things, to each other, or to whatever we're doing, without thoughts and images and forms intruding. We can just be there, receiving and seeing in a nonjudgmental way.

JOSEPH GOLDSTEIN: I would just like to add that I don't think it is a matter of *not* thinking. It is more a matter of not entering into dialogue with thought. In other words, it is possible to be aware of thought in the same way that one might be aware of a sound during meditation: there is no identification with it; it is just a mind bubble. Seeing thought in that way, it is no longer a hindrance or a problem. It is just another phenomenon. That simplifies the whole process, because then there is not the extra effort to stop thinking.

FATHER TIMKO: Yes. The way to deal with thought is to watch the mind. It is just like watching a child who is about to put his hand into the cookie jar. If you are watching the mind, it can't fool you. It can't con you into something. But you can't really stop it. When the mind is restless and jumps all over the place, the tendency is to try and trap it with some technique. But then what happens when you stop the technique? Mind just starts jumping again. But by contemplating, by simply watching, the mind naturally becomes quiet and stills itself.

REGGIE RAY: Father George, is this practice of watching the mind dominant in the Orthodox church? I haven't heard Christian contemplation described this way before.

FATHER TIMKO: Well, I don't really know how to answer that. It is dominant in the writings of the Fathers and the tradition of the Church. You can find it in great detail in the *Philokalia*. But it isn't a dominant practice in our current religious life. These days most people say that really practicing and experiencing these things is for the monks in the monasteries, and for everyone else spirituality just involves going to liturgy. Somehow I discovered it isn't necessary to leave the world in order to practice the exercises of spiritual training devised by the ascetics, to acquire a certain degree of dispassion, and to achieve a certain state of inner spiritual growth and being and transformation of the psyche.

REGGIE RAY: Have you had support from your church?

FATHER TIMKO: Well, I have had to reassure some of the authorities from time to time. They assumed that if you began working too much with the mind and the interior life you'd end up being Buddhist. When I began doing hatha yoga, just for health reasons, some became very uncomfortable. I had to explain that it had nothing to do with any religious beliefs, that I wasn't bowing down before a statue of the Buddha or worshipping some Hindu divinity. All the teachings I have described which deal with the important work of the mind are in the original tradition of the Fathers, and they provide the key to spiritual guidance for the interior life. For example, Saint Maximus the Confessor says, "How do you know when you're greedy? It's very simple. If you are asked to give money, and you find resentment awakening in your inner being, in your heart and your thoughts, then you're greedy!" If you're watchful and aware, you will actually see the process of greed in operation within you. So by relying on the writings of the Fathers and being nurtured by their insights and being guided by their spiritual directives, I have learned to be watchful and know myself and to have a deeper experience of that holy and blessed Divine Presence.

DOING Nothing

Tessa Bielecki
Eido Tai Shimano Roshi
David Steindl-Rast O.S.B.

QUESTION (from audience): I think a lot of people could get the impression from listening to these presentations that the main point of contemplative practices is to attain some special state of mind—that by meditating or praying, something very extraordinary is going to happen. But I would suggest that you can find contemplative states of mind in people's most common experiences. For example, I enjoy watching the sun set. As soon as the sun touches the horizon, my mind becomes quiet. That is a natural kind of prayer which everyone does. You can just relax and watch the sun set, and you will find yourself becoming aware of your breath and so on. So meditation doesn't have to be anything so special or different.

MOTHER TESSA: I sympathize completely with what you're saying. I've always had difficulty talking about spiritual practices as those specific things we do when we walk into a chapel or meditation hall. I personally feel that it's much broader than that. Certainly in my community, a lot of our prayer is practiced out of doors—up in a tree, out in a canoe, on a mountaintop, in the garden. We refer to this kind of prayer as "earthy mysticism," or "incarnational contemplation." I think that this, as well as the more formal option, is important. We need to make a special effort to remind ourselves of the ordinariness of prayer, especially in a context such as this discussion. I'm glad you raised that point.

EIDO ROSHI: There is this saying in the Zen tradition: "However wonderful something may be, it is not as good as doing nothing." But it is important how we place the emphasis. It is not "doing *nothing*;" it is "*doing* nothing." (Laughter.) These are two different things. Just as Christianity originated with the crucifixion and resurrection, Buddhism started with Shakyamuni Buddha's enlightenment experience. In other words, it started with meditation practice. As long as we are Buddhists, we cannot forget that. If we did, and we just watched the sun rise, sun set, that would be a good excuse not to sit.

BROTHER DAVID: There is a beautiful parallel to this, Roshi, which is a Christian blessing we give to someone who is leaving on a journey. We say, "May nothing happen to you." Actually, one doesn't wish that nothing may happen, but one wishes that many good things will happen. And yet we say, "May nothing happen to you" because, when nothing really happens, that nothing which is God, then that is truly the greatest thing that can ever happen to anyone.

Relatively Speaking

H. E. the Tai Situpa Rinpoche
Eido Tai Shimano Roshi

QUESTION (from audience): Rinpoche, when I supplicate the
buddhas and bodhisattvas I sometimes have the experience of
actually receiving their compassion and blessings. How can we
say this is nontheistic meditation?

SITU RINPOCHE: Yes, what you say is true on a relative level. But we
should not mix the relative and ultimate. First we have the
relative, and then the ultimate. And ultimately, you know,
there is no reason to pray to the buddhas. The essence of the
buddhas is the essence of oneself. But relatively speaking, we
definitely do have to pray and to meditate.

QUESTION (cont.): Well, it certainly feels like I'm reaching out to
something beyond myself, and that I'm being blessed by
something greater and beyond me. And I've always felt that to
be very much like Christian prayer. This feeling may be just
relative level, but I'm just relative level, you know. (Laughter.)

EIDO ROSHI: We have a saying in the Zen Buddhist tradition, which
is, "You are fifty percent right!"

SITU RINPOCHE: That means, relatively right.

EIDO ROSHI: At the same time, relative and absolute are inseparable;
it is one thing. So in that sense, you are one hundred percent
right. But when you only see one side, you cannot see the other
side, so this could be a problem. We are almost always fifty
percent right, despite the fact that we are one hundred percent
right.

High Creativity

William McNamara O.C.D.

For years I have been looking forward to coming to this conference, and now I look forward to the transforming effects of being here. That is why all of us have come: to be transformed. The dialogue we engage in must grow out of such silence and God-centeredness that we will indeed be transformed. I have watched with great interest the transformation that has already begun to take place in the life of Mother Tessa, who has been coming here for four years. It has been a phenomenon! Once a year in our community we renew and reformulate our vows. This year, Tessa said something about her buddha-nature! (Laughter.) This was rather alarming. The community spent years and years trying to cope with her Polish nature . . . (laughter) . . . and now we've got to cope with her buddha-nature as well. So do pray for us!

The transformation that I look forward to is an open-ended one. Strangely enough, what I think has to happen for myself and my community is the total acceptance of two poles. (Laughter.) As you may know, Tessa's sister is also with us, so we do live with two Poles. . . . But what I mean to say is that when you live in tension, that's the best possible atmosphere for high creativity. That's where the infinite possibilities of the human adventure are. That's where the void is, and that's where God is: in between. We need a two-eyed view. We need to be bipolar or even multipolar in our perceptions of Buddhism, Hinduism, Christianity, Judaism, and other traditions. I think our high ecumenical aspirations are hindered and perhaps even repudiated when we cling tenaciously to one center. It is important to see, to accept, and to learn to be at home in many centers, so that we can be multipolar about the whole spiritual adventure, the whole thrust toward the fullness of life. Then, if we are Christians, we can move into the very heart of Christianity, which is a movement into other and deeper dimensions of being, until we are swept away and overwhelmed by the Spirit himself.

When we listen to a Buddhist speaker and then to a Christian speaker, it may sound to us as though one is contradicting the other. But I don't think that's actually true. The mystical life itself reconciles opposites. And that makes life interesting. There is no room for boredom or majestic trivia when you live in the kind of high creativity where you have to cope intelligently, lovingly, and peacefully with various kinds of opposing centers. Otherwise there will be no charge, no electricity; there will be no joy.

Prayer

New Language of Prayer

We are going to have to create a new language of prayer. And this new language has to come out of something which transcends all our traditions, and comes out of the immediacy of love. We have to part now, aware of the love that unites us, the love that unites us in spite of real differences. . . .

Oh God, we are one with You. You have made us one with You. You have taught us that if we are open to one another, You dwell in us. Help us to preserve this openness and to fight for it with all our hearts. Help us to realize that there can be no understanding where there is mutual rejection. Oh God, in accepting one another wholeheartedly, fully, completely, we accept You, and we thank You, and we adore You, and we love You with our whole being, because our being is in Your being, our spirit is rooted in Your spirit. Fill us then with love, and let us be bound together with love as we go our diverse ways, united in this one spirit which makes You present in the world, and which make You witness to the ultimate reality that is love. Love has overcome. Love is victorious. Amen.

THOMAS MERTON[8]

Chapter 7: Notes

1. Epigraph: *Christian Zen* (San Francisco: Harper & Row, 1971), p. 7. Reprinted with permission.

2. Fenelon, Guyon, and Molinos, *A Guide to True Peace or The Excellency of Inward and Spiritual Prayer* (Wallingford, Penn.: Pendle Hill Publ., 1979).
3. The twelve "links" or *nidanas* describe the chain of habitual reactions which maintains and reinforces the sense of self or ego. By meditating on these components of the psychological process, one sees that they do not have, or come out of, an independently-existing nature.
4. In this case, *vajra* refers to the symbol or ritual scepter used in tantric practices.
5. In *The Collected Works of St. John of the Cross*.
6. For a description of the historical factors that have obscured the contemplative element of the Western Church, see Thomas Keating's "Contemplative Prayer in the Christian Tradition: An Historical Tradition," in *Finding Grace at the Center*.
7. This quotation has been translated and compiled by Father Timko from *Chapters on Prayer*. See also *The Philokaliah* Vol. 1 and Evagrius Ponticus, *The Praktikos & Chapters on Prayer* (Spencer, Mass.: Cistercian Pubns., 1970).
8. From a "Special Closing Prayer" offered at the First Spiritual Summit Conference in Calcutta, 1968. Reprinted with permission from *The Asian Journal*, copyright by New Directions Publishing Corporation.

Part Three

Everyday Journey

How to bring silence into everyday life—or rather, how to awaken to its already-present dimension—is a concern shared by people of all traditions.

In Chapter Eight, compassion is defined as the natural and spontaneous expression of meditative awareness. Chapter Nine, "The Spiritual Teacher," acknowledges the need for direction and guidance along the way and raises questions regarding availability, hierarchy, and trust. Chapter Ten, "Time, Place, and Silence," looks at lifestyle: the role of the monastic community; the challenges of being a contemplative householder; and how to balance silence and activity, contemplative practice and worldly responsibilities.

8

Compassion

True love hurts. It always has to hurt. It must be painful to love someone, painful to leave them, you might have to die for them. When people marry they have to give up everything to love each other. The mother who gives birth to her child suffers much. It is the same for us in the religious life. To belong fully to God we have to give up everything. Only then can we truly love. The word "love" is so misunderstood and so misused.[1]

TERESA OF CALCUTTA

It is not by closing your eyes that you see your own nature. On the contrary, you must open your eyes wide and wake up to the real situation in the world to see completely your whole Dharma Treasure, your whole Dharma Body. The bombs, the hunger, the pursuit of wealth and power—these are not separate from your nature. . . . You will suffer, but your pain will not come from your own worries and fears. You will suffer because of your kinship with all beings, because you have the compassion of an awakened one, a Bodhisattva.[2]

TICH NAHT HANH

Noble Heart

Ven. Chögyam Trungpa Rinpoche

In the Vajrayana Buddhist tradition, we talk about how we can discover wisdom behind our passions and delusions. If you simply cut out your passion or your desire, you can't work with the world of non-compassion. It would be equivalent to going through surgery and removing your eyeballs, tongue, heart, and sexual organs. Some people might think that is the way to become a monk or nun, but I'm afraid such an approach doesn't quite work. Compassion is not so much a matter of removing the organs of passion, aggression, and delusion; compassion means working with what you have. If you are hungry, you need your tongue and teeth to eat with. It is a natural thing. We don't punish ourselves because we have a tongue and teeth. Instead, we work with them. When we have a problem, we don't throw it away as if it were a piece of garbage. We pick it up and work with it. Then we find that we have a working basis.

According to the Buddhist teachings, the practice of sitting meditation is a way to work with what we have. Meditation is very practical: We learn how to wash the dishes, how to iron our clothes, how to be. That is compassion. When we know how to be, we don't create chaos for ourselves, to begin with, and subsequently we don't create chaos for others. As it is said in Christianity, "charity begins at home." Perhaps we could also say, "compassion begins at home."

Basic virtue comes from learning how to be. If we have no idea of how to be, then we commit sin and crimes of all kinds. When we know how to be, our hearts are softened, and compassion naturally comes along with that. We learn how to cry, how to smile, and how to experience other people's wounds. We also begin to appreciate joy and pleasure. Perhaps we haven't ever really explored pain and pleasure in our whole lives. When our hearts are softened and we feel pain, it is excruciating. And when we experience pleasure, it is wonderful. Compassion means exploring pain and pleasure properly, thoroughly, completely. The Sanskrit word for compassion is karuna, which means "noble heart." It is not just a matter of feeling sorry for someone: when we experience noble heart, we are able to have a good time, and we are able to identify with others' pain and pleasure.

We need to learn how to be decent human beings. That is the basis for what we call "religion." A decent human society brings about spirituality. It brings about blessings and what could be called the gift of God. This is an extremely simple-minded approach. I'm sorry if I disappoint you, but it is as simple as that. We have to be just as we are. This is not necessarily a Buddhist message; for that matter it is not even a particularly spiritual message. Compassion is simply a matter of experiencing reality properly.

Mother's Love

Eido Tai Shimano Roshi
David Steindl-Rast O.S.B.

QUESTION (from audience): Roshi, how do you understand the Christian statement "God is love"?

EIDO ROSHI: I think it is a fabulous, excellent expression. (Laughter.)

QUESTION (cont.): And what is your interpretation of the word "love"?

EIDO ROSHI: How do I define "love" in Christian terms? (Laughter.)

QUESTION (cont.): No, how do Buddhists understand what love is?

EIDO ROSHI: Years ago, Brother David and I had this kind of discussion. Buddhism translates karuna as "compassion." We had a discussion about the difference between love and compassion. It went on and on and on and on and on.

QUESTION (cont.): I see. Perhaps I'll sit down. (Laughter.)

EIDO ROSHI: But this time I'll just say that, to me, this word "love" has romantic implications. Of course sometimes I feel warmth, gentleness, harmony, peace, etcetera, etcetera. But nevertheless I prefer the term "compassion." This is just my personal preference.

BROTHER DAVID: I think it is important to add that you also have to take the emphasis off the romantic notion before you can come to a true understanding of what the Christian tradition means when it speaks of the "love of God": both God's love for us and our love for God. It is interesting in this context that God's loving-kindness, as it is described in the Old Testament, is a *mother's* love. The term used is *rachamim*, which is the abstract form of *rechem*, which means "womb." So the masculine notion of God, which has been so overemphasized in the Christian tradition, is very much balanced by remembering that God also loves us with a mother's love. I think that image comes much closer to the Buddhist definition of compassion than it does to the usual Western notion of romantic love.

Where the Clouds Crop Up

Tenshin Reb Anderson Roshi

All the buddhas and ancestors are sitting at the heart of suffering. By sitting at the heart of suffering they develop their unshakable vow to drop body and mind and save all sentient beings.

Depending on how we conduct our lives, we find ourselves in one of a variety of forms of existence. The varieties are endless, but there are six major categories, called the "six worlds." These worlds, which we create for ourselves, have nicknames: the human realm; the realm of divine bliss; the hell realm of extreme torment and isolation; the insatiable realm of the hungry ghosts; the animal realm of fear; and the realm of the fighting gods. The human realm is the center of gravity of the other five. As human beings we tend to return here. And at the very heart of the human realm is Jambudvipa, a Sanskrit name which means "Rose-apple Island." It is the place where we are right now, and it is where we feel connected with all forms of suffering.

When we are in the realm of bliss, it is difficult to empathize with extreme isolation and torment. And when we are in a state of great torment, it is hard to appreciate bliss. But in Rose-apple Island, all manifestations of suffering are close at hand, from the most gross to the most subtle. Here at the center of the range of suffering, we can sense the suffering that is present within blissful experience, within torment, within insatiability, within fear and numbness, and within power-seeking. The human realm could be basically described as the state of dissatisfaction, as the frustration of all our desires and strivings. Yet it is only in this realm that there is also the possibility of seeing things just the way they are. There is no point in looking to another realm for comfort. The only real comfort is to be found by settling in deeply, right here and now.

Our sitting practice is to simply settle in and make ourselves at home at the heart of all sentient beings. How do we do this? Actually, there is nothing to do, because we are already at this place. But because of our accumulated opinions, philosophies, and striving human nature, we are obstructed from this simple practice of paying attention to what is right under our feet at this very moment. Great effort is required to be free of our ideas of effort. It takes courage to give up our personal views and to attend to life, just as it is.

One description of this process which I find very helpful is by Wang Wei, a Chinese Buddhist poet of the T'ang Dynasty:

> In my middle years I became fond of the way,
> And made my home in the foothills of South Mountain.
> When the spirit moves me, I go off by myself
> To see things that I alone must see.
> I follow the stream to the source,
> And sitting there, watch for the moment
> When clouds come up.
> Or I may meet a woodsman;
> We talk and laugh and forget about going home.

At first, sitting meditation is a settling down and a retiring to the foothills. Then, when the spirit moves us, when something happens, we follow the stream to the source: to the heart of all sentient beings. We sit still and observe the time when the clouds crop up. To be present at this moment is to witness the inevitability of thought and its illusory nature. This is the birth of compassion: we observe the production of phenomena and understand their source.

The source of the stream of experience is completely calm and serene. Still, something crops up. For example, when Suzuki Roshi's second teacher, Kishizawa-Ian, was a young monk, he was sitting in meditation one rainy day and heard the sound of a distant waterfall. The han[3] was hit. He went to his teacher and asked, "What is the place where the sound of the rain, the waterfall, and the han meet?"

His teacher replied, "True eternity still flows."

Then he asked, "What is this true eternity that still flows?"

"It is like a bright mirror, permanently smooth."

"Is there anything beyond this?"

"Yes."

"What is beyond this?"

"Break the mirror. Come, and I'll meet you."

When we are at this source, sitting completely still, all buddhas and sentient beings are there with us. Then this calm mirror experience breaks, and clouds of thinking crop up. Just being willing to give up great calm and to become involved again in particular thoughts is compassion. In this way we knowingly and willingly re-enter the world of confusion and suffering. We become an openness that participates in the world. This is our authentic self, the self which feels connected with all the different varieties of suffering.

We sit calmly without fear. We are open and at ease. We could stand up from our sitting and walk to hell, walk to heaven, or walk to the animal realm. We can also welcome them if they come to us. Compassion is not dualistic: we do not do it, and we cannot stop it. Our body interacts fearlessly with all forms of suffering. This does not mean that the fear does not exist—or that it does exist. It means that we are open to all varieties of fear, so that the forces around us are balanced. We do not have more friends in heaven than we have in hell. If we have too many friends in heaven and not enough in hell, then there will be fear. If we observe our own body and mind as we are sitting, and find that we are leaning more toward heaven than hell, or more toward hell than heaven, we have not yet realized the calm of buddha's mind. Whenever our mind is completely open and we are not trying to control what we are exposed to, the body and mind can sit still in the heart of all suffering beings. That is all we have to do. Everything else will take care of itself.

But even for the ancients this process of harmonizing body and mind was difficult. Buddha asked his ordained disciples to beg for their food from house to house, without prejudice toward the rich or the poor. Mahakasyapa, the first ancestor in our lineage, preferred to beg only in the poor neighborhoods. Buddha told him that he should not beg just from the poor, even though that was his tendency.

So we have tendencies to lean this way or that way, forward or backward, and occasionally our teachers may adjust our posture and show us what it feels like to be in the middle. We tend to go back to the way we were, until we find out that being off-balance is painful. That is why sitting is very good: if we are off-center, and sit long enough, we will find out that it doesn't work. The most comfortable way is upright sitting, where we don't emphasize one direction more than any other. Eventually our own experience will bring us back to the middle—if we sit again and again. But if we are not paying attention to our experience we may not be able to learn from it and find our way home.

I personally need to sit every day. Although I have been sitting for a while, it is still difficult for me. When I get up in the morning I am often aching and slow to get going. I take this sore, resistant body, and I put it on a black cushion. As I stretch and settle into the sitting position, the resistance falls away, and I am prepared to meet the other kinds of suffering that arise later in the day. This body and mind settles into itself, empty and open, and I am ready to meet all of you.

It is like bamboo in the falling snow. Snow piles up on the leaves, and the bamboo bends. It bends and bends and bends. It keeps bending all the way down, until finally the snow drops off and the branches spring back. When we accept that we are what we are, then we are free of what we are.

When I look at that picture on the wall of my teacher, Suzuki Roshi, I feel that he is very happy that we came and sat with him today. This sitting is a great joy for all the buddhas and ancestors. But we don't just sit with them. We also bring the heart of suffering and compassion into all the activities of our daily life. In this way, true eternity flows, wherever we are.

QUESTION: When I was sitting and doing the breathing technique, for brief moments at the end of the outbreath there would be no thinking. It was just a feeling of being there. And then the thoughts would start again. But when I was in that no-thinking moment, there was no idea to get up and do something compassionate.

TENSHIN ROSHI: There shouldn't be. Compassion is not an idea.

QUESTION (cont.): Then where does the compassion arise, and what would make you do something?

TENSHIN ROSHI: You started thinking again. That is compassion. You were kind enough to become involved in delusion again, with all of us. (Laughter.) You got to a place where there is no thinking: congratulations. And then you were willing to throw that away and come forth, and you were willing to enter into the world of suffering, where all the various thoughts are. The particular thought you had may not have bothered you, and that is because it was just a few seconds away from that center. If you go to the calm source, and you come forth just a few inches, or a few seconds, there is no problem. You feel quite at ease, quite calm. Even though you are thinking, even though your delusory thoughts are coming up again, still you are quite calm. You can feel the calm even though you are getting involved in agitation. But if you keep going and going and going, and you don't go back to the source for a long time, you will find yourself quite isolated from that place, and you will become upset. If you lose all your composure, you should go back. But at first, there is no problem; the very thoughts are compassion. There is no more you have to do than that.

QUESTION (cont.): But it's not as though I did anything. The thoughts just came back.

TENSHIN ROSHI: You didn't have an "I" yet. If you kept going you would get an "I" again. "I" will come back, along with various other things. But at first the thoughts are even more primitive than a concept of self. At first they are just tiny outcroppings. You have to have them. If you're alive they naturally come forth. You can't stop them.

QUESTION: My understanding of Buddhism is that suffering is illusory. If so, what is the point of compassion? Is compassion itself also considered illusory?

TENSHIN ROSHI: Suffering is the stream of our lives, and it is illusion. Walk back up the stream, in the opposite direction of the flow of suffering—which is to say, walk up the stream of delusion. When you get to the source, you will be grateful to the suffering and the illusion, because they showed you the way to the source. You can't get to the source without delusion. When you arrive there, you might ask, what is the point of compassion? But there *is* no point to compassion. It just naturally arises. If you're alive, it naturally comes forth, and you return. Some people think that they could stay at that place, but fortunately the buddhas are there, and they say, "Let's go!" (Laughter.) There is a famous koan: does a dog have buddha-nature? One of the answers is: No, it doesn't. And another answer is: Yes, it does. When the master Jao Jo said, "Yes, it does," a monk asked, "But why would a bodhisattva choose to be in a dog skinbag?"

Jao Jo answered, "Because he knowingly and willingly transgresses." The boddhisattva sits with all the buddhas at the source and then knowingly and willingly gives rise to delusion and becomes involved in the world again. This is compassion.

On Saints and Sanctity

Tessa Bielecki

In the Christian tradition, there is no one model for a life of compassion; there is no blueprint. Because each person in this world is unique, distinct, and unrepeatable, each person's sanctity is expressed in a unique, distinct, and unrepeatable way. The Christian communion of saints is therefore made up of an incredibly colorful and captivating variety of individuals. There are ardent scholars like Thomas Aquinas and dumbbells like John Vienny, the curé of Ars. We find cenobites like Benedict who live in community and solitaries like Antony of the Desert; kings like Louis of France, and handicaps like Herman the Cripple. We find soldiers like Joan of Arc and pacifists like Martin of Tours. There are public figures like Pope Leo the Great, who rode out single-handedly to encounter Attila the Hun and keep him from sacking Rome, and there are many hidden faces, like Saint Claire of Assisi who, after a certain point in her life, never went out of her convent cloister. There are people who were models of virtue from a very early age, such as John the Baptist, and there are such profligates as Saint Augustine, whose prayer was, "Lord, give me chastity—but not yet."

Although the saints manifest in all these unique ways, when we get to know them intimately, we find that they do have certain traits in common. I have chosen ten such traits, which could be called marks of Christian compassion. First of all, we find in all the saints a heroic *fidelity to the details of ordinary, everyday life*. Although I am personally more attracted to flamboyant personalities, and the saints I will present as examples reflect this bias, I would like to begin by calling to mind all those whose lives were quiet, hidden, and unobtrusive. In essence, Christian sanctification requires no glittering achievements and no spectacular successes—only fidelity to a hundred little things.

The second quality is *God-intoxication*, and this is also not necessarily a visible trait. Nevertheless, if you look closely, you will find that every Christian saint is madly in love with God, and is in fact becoming ever more consumed by his or her passion for God, as we see in Saint Augustine's magnificent prayer:

You called and cried to me, you even broke open my deafness: Your beams shone on me, and You chased away my blindness: You blew on me most fragrantly and I drew in my breath and now I pant after you; I tasted you, and now hunger and thirst after you; You touched me, and I burn again to enjoy Your peace.[4]

The saints are burning with their love of God. But this love does not take place in a vacuum, nor in abstraction. It is expressed concretely and specifically, and this brings us to the third quality, which is the saints' *zest for life*.

Their passion for God is lived out in vitality, energy, and fecundity. Jesus said, "I came that they may have life, and have it abundantly" (John 10:10). The fullness of life is what Christian sanctification is all about. Saint Ireneus said that we glorify God most when we are fully alive. Because, according to John the Evangelist, "the Word was made flesh," and because God became incarnate in matter, the saints' passion for God is expressed in their passion for the materiality of the universe. Saint Joan of Arc, for example, was crazy about her horses, and Saint Charles Borromeo was wild about chess. John of the Cross was utterly enamored of the Spanish landscape, and he also had a passion for asparagus. When he was dying, he was asked what would help alleviate his pain, and all he wanted was asparagus.

I recently read something about Saint Alphonsus Ligouri that greatly endeared him to me. I had always found him rather lugubrious, but it turns out that he had a great love for music and the theatre. It so happened, however, that one of the performances in the Naples theatre featured a half-naked chorus line. Alphonsus felt that this was inappropriate for him, but he so wanted to hear the music that he went anyway. He sat in the back row, and when the presentation began, he took off his glasses. Because he was so near-sighted he couldn't see a thing! This was an act of great compassion, because through his own purity of heart he did what was appropriate for him, and yet he never made a fuss about what the other people in the theatre should or should not be doing.

Teresa of Avila had a passion for absolutely everything. There wasn't anything in life that she did not passionately enjoy. As a popular story goes, one day the sisters walked into the kitchen and found her gorging herself on partridge, and they were scandalized. She looked up, astonished that they would even question this. She said, very simply but with great enthusiasm, "When I pray, I pray; and when I eat partridge, I eat partridge!" The important thing is that all of Teresa's passions were purified, refined, and unified into her one great passion for God: there was no dispersion or fragmentation.

The Celtic saints were particularly zestful—especially Brigid, who happened to love beer. She wrote this wonderful poem:

I long for a great lake of ale.
I long for the men of heaven in my house.
I long for cheerfulness in their drinking.
And I long for Jesus to be there among them.

And of course Jesus should be there among them. He would be the first to raise a toast. His first public miracle was to change water into wine, and the gospels are full of passages of his eating and drinking—so much that he was sometimes criticized for being a glutton and a drunkard.

Along with this passion for life necessarily goes a *passion for suffering and death*, particularly in the higher realms of realization. The saints suffer willingly, and this is because they understand it as growing pains, or as labor pains. It is clear to them that death is not in opposition to life; it is an integral part of life. Saint Paul, for example, made lists of his sufferings: he was shipwrecked, flogged, imprisoned, and so on. And yet he had a tremendous resurrection spirit. In his letter to the Corinthians he says, "We are . . . always carrying in the body the death of Jesus, so that the life of Jesus may also be manifested in our bodies. For while we live we are always being given up to death for Jesus' sake, so that the life of Jesus may be manifested in our mortal flesh" (2 Cor:10-11). Later he says that there is absolutely no suffering in this life that can be compared to the glory that comes when one has gone through all the way to the other side of that suffering.

John of the Cross, after being imprisoned for nearly a year and very badly beaten, said, "One single grace of all those which God granted me could not be repaid by many years of imprisonment." When John was dying after a long and excruciating illness, his brother sent in a group of musicians, because he knew John had a great love for music. But John sent them away, saying, "If God has given me the great sufferings I am enduring, why wish to soothe and lessen them by music? Thank these gentlemen for the kindness they have wished to do me; I look upon it as having been done." For us, his response may at first seem morbid, but if we look more deeply, we will see that it is a most human, most healthy, and most holy response.

When Ignatius of Antioch, one of the earliest of the Christian martyrs, was condemned to be fed to the lions in the Colosseum, he responded to his disciples, who were of course intent on rescuing him, with long letters that begged them to stop their efforts, saying, "Do not hinder me, and show me no false kindness. Let me be the food of these wild beasts, for they shall bring me to God." And of course, when he says "to God" he means that they shall bring him into the fullness of his realized being. For the Christian saints, death is ultimately a love-act, the consummation of a love affair, and they speak tenderly and lovingly about embracing the cross.

The fifth quality of the Christian saint is a *passion for people*. Jesus said, "By this all men will know that you are my disciples, if you have love for one another" (John 14:35). There is an extravagance to the compassion that the saints manifest: they squander themselves for God and for the people of God. John of the Cross' advice is, "Where there is no love, put love, and you will find love." By their very love, the saints make lovable what or who is unlovable. The essence of sanctity is heroic charity and an utterly generous heart. Saint Thérèse of Lisieux was a good example of this. She singled out the most unloved and unattractive sister, for whom she felt a natural antipathy, and she loved her with such compassionate effort that the nun believed she was Thérèse's best friend.

This sanctified self-giving can either be simple or it can be spectacular. It can be the humble gesture of Saint Pius the Tenth, who gave his last pair of socks to a poor beggar. Or it can be the dramatic activity of Princess Elizabeth of Hungary, who opened up the doors of her palace and fed all the poor, and on her wedding night put a leper in her wedding bed. Father Maximillian Kolbe, a Franciscan priest, exchanged his life for another prisoner's in Auschwitz. Father Kolbe took the place of a man who had been singled out to be executed, and he subsequently starved to death in solitary confinement. When Catherine of Siena heard about a political prisoner who had been sentenced to die, she went to visit him. She took him in her arms, and he rested his head on her breast and, according to her own account, she felt the scent of his blood, which seemed to flow with her own, and she could feel his fear within her. She was so identified with his suffering that she felt it in her own body as well. I was thrilled to hear Father Timko speak recently about the "visceral dimension" of compassion. Because when you are really experiencing another human being's suffering, you don't feel it merely with calm.

The saint's passion for people manifests itself not only in action, but also in *contemplation* or *stillness*. The scriptures are full of allusions to the mysterious disappearance of Christ, who regularly retreated into the hills to be silent. If you look at a photograph of Mother Teresa of Calcutta, you recognize the source of the dynamism for her heroic charity. It is not the product of a lavish funding and influential friends; it comes from her prayer. According to her own direction, the more we receive in silent prayer, the more we can give in our active life. Mother Teresa gets up to pray every morning at 4:30, no matter where she is in the world or what time she went to bed the night before.

In other words, the Christian saints are not only passionately engaged with people, they also exhibit a "holy indifference." They have learned, in the words of T. S. Eliot, "not only to care, but also not to care." They begin by just being there, open and available. And then, out of their stillness, they are sent out. The word "apostle" actually means "one who is sent." The terrible problem for many Christian apostles today is that they have not really been sent. Therefore they are not true apostles who are spirit-led; they are self-propelled. So compassion is first and foremost a mode of being. It is an extravagance of being which overflows into doing. Any action without contemplation is blind. No one should be extremely active in the world unless he or she is also extremely contemplative and prayerful. A venerable spiritual guide among the Jesuits, the seventeenth-century Father Louis Lallemont, said that if we have only a very little inwardness, we can give nothing at all to what is external; if we have gone a little distance in the inward life, then we can give ourselves moderately to the outward life. He concluded that a man of prayer will accomplish more in one year than another man who does not pray will accomplish in an entire lifetime. If you rush headlong into action without first finding the power, vision, and wisdom of discrimination in your prayer, you will do little more than nothing. Sometimes you will do nothing at all, even though you seem to be very busy, and other times you will do nothing but harm.

It is actually not fair to call some saints active and others contemplative, because each one is engaged in both, and in fact the seventh quality a saint must possess is the ability to hold a delicate *balance* between polarities. For some, action may predominate, and for others contemplation is dominant. But always there is the tension of trying to hold a balance, of trying to come, in Eliot's words, to "the stillpoint of the turning world." It takes a muscular kind of personality to hammer out this polarity, and often the strain takes a terrible toll on the nerves and bodies of the saints. The one who expressed this struggle best was Saint Ignatius of Loyola, who said that we have to work as though absolutely everything in the world depended on us, and we have to pray as though absolutely everything in the world depended on God—a Christian koan for all of us.

The next mark of sanctity is *human frailty*. This is important to remember, because the statues, pictures, and stories of the saints tend to gloss over the real human beings and give us a terribly wrong impression, leading us to think that the saints are all stuffed-shirts. In fact that is not at all the case. The saints are thoroughly human and completely natural—which means that they are also imperfect. For example, Saint Augustine was given to rages, and little Saint Thérèse of Lisieux suffered incredibly from bouts of depression. Saint Vincent de Paul, who was so heroically generous, was actually a bilious character subject to fits of anger. Saint Jerome was downright nasty, although still quite lovable. He was insulting to his theological opponents and known to attack not only their arguments, but also their persons. Saint Francis suffered throughout his life over his chastity. One day he was seen building a family out of snow: a mother, a father, and a child. When asked what he was doing, he said "I may father a child yet." His chastity was not something that came easy to him.

The secret of realization in all these people is that they never gave up struggling and working on their human weaknesses. They knew that what counts is not triumphant victory but endless persevering effort. Teresa of Avila said that we should strive and strive and strive, for we were meant for nothing else. Saint Paul said in one of his letters, "To keep me from being too elated by the abundance of revelations, a thorn was given me in the flesh, a messenger of Satan, to harass me. . . . Three times I besought the Lord about this, that it should leave me; but he said to me, 'My grace is sufficient for you, for my power is made perfect in weakness'. . . . For the sake of Christ, then, I am content with weaknesses, insults, hardships, persecutions, and calamities; for when I am weak then I am strong" (2 Cor. 12:7-10). Because of the imagery of Saint Paul, we often refer to our imperfections as "thorns in the flesh." In fact, it is these very flaws that make our favorite saints saints.

Another characteristic related to imperfection is *bounce*. As we say in my community, "It's the bounce that counts." Whenever the saints fail, whenever they fall, they pick themselves up and keep going. Saint Peter is the perfect example of this. He bumbles all the way through the scriptures until the biggest bumble of all, which is of course his betrayal of Jesus. The third time the cock crows, Peter remembers Jesus' prophecy, and he fills with remorse. What happens next is one of the most wrenching passages in all of scripture: "And Peter went out and wept bitterly" (Matt. 26:75). But after the bitterness came the bounce. He became one of the greatest of the disciples—in fact the one upon whom the church is built—simply because in addition to being the biggest bumbler, he had the best bounce.

This brings us to the last of the ten characteristics of the realized Christian, which is *hilarity*. I am not just referring to a quiet kind of joy: I mean an uproarious hilarity which wells up out of the depths of stillness. Hilarity makes it possible for the saints to exhibit such bounce in the midst of frailty. It is why it is possible for the Christian saint to face suffering and death in his own life and in the world around him. As Francis de Sales said, a sad saint is a sorry saint. Philip Neri played football with the red biretta that the Pope had sent him as a sign of prestige and privilege. When Saint Simeon came into the city after spending forty years fasting and praying in the desert, it was Good Friday, the most solemn day in the church year. What did Saint Simeon do? He ate sausages and danced with the harlots! As Nikos Kazantzakis so aptly said, "every one of us needs a little madness in order to cut the rope and be free."

There is an old Hassidic story about a rabbi who used to go to the marketplace to meet the prophet Elijah. They would talk together about who was living the life of God. On one particular day, the rabbi asked Elijah, "Well, is there anyone here who is on the way? Is there anyone here who has really awakened?"

Elijah looked around and pointed to two men in one corner and said, "Those two."

Immediately the rabbi went over and asked, "What is your occupation?"

"We are clowns," they said. "When we see people who are depressed, we cheer them up."

If ever our world needed jesters, it is now. We have forgotten how to relax, how to laugh, how to play. We have forgotten how to be. In our world today, laughter can be a sign of deep faith, deep love, and deep hope. It may be our highest manifestation of compassion.

These ten qualities are not only a description of Christian saints; they also give us an outline of how we can cultivate compassion in our own lives. So, in conclusion, I will simply shift them a little, to give you ten practical guidelines. First, work diligently with the ordinariness of your day-to-day existence. Second, love God. Of course, you can't love what you don't know, so succinctly speaking, get to know the historical Christ through the scriptures; get to know the cosmic Christ through nature and through his manifestation in the entire universe, including other people; and get to know the mystical Christ through prayer and meditation. The third step is to love life. Immerse yourself in it, celebrate it, enjoy it, and as Brother David says, be grateful for everything. Gratefulness sounds so simple. I know people keep badgering Brother David to say "something practical." But every time he speaks, he says something practical; it's just usually so simple that we miss it. Fourth, embrace every small suffering and every small death that comes your way. If you do that every day, you will be ready for the bigger challenges later on. Next, love one another. And then, when you are called upon to express that love in some kind of action, do it—appropriately and generously. Sixth, sit still and empty yourself for some part of each day. It doesn't matter whether you practice Buddhist meditation or Christian prayer: just do some kind of sitting with great fidelity and regularity. Seventh, keep your balance. And then, eighth, work perseveringly and creatively with your human weaknesses. Ninth, remember to bounce right back immediately after each fall. And lastly, laugh! No matter what happens, keep your sense of humor and keep on laughing, especially at yourself. We must take God alone so seriously that we take everything else—including ourselves—light-heartedly.

Good Intentions

Judith Lief

QUESTION (from audience): In the West, people often have the idea that Buddhism is a somewhat introspective and apathetic tradition, and that it isn't particularly creative or productive in terms of working with human problems. However when I began studying Asian history, I was quite surprised to discover that, in the cultures where it has been the dominant religion, Buddhism has been most active and supportive in terms of the arts, cultivating humanistic ethics, building human service institutions, and so on. Perhaps one reason Westerners aren't aware of this is because when Buddhists talk about compassion, they don't say much about activity; they talk about working with the mind. Why is it that there is generally so much focus on the individual in Buddhist literature, rather than on social contributions?

JUDY LIEF: I think there is a good reason for that focus, which is the understanding that the quality of one's motivation is critical. Actions can be extremely deceptive: seemingly good activities may not really be so, and seemingly bad activities may also not really be so—which is wonderful. Acknowledging this cuts through our tendency to judge ourselves and each other too quickly. The point is that, no matter how hard we strive, if we don't work on the inner force behind our actions, we don't seem to fundamentally change or progress.

For many centuries, innumerable well-intentioned people have been accomplishing all sorts of things, but how many people have actually lit the flame of wisdom everyone needs? How many people have truly inspired a vaster view and have successfully propagated a sense of human family? That can't come about merely through one's actions; it requires a change of mind and heart, and that takes great patience and effort. There is always the temptation to drop the larger intention and to just try and do what one can—everywhere at once. But that approach, no matter how heroic, always seems to lead to terrible frustration.

I think it is most important, especially in this era, to work with the root cause of the problem, which is aggression. That root goes very, very deep. I am not saying we must wait until we're fully enlightened to be involved in social or political action, but we must at the same time also be working at this deeper level.

Finally, each of us should start with some sense of what we actually can accomplish. What is our capacity, and what are our talents, realistically speaking? Often when we read the newspapers we think about the suffering in the world, and we feel that something should be done, and then we congratulate ourselves for being involved, for not being indifferent. But we might as well face the reality of what we really can do, and then try to carry that out to the best of our ability. Otherwise we end up either feeling righteous about our grand schemes to help everyone in the world or feeling guilty because we haven't yet managed to do so. Buddhism presents a realistic approach. We work with the immediate situation, with what we can do effectively, and at the same time, through our practice we continually undermine the aggression which is at the root of all suffering.

Well-Balanced I

David Steindl-Rast O.S.B.
Eido Tai Shimano Roshi

BROTHER DAVID: Roshi, is there some particular aspect of zazen practice that helps you to cope with this world we live in, this world which finds itself not only in a state of crisis—we have had many thousands of crises in our history—but which is actually on the brink of self-annihilation? What can be acquired through zazen that will help people to deal with this situation effectively?

EIDO ROSHI: Very few people are able to do something, realistically speaking. Some people may have the desire, but then the situation does not allow them to take action. We all need to have good faith that when we are doing our spiritual practice—even though we might be sitting alone, deep in the mountains—we are radiating a kind of spiritual vibration. I am not saying this with an arrogant attitude, but it is important for us to have faith that if one person sits, the whole universe goes into great samadhi.

BROTHER DAVID: Yes, this is a strong belief in our tradition, as well;

it is usually called "praying for the world," or "suffering for the world." But from knowing you personally, I think you would agree that there is something else we can also do. I am recalling, for example, that we participated together in one of the early Vietnam war protests, in 1965. What little weight we had, as one Buddhist and one Christian monk, we were throwing around even then. Of course, there can be a problem if someone is only an activist and he or she is too busy to spend time in contemplation. But it seems that some people are so intent on sitting that perhaps they overlook opportunities to respond in a helpful way to this present situation of crisis.

EIDO ROSHI: Well, I think we need different kinds of people: some people need to sit, some people need to act. This will make a good balance.

BROTHER DAVID: And what about the people who sometimes sit and sometimes act?

EIDO ROSHI: That is another balance.

BROTHER DAVID: Then you are saying that the solution is to find out where we belong.

EIDO ROSHI: Well, actually, the world itself is well-balanced from the very beginning. (Pause.) Don't you think so? (Laughter.)

BROTHER DAVID: From the beginning, yes. I'm more concerned about the end. (Laughter.)

EIDO ROSHI: It really is my conviction that the world is well-balanced: from the beginningless beginning to the endless end. It is always well-balanced.

BROTHER DAVID: Yes, I really believe that too. This is what we call "trusting in God." But there is a way of understanding this that is superficial, so that something else that is also important is bypassed, namely, our sense of responsibility. Even though the world is well-balanced on one level, on another level we need to rise to the responsibility of keeping it in balance. We have the ability to act, and also to fail to act, in ways that will affect the world's state of balance.

EIDO ROSHI: But whether we sit or not, the world is well-balanced. Remember a few years ago, we had an oil shortage, and the world was shocked. Today, everyone just continues on. Right?

BROTHER DAVID: Well, that is just because we can afford to pay more, but that may not always be the case. . . .

EIDO ROSHI: Brother David, if you start to think that way, you have to worry endlessly.

BROTHER DAVID: Well, there is a way of thinking about it that is not worrying. But there is a way of not thinking about it that is irresponsible.

EIDO ROSHI: No, I really think we are responsible to realize that the world is well-balanced from the beginningless beginning to the endless end. That is our responsibility.

BROTHER DAVID: Yes, I believe that . . . (laughter) . . . but I also realize that, because we are spending more money for oil and gasoline, farmers in the Third World who cannot afford to do so are dying by the score and by the thousand. Every day 50,000 people die of starvation. That is a tragically large number, especially when you consider that these people are dying because we have channeled funds and resources in a way that is not well-balanced in terms of the entire human family. All of us here belong to the small percentage that uses most of the world's resources, so we have a certain responsibility. I don't think we should worry, but I do think we should be deeply disturbed. If we are part of a family where something terribly unjust is taking place, we have to do something about it or we are not living up to our practice.

EIDO ROSHI: I feel the same way, and at the same time I feel powerless. No matter how much I think and I do, I alone cannot do anything for those 50,000 people. And suppose 50,000 people did *not* die every day: there would be other kinds of population problems. I am saying, fundamentally, that I am very much aware of this problem, but it is more important to be aware of the nature of the universe, so that we are able to accept, as Walter Cronkite often said, that "that's the way it is." (Laughter.)

BROTHER DAVID: But I often see a reckless kind of trust in God's power, a reckless presumption that God will make everything come out alright, because God "knows best."

EIDO ROSHI: Do you think that by doing something, a solution can be found?

BROTHER DAVID: Yes, I do.

EIDO ROSHI: Oh . . . oh. . . . (Laughter.)

BROTHER DAVID: But what to do is the great question. I would say that the answer is: Do whatever it is time to do. For some people that may be very little. But if we really do trust in the balance of the world from beginning to end, and at the same time we are aware of our responsibility, we will do the little thing that we can do, and that will be our contribution. No more is asked of us.

EIDO ROSHI: But don't you think that contemplative practice is one of these deeds?

BROTHER DAVID: Yes. And in exceptional cases it may be the only thing that is asked of someone. But I think that contemplative practice usually alerts us to the other things that are also being asked of us.

EIDO ROSHI: (sucking in breath loudly) You know, Brother David, I have known you for so many years, and you are so romantic. (Laughter and whoops from the audience) Whether in front of the public or just between the two of us, our conversation has been this way for the past twenty years. I am not a pessimist. I think I am a realist. Perhaps you are a realist too, but with romantic inclinations. (Laughter.)

BROTHER DAVID: Well, don't you think there must be a way for a realist with romantic inclinations to do the right thing in the world today? (Laughter.) What would you say it is?

EIDO ROSHI: Well, for myself, somehow I am karmically engaged with the practice of intensive zazen meditation. I can do without consulting others, making telephone calls, writing letters: I just shut up and sit down. This is what I have been doing, and through this I came to a spiritual conversion, and I realized the fact that I don't need to worry, because the world is well-balanced from the very beginning. And that is why I can talk to you, or to these other intelligent people, with great confidence. Perhaps you have different attitudes or ways or answers, but this is certainly one way. It may sound inactive, but zazen is a very active job.

BROTHER DAVID: And I know you well enough to respect that this is your contribution. But it is not the only one. For others there may be other contributions.

EIDO ROSHI: Oh, yes. If all the people in this city were practicing intensive zazen, that could be a problem. The airplanes wouldn't fly; the stores would be closed, and so on. That is exactly what I mean: the world is well-balanced. (Laughter and applause.)

Well-Balanced II

William McNamara O.C.D.
Eido Tai Shimano Roshi

FATHER MCNAMARA: After pondering Roshi's statement that the world is well-balanced, I would like to propose a distinction. I certainly do believe that the earth is, from the beginning to the end, marvelously well-balanced—but not so the world. We have un-balanced it, by our greed and our anger and our lust, and I believe we have to come to terms with that. We must have a courageous trust in life, knowing that God is God, but we must also take the responsibility of being his partners, his co-creators. Therefore, we have to cope with the obvious evil in the alienated world we have created, and with the alienated selves we have come to be. We have to be always healing, purifying, and reordering that world through our prayer, our love, and our disciplined lives. So I would distinguish between the forever well-ordered earth that God created and the alienated world of sinful humanity.

   The one thing I noticed that both Eido Roshi and Brother David strongly agreed upon was that one should never worry. I want to talk to them both about that. (Laughter.) I think that there is a place in the human adventure for existential anxiety. There are some things I think we should worry about. I worry, for example, about the fact that our leaders, both political and ecclesiastical, seem seldom contemplative enough, even though Plato, Aristotle, Saint Thomas Aquinas, Saint Bonaventure, Sir Thomas More, and Louis L'Amour (laughter) all said that the end and the goal of all society is contemplation. I also worry about the extent that I, one tiny little creature, can change things significantly. And so I worry about my vocation. I am never finished becoming a monk. I have been a monk for over forty years, but I am still becoming a monk. I am trying to become a human. But I worry about the fulfillment of my vocation, and about how adequately I respond to the divine call, to the challenges of love, to the devastating demands of absolute, total love. Theoretically I know that there is only one way to respond to the absolute, and that is absolutely. I know that I have to come up with a life of such simplicity that the cost is no less than everything. And so I worry about my capacity for God. I worry about my capacity to do the most important thing, which is to be. Look at Mary of Nazareth. One little Jewish girl learned how to be still, and how to cling to nothing, so that there was nothing in her mind or in her heart to impede the onslaught of the passionate presence of God. That one little girl changed the world. Look at Joan of Arc, who changed the history of France, England, and America. Christians in America today owe their faith to the fact that when Joan of Arc was out taking care of her sheep centuries ago, she listened carefully and contemplatively to the word. She listened to the word she could not dream of, could not pronounce. She heard, and she was saturated, and she did what she was told. And so she became a saint by riding horses with soldiers, fighting battles, crowning kings, and being burned at the stake. That, by the way, is one of the few valid ways of becoming a saint. If you are burned at the stake, you know you are not being narcissistic. (Laughter.) I highly recommend it.

EIDO ROSHI: Father, I think you are a real Zen man—more than a Zen master. (Laughter.) True! I am quite impressed by your presentation. Now, about this distinction between the earth and the world . . . perhaps I should have used a different word in my earlier discussion with Brother David: universe. How would you respond if I said that the universe which is created by God is well-balanced from the beginningless beginning to the endless end?

FATHER MCNAMARA: I would say, bravo. (Laughter and applause.)

Chapter 8: Notes

1. Epigraph: *Mother Teresa: Her People and Her Work* (New York: Harper & Row, 1976).
2. Epigraph: *A Guide to Walking Meditation* (Nyack, N.Y.: Fellowship Pubns., 1985).
3. A han is a wooden sounding-board used in Zen monasteries.
4. From "The Conversion of Saint Augustine" in *The Living Testament*, p. 83.

9

The Spiritual Teacher

The *starets* (spiritual father) does not apply abstract rules learnt from a book, but he sees on each occasion *this* particular man or woman who is before him; and illumined by the Spirit, he seeks to transmit the unique will of God specifically for this one person. . . . To each one he shows his or her true face, which before was largely hidden.[1]

KALLISTOS WARE

All in all, the desire for enlightenment, for fulfillment, for realization, abides in the image of the guru. Even when we see a painting or a statue of the Buddha, longing for the awakened state of mind is kindled in us. We cannot manufacture this longing; we have to experience it. That can happen only when we encounter someone who presents the truth without apology. Longing for the guru is the same as longing for the extinction of ego. Such longing produces great practice.[2]

OSEL TENDZIN

Obedience

Ven. Chögyam Trungpa Rinpoche
Reginald Ray
David Steindl-Rast O.S.B.
Thomas Keating O.C.S.O.

Tessa Bielecki
Judith Lief
Joseph Goldstein
Eido Tai Shimano Roshi

TRUNGPA RINPOCHE: It seems that the main point of having a teacher is that we need to develop a sense of humbleness. Usually we hold onto our egotism as a way of displaying our strength, beauty, knowledge, or wealth. Such egotism is a kind of blockage: we don't hear other people's messages, and we become deaf and dumb. We only hear and see what we want to, rather than opening ourselves. On the spiritual journey, it is important to overcome this deaf and dumb quality. We need to develop a connection with the world, the world other than ourselves. Therefore, devotion is very important.

When I was a child I used to think I was an important person, a specially-chosen lama. That particular blockage was slowly and thoroughly broken down by my teacher. Sometimes he criticized me, and sometimes he joked with me. Humor is actually one of the most powerful aspects of such a relationship. I think whether we are in a Christian, Buddhist, or Hindu tradition, it is necessary for us to have a spiritual teacher we can talk to: someone who will relate to us directly. Otherwise there is no chance of a real journey taking place. Sometimes you might feel you want to run away from such a person, and sometimes you feel great love for him or her. Nonetheless, such a relationship based on devotion is always important.

Devotion to a spiritual teacher is different from relating to your college professor. You are not simply trying to snatch whatever he or she knows for yourself, with the hope that you will become better than your teacher some day. In this case, you become continually more humble. The teacher represents the whole lineage of spiritual teachers of whichever tradition you belong to. Once you begin to be devoted to such a teacher, a sense of grace or blessings descends on you, so that you become softer and softer. You become a more decent person. In fact, you become much happier, because you don't have to hold on to yourself so tightly. There is less strain involved, and you can afford to relax. Then you begin to grow beautiful flowers of wisdom in your heart.

REGGIE RAY: Thank you, Rinpoche. Brother David, would you like to address us from a Christian perspective?

BROTHER DAVID: In terms of the Christian tradition, I think the image that best describes the historical Jesus is that of someone who gave spiritual direction to a small group of people. We could also say that the spiritual direction of the early Fathers, during the first centuries of the Christian tradition, closely parallels what we hear about the guru-disciple relationships of Buddhism. We can read many stories about the novice or monk going to one of the Desert Fathers in order to confide in him and seek advice. Many people don't realize that the form of confession now practiced in the Roman Catholic Church is a relatively late development, which grew out of the relationship between monks and their spiritual guides. In our own time there is once again a great upsurge of interest in spiritual direction—not only in monastic circles, but among lay people as well. We can see this interest reflected in the recent proliferation of books, workshops, and audio tapes offering spiritual direction.

As a more personal confession on this issue, I have to tell you that I speak as someone who has not been particularly successful either in receiving or giving spiritual direction. I'm an expert at what *not* to do, and that might also be a helpful perspective. In the monastery I live in, every monk has a spiritual guide, which, according to the Benedictine tradition, is the abbot. I was privileged during the first twenty years of my spiritual life to have had a great spiritual master as my abbot. I totally entered into this relationship with him, to the best of my ability, but for some reason it just never really worked. It must have had some effect on me, but in a roundabout way that I was never really able to assess. Our relationship took place within a framework that was already set up for us, and we both tried, as abbot and monk, to fulfill what this framework demanded of us. Humanly speaking, however, it only sporadically felt warm and supportive. I'm not talking about the difficulties and challenges one should, of course, expect from one's teacher; the relationship itself just never seemed to get off the ground. Whenever a real crisis occurred in my life, the guidance would always come from somewhere, but it never came from the quarters I expected it to come from.

For my part, I personally do not give spiritual direction to anyone, in spite of the fact that I constantly receive letters from people seeking spiritual guidance. But the most important ingredient of spiritual direction is continuity, and these days I have so many commitments outside the monastery that even my cactus die between the time I leave and when I come back home. So if I can't take care of a cactus . . . (laughter) . . . how can I possibly take care of anyone else? So from my perspective, the important question is, how does one manage without spiritual direction? I think the majority of people will never find it. Even Mahatma Gandhi living in India, which I've heard is teeming with gurus, said in his autobiography that although he was looking for a guru all his life, he was never able to find one. Now, if Ghandi, who was surely ripe for such a relationship, wasn't able to find a teacher in all of India, what can we expect, living in the United States? (Laughter.)

In the Christian context, the primary insight is that God speaks. He speaks not only through a guru, but through everything: every situation, every person. We have to take this to heart. If I start a car and I don't listen to the noises it makes, I am not being obedient to this car. But if I do listen, the car will teach me something. And God speaks very loudly to me through cars, because I have such a hard time with them. (Laughter.) God also speaks to me through animals. I like to feed the birds, for example, and God has taught me an awful lot through them. He also teaches me through children—even more so than through adults. In general, if we haven't learned to listen, nothing and no one will speak to us. If we have, God will speak to us through everything. So, at least that's how I console myself, and maybe this will console some of you. (Laughter and applause.)

FATHER KEATING: I'm happy to see that Brother David is renewing the ancient tradition of the wandering monk! (Laughter.) Of course, if any of us wander as much as Brother David says he does, it is true that we will not be in a position either to give or receive spiritual direction. However, I think in this discussion we could try to define what, if we do find a spiritual director, such a relationship should be like. It is my opinion that, in whichever tradition one follows, the more the practice is directed toward the surrender of the false self and the release of what is in the unconscious, the more important it is to have spiritual guidance. Certainly, some meditative practices require an expert teacher; otherwise we should not do them. And even when guidance is not absolutely necessary, the great advantage of having such a relationship is that it gives us the opportunity to express ourselves to someone who holds a sacred place in our lives, and who has an objective judgement about what is going on in us—which is something a friend can never quite do. We may go to a friend looking for sympathy when what we really need is a good kick in the behind. Or sometimes our thoughts and feelings build up such an incredible energy and importance that we become enslaved by them. As soon as we reveal these in the context of a sacred relationship, by which I mean a relationship of faith, then a spirit of openness enters in and we can be freed from the fascination of our thoughts and passions.

A sacred relationship doesn't work unless we totally commit ourselves to obeying our teacher. In the monastic experience, obedience is an essential element in establishing a deep foundation for one's spiritual growth. It is a concrete way of giving up one's own will and judgement. However, for many people in this culture, "obedience" is a difficult word. No one wants to do anything unless he or she can see the reason for doing it. But if you see the reason to obey, the sacred relationship ceases to do its subtle work. In the long run, it is more important to be detached from our own judgement than to know that what we are told to do is "right." We need to be free of the interior dialogue that is constantly judging our interior states, and especially our prayer.

When I was a young monk at Saint Joseph's Abbey, I was eager to follow all the ascetical practices. One day, out of the blue, my abbot conceived the idea that I was too thin. He said that if I was going to persevere in the Trappist life, I needed to put on some weight. He told me to drink one glass of cream and to eat three Hershey bars between meals. (Laughter.) The problem I then faced was how to do this without my peers seeing: I was supposed to be an ascetic, after all. But there is no way of hiding anything from anyone in the common life. And so for six weeks I sheepishly stuffed myself with cream and Hershey bars. I can't remember whether I gained any weight, but I do know that I experienced a tremendous grace of interior freedom. My abbot had perceived that not only did I need to put on weight, but that I needed to be dislodged from my ascetical self-image. It was his idea, not mine, and I had the grace and insight to throw myself—as I then saw myself—away.

Saint Benedict gives monks this succinct advice: "Obey without delay." In other words, don't reflect on the command; just do it. Nobody is asking you to decide whether it is a good idea, whether the superiors are wise or foolish, or whether the orders should be changed around to suit your ideas. Just do it, and keep doing it. That frees you to be present to what you are doing, which is one of the great ways of liberation. There is a greater freedom available in obeying one's spiritual director than in any kind of independence. The ability to obey a human voice is also an apprenticeship, in which we learn to obey the more delicate movements and inspirations that are interior and come from the Spirit of God. Obedience is ultimately a way of training and refining our own conscience.

MOTHER TESSA: Father Thomas, I agree with everything you say, but I think that for many Christians discussions such as this can be extremely frustrating. The theory is magnificent, but there are so few spiritual directors around. It might be more realistic to look at what we can do if we don't have a living master. I certainly agree with Brother David that everyone and everything around us can teach us. Also a somewhat derivative but nevertheless effective source of spiritual direction can be found in books. Thomas Merton is a spiritual teacher for a great many people, and so is John of the Cross. And obviously Christ himself is our teacher. As Christians we should always be looking to him. I could also say something specifically to the Catholics, which is that confession can be a tremendously positive situation of spiritual direction. As Father William is often telling us, confession is not a "sin bin" but a "grace place." Rather than unloading something bad, the major value of the sacrament of confession is spiritual counseling. Now again, if it's hard to find good spiritual directors, it is also hard to find good confessors. Still, a bad confession experience, or even a bad spiritual direction experience, can be a powerful teaching. It is often said that Teresa of Avila suffered many years from very poor spiritual direction, and yet that difficulty was in itself spiritual direction for her.

I could also add that, from my own experience, the humiliation which is often the byproduct of spiritual direction can be fun. It's especially fun for other people. (Laughter.) In my community, Father William is a genius at entertaining us through the penances he gives. One person's penance, for example, was to dance an Irish jig on Saint Patrick's Day, at the very moment we were all filing out of the chapel. Another had to stand on the roof and shout Psalm 51, which is the main penitential psalm, at the top of his lungs. The best penance I ever received was when he instructed me that the next time I went down to the lake for a canoe ride, I had to get into the canoe backwards, hold the paddle upside-down, and then try to paddle. For awhile I deliberately stayed away from the lake when I saw anyone else around, so that I would not have to make a fool out of myself. But then one morning I woke up to such a magnificent sunrise that I couldn't resist; I dashed down to the lake and hopped into the canoe. Suddenly I remembered my penance, but it was too late. I looked around and—fortunately or unfortunately, depending on your perspective—there were all kinds of people around. And so I proceeded to try to paddle, sitting backwards in the canoe and holding the paddle upside-down. If you've ever tried such a thing, you know that it gets you absolutely nowhere. (Laughter.)

REGGIE RAY: Thank you, Mother Tessa. Judy, would you like to add anything?

JUDY LIEF: In this discussion I seem to be representing the students who try to manage *with* a teacher. In my case, I was going blithely along with no intention at all of looking for a teacher, when, through some quirk of chance, I happened to run into a genuine teacher, years ago in New York City. Now I am in the further unlikely situation of having to talk about that relationship in his presence. (She looks at Trungpa Rinpoche, who looks back over his glasses.) I suppose this is my Buddhist penance. (Laughter.)

As any typical American, I was always suspicious of any kind of hierarchical relationship, whether it involved my parents, teachers, or anyone else in a position of authority. During the 1960's and 1970's there were many spiritual teachers in this country who were presenting all kinds of spiritual teachings and offering many varieties of promises. In the midst of all that, I happened to run into Trungpa Rinpoche, who didn't offer any promises at all. Somehow that intrigued me. So I became his student and decided to follow the basic instruction, which was to practice meditation. I don't think I realized at the time how extremely fortunate I was to have encountered such an uncompromisingly genuine teacher. All I knew was that I suddenly had a new element of discomfort in my life.

In my practice, and in my relationship with my teacher generally, I have found that I am continually thrown back on myself. Often when I would ask a question, it would simply resonate hollowly in space. I'd be left hanging there, waiting for the clarifying response. As I went on, I found that my questions became more and more intensified and constant. I was becoming enlivened, in fact. On the one hand I experienced the discomfort of contrast: the more I perceived my teacher's wisdom, the strength of his tradition, and the depth of his understanding, the more I felt stupid, awkward, lacking in understanding, and totally hopeless as a student. And yet, on the other hand, I also felt tremendous inspiration. His world wasn't really alien to me, but was actual proof that it is possible to achieve realization; it is possible to manifest gentleness, compassion, and enlightenment.

My relationship to my teacher is simultaneous pain and pleasure: the pain of contrast and the delight of discovering that there is something real to spiritual traditions, that it is possible to become a genuine human being. I suppose that is the combination of qualities which forms the basis of real trust—it is a trust that is by no means based on blindness. In fact, I personally feel that the mark of a true teacher is that the student's inquisitiveness and interest in the world is heightened, rather than satisfied. At the same time, to be a student means simply that one follows the teacher's instructions. If he or she tells you to go on retreat and meditate for a month, you do it. And then you find out the reasons for yourself.

BROTHER DAVID: If I may, I would like to ask Trungpa Rinpoche a question. There is presently a great deal of discussion in the Roman Catholic Church as to whether a spiritual director is responsible for expanding people's political horizons in relation to the spiritual life. In a world in which every day as many men, women, and children die of hunger as if a city of 50,000 inhabitants had been wiped off the map, it seems a little strange to be preoccupied with whether you are eating a little more than you should, or fasting as much as you should. And although it is of course important to be kind to people and to help them, that attitude may or may not naturally extend to a concern about the arms race. So my question is, to what extent do you think the spiritual director is responsible for these political dimensions of the disciples' development?

TRUNGPA RINPOCHE: I think he or she is very responsible, very much so. Nevertheless, relating to a spiritual teacher is a matter of personal discipline to begin with, rather than just being a way of jumping into a social club. Preparation of oneself through contemplative practice is important. Then you begin to see clearly, and you start to become helpful, so that at least *you* don't have to be helped.

REGGIE RAY: Rinpoche, I have a question that concerns the apparent discrepancy between the situation in Tibet, where anyone entering the spiritual life would have a teacher and work with him closely over many years, and the situation in the West, where there are probably tens of thousands of people who would love to find a good teacher and who would benefit greatly by that, but who are unable to do so. In terms of your situation now, you have the responsibility of being a spiritual director for over 3,000 students. I wonder if you could say something about how you have extended your role of teacher so that you, personally, don't have to see every student every week, but yet the same process of teaching is still maintained.

TRUNGPA RINPOCHE: That is an interesting question. The teacher is not just in the role of behaving like a mother with her baby: changing diapers and bottle-feeding. The teacher creates a whole world. In the Christian tradition, you have churches and cathedrals. As soon as you go inside, you begin to feel the presence of God. Someone doesn't have to stand at the door and whisper to each person who enters, "There is God up there." (Laughter.) It is a question of creating the general environment, and then that environment teaches a lot to whoever enters. Also, in our sangha older students sometimes act as teachers. It is not that they are necessarily empowered or regarded as enlightened, but teaching others is considered part of their training. In that way a whole society can gradually be created. It is not just a matter of one man working hard all the time. So I think that is an important point here.

REGGIE RAY: Father Thomas, is there also an understanding in the

Christian tradition that the spiritual community, such as the monastery, is an extension of the teacher, so that the openness and learning you experience in that relationship extends into other situations? Do you have that expanded idea of what the teacher actually embodies?

FATHER KEATING: Oh yes. As Rinpoche said, spiritual direction isn't just a matter of bottle-feeding. The teacher tries to awaken the student's own capacity to hear the will of God. The abbot is believed to hold the place of Christ in the monastery. As that faith grows, it extends to other situations, because God is not only in the abbot; he is also in everything else, as Brother David said earlier.

JUDY LIEF: Once again from the perspective of a student, it seems that part of the teacher's role is to transmit an understanding of how to hear teachings altogether. I think many of us start out with a fixed and narrow sense of what teachings are, and we tend to be focused on the literal words. Over time, the teacher expands what our ears are able to pick up, and what our eyes are able to see. We begin to perceive his display of teachings through all the sense organs. Then we are also able to go back and rediscover what we thought we learned years ago. Because of having heard one teaching clearly, all the other teachings begin to shimmer and glow.

JOSEPH GOLDSTEIN: This brings another dimension into this discussion, which may be especially appropriate for the many people who do not have a spiritual guide. Without even realizing it, very often in our search for a teacher we are looking for a personality that seems compatible with our own. Sometimes it may be more possible to initially connect with a particular set of teachings than with a teacher. That was very much my own experience. When I first went to India looking for a master, I met Munindra-ji, and what inspired me from the very first moment was the quality of his teachings. This was what motivated me to continue the practice. Out of that, I later developed a relationship to him as a teacher.

REGGIE RAY: Roshi, earlier today you said that the main difference between Japanese Zen students and American Zen students is in their attitude toward obedience. I wonder if you would say a little more about that intriguing comment.

EIDO ROSHI: Actually, that was what one of my students said to me. When my teacher, Soen Roshi,[3] was visiting me in New York, my students watched me serving him, and they saw the loving kind of relationship we had. After a few weeks, one of my students said to me, "Roshi, I must say that, watching you and Soen Roshi together, and then seeing ourselves and you together in America, there are a lot of similarities, but there is one big difference. The difference is that, in our case, there is a basic deficiency of obedience." (Laughter.) In Japan, obedience is not spoken about very much, but it has been performed by students for centuries. I, myself, had two teachers. My first teacher I tried my best with, like Brother David, but there was some kind of chemical reaction: somehow it didn't work out. It wasn't a deficiency of obedience in that case, but a chemical reaction. When I met my second teacher, Soen Roshi, for the first time, I felt a great congeniality, and this feeling silently conveyed to me that I could be happily obedient. He has been my teacher for about thirty years now. So, it is my own feeling that, if there is a deficiency of obedience between myself and my students, perhaps there is a difficult chemical reaction between us. (Roshi laughs, laughter.)

FATHER KEATING: Frankly, Roshi, I don't think it is just a chemical reaction. I think Americans generally prefer not to obey if they can possibly get away with it. (Laughter.) In particular, they like to get rid of abbots from time to time. (Laughter.) It doesn't mean Americans aren't great people; but, in this democratic society of ours, they like a change of administration once in a while!

QUESTION (from audience): I also have a feeling that many people in America are turning to therapists for the kind of relationship they haven't been able to establish with spiritual leaders. I am

personally concerned about this, and see it as a potential
perversion of psychotherapy. Rinpoche, at what point would
you say therapist should refer his or her clients to a guru?

TRUNGPA RINPOCHE: I think that, in the therapeutic world, color
and individuality can become very important. One is often
listening not so much to the message as to the therapist's
colorfulness and congeniality—which is problematic. Therapy
often becomes a personality cult. In working with a spiritual
teacher, it is not the teacher himself who you are following, but
the teachings. And I think the point at which you should leave
therapy for spiritual practice is when you are more or less
together: you are capable of looking after yourself, roughly
speaking. (Laughter.) Then you should go to a spiritual teacher
and begin to practice. At first you may find that you are almost
regressing. You are going back to the previous state. You may
find that the practice is not easy, and the general conditions
may not seem helpful. Nonetheless you should go on. At a
certain point that situation will become at least congenial, and
you will begin to realize that your ego has been playing a game
on you. When you realize that, then the kind of personality
worship you had for your therapist begins to fall apart. You
realize how much you have been trying, very badly trying, to
take care of yourself. We always feel we need help and
comfort, and we are horrified by discomfort. But when we
practice, and we begin to be more reasonable, discomfort isn't
seen as all that bad—or pleasure as all that great—and we begin
to find our way.

QUESTION: Father Keating, wouldn't you say that your interpretation
of obedience is particularly Cistercian? I am a Catholic nun,
and I very much treasure the monastic tradition within our
church. But I would also like to say that in the context of the
present renewal within the Roman Catholic Church, we are
discovering that there are other ways to interpret obedience
and to respond to that movement of the Spirit we all feel. I
have had many spiritual fathers in my life, but I am grateful
that I have not had *too* many. Otherwise I may not have looked

as much to the resources of my own spirit, my own being. By relying on our own experiences, and also by reaching back into our tradition, we can find different kinds of resources than we might be accustomed to. For instance, the Way of Friendship, which is actually part of our tradition, is a way to God. We have recently rediscovered such riches *because* we have lacked the direct relationship to a teacher that has been enjoyed in the Buddhist tradition.

FATHER KEATING: Sister, you have touched upon a controversy that is important within the Roman Catholic community at present. The description of obedience that I gave belongs primarily to a monastic context, and might be called "ascetical obedience." I heartily agree that the concept of obedience has at times been confused with relationships that do not provide the proper context for it, such as obedience to superiors who reside far away and do not know you. Ascetical obedience has to be practiced in the right context, and with the ultimate goal of assuming more and more responsibility for oneself. If you cannot find the right milieu for ascetical obedience, then I agree that it would be a matter of cultivating obedience to the Spirit, and of being faithful to your own conscience.

REGGIE RAY: Would anyone like to offer some final comments?

BROTHER DAVID: Well, it's not so much a comment, but an image we can take away. Actually I have two images, and I think we have to make a choice between these two when we go in search of spiritual direction. The first is of a model airplane. As we are soaring along on our spiritual flights, we entrust the master with a remote control. He pushes little buttons to make the airplane fly, and to give it direction. The other image is that of a homing pigeon. All the spiritual director has to do—although this is also quite a challenge—is to let the pigeon out of its cage, and it will find its own way home. And I personally prefer the second image. (Applause.)

REGGIE RAY: Rinpoche?

TRUNGPA RINPOCHE: Well, I think the whole thing boils down to a question of needing discipline and some sense of joy, and also of having a true and real spiritual friend who will speak to you and help you. Sometimes he will encourage you, and sometimes he will punish you. Such a guru or teacher is always necessary. That seems to be the contemplative tradition altogether. Without that, we are completely lost. However clever we may be, however devoted we may be, still we are lost. Thank you.

Trust

Loppön Lodrö Dorje
Thomas Keating O.C.S.O.
David Steindl-Rast O.S.B.

Joseph Goldstein
Reginald Ray
Judith Lief

QUESTION (from audience): One of the difficulties I encounter on the path is that I am unable to trust in the reality of spiritual transformation. How does one develop confidence that there is such a reality? How do you know that the teacher or the path is valid, and that it is right to trust?

LODRÖ DORJE: In Buddhism, trust always begins with trusting in oneself and one's experience. When we come to the path, our initial experience is of personal pain, discomfort, insecurity, anxiety, alienation, and so on. In other words, we start with the experience of suffering. The teacher responds to that with the instruction to practice meditation and to acknowledge and accept one's experience for what it is. On that basis, we quite possibly begin to feel that it is worthwhile to practice, which then leads us to develop trust in the teacher and the tradition that suggested it was a good idea. And then the relationship goes on from there.

FATHER KEATING: Yes, I would agree that it takes time to develop trust. It is a help to know one's tradition well enough to realize that the difficulties one is going through are also everyone's difficulties. They are nothing new. And in a monastery, it is a great help to see that someone in his eighties is still toddling around. He has made it through the discipline and is still there. Entering a monastery is like entering upon an apprenticeship. No one can learn to be a cabinetmaker overnight. In the course of two or three years you may feel many times that you are never going to make it; it is hopeless. But your teacher, your elders, your guide, and the community that supports you tell you to wait a little while and keep trying. Little by little, your experience begins to yield to the fact that you do get through certain tough spots. Thus you develop confidence. Also in the Christian tradition we put our confidence in Christ; what we don't have he can give us. So the dimension of prayer is also extremely important for developing trust.

BROTHER DAVID: Of course, the kind of trust we must give one another, including our teachers, is not a trust *in* this and that, but an unconditional trust. When our trust is based on the condition that the other person will do this or that, then we are already on the wrong track. When we trust unconditionally, we trust in the seed within the other person. We don't know yet how it will manifest, but we trust that it is a good seed.

JOSEPH GOLDSTEIN: I think there is often a fundamental misunderstanding about trust. As an experiment, I would like to ask you to feel yourself sitting on your chair—just feel that sensation. Is there any lack of trust in that experience? It is so simple. The person who doubts or has a lack of basic trust is actually lost in thought, lost in concept. As soon as we drop down to the level of actual experience, we discover that the trust is already there. It is not an exotic or metaphysical experience. It is not even something that has to be developed. Instead, it is something accessible to all of us, which can be remembered in each moment.

REGGIE RAY: Another side of this issue is the question of how we can create social or political institutions that encourage people to have their own integrity and sense of trust, so that they can find their own way. Both Judy Lief and I have been working on the development of Naropa Institute as a place that provides such an educational environment. Judy, could you say something about trust in an institutional context?

JUDY LIEF: Well, lately I've been thinking a lot about how important it is *not* to trust, because so often people naively place their trust in leaders or traditions and get badly burned in the process. Then they become cynical and hardened. So I think the starting point is distrust, by which I mean constant questioning. Otherwise trust that is based on an external object can reinforce a feeling of duality.

I feel that a good educational system provokes the spirit of inquiry, which gives rise to a level of trust that is real and simple and quite different from our need for feedback or for confirmation of our experience. I think a lot of people can't and shouldn't be trusted; in fact, we can't even trust our own thoughts and perceptions, because they are so colored by hopes and fears and desires. So I would like to suggest that distrust is the foundation for real trust.

Chapter 9: Notes
1. Epigraph: *The Orthodox Way*, p. 128.
2. Epigraph: *Buddha in the Palm of Your Hand*, p. 89.
3. Soen Nakagawa Roshi died March 11, 1984.

10

Time, Place, and Silence

He who truly attains awakening knows that deliverance is to be found right where he is. There is no need to retire to the mountain cave. If he is a fisherman he becomes a real fisherman. If he is a butcher he becomes a real butcher. The farmer becomes a real farmer and the merchant a real merchant. He lives his daily life in awakened awareness. His every act from morning to evening is his religion.[1]

SOKEI-AN

We are fellow-helpers with God, co-creators in everything we do. When Word and work are returned to their source and origin, then all work is accomplished divinely in God. And there too the soul loses itself in a wonderful enchantment.[2]

MEISTER ECKHART

Called into Solitude

Reginald Ray
William McNamara O.C.D
David Steindl-Rast O.S.B.
Thomas Keating O.C.S.O.
Eido Tai Shimano Roshi

REGGIE RAY: Father William, how would you assess the overall health
of the monastic element in the Catholic tradition? Is
monasticism on the rise or on the decline?

FATHER MCNAMARA: There is presently an effort to renew the
monastic tradition of the Western Church. I personally see the
life of the whole Church, and of society itself, depending to a
very large extent, as it did in the Dark Ages, on whether or not
monasticism is indeed profoundly renewed. I must say that I
do not think it is presently being profoundly renewed. I feel
the changes to date have been rather superficial adaptations
and accommodations which have come about as survival
measures. There are of course some refreshing exceptions to
this general trend of mediocrity, and hopefully there are
enough exceptions to indicate that more positive developments
will happen in the future, so that we will be able to pass
through this new Dark Age with the great assistance of
monasticism, as we did in the past.

I find it difficult to imagine a renewal of the spiritual life
of the laity without a healthy monastic tradition. Monasticism is
a symbol which lay people need. It is a wonderful sign of God
exerting his sovereign claim on human beings. Here are men
and women who so carefully regulate their lives that they are
always watching. Here are people who are God-filled, God-
intoxicated, and whose lives make no sense except for God.
The laity needs to know that those monks are always there;
then they can go about their business in the fray and in the
marketplace buoyed up by the knowledge that those monks are
willing to waste their lives and be fools. (Laughter.)

BROTHER DAVID: To hear you speaking about wasting time reminds me of a talk Suzuki Roshi once gave to the Tassajara community. He said, "You ought to waste time . . . " and of course everyone was very surprised at this, until he added, " . . . conscientiously." I think that's the kind of "waste" you had in mind, too.

FATHER MCNAMARA: Conscientiously and creatively.

QUESTION (from audience): I can't help thinking that in the West monasteries are so cut off from the rest of society that whatever inspiration the monks and nuns might generate through their contemplative practices never reaches the rest of us. Although I think a life spent in retreat and solitude is valid, I don't really see, if the monks and nuns never come out, how monasticism is playing such a critical role in society at large.

FATHER MCNAMARA: Some of the people who convey the most truth, the most love, and the freshest dimensions of being never come out. Look at the effect Thomas Merton had on the whole of American society before he ever physically came out. And even when he finally visited the East, he came to the conclusion that he didn't need to go, after all. I would say that a lot depends on personal vocation. Some will come out in order to speak; some will stay, but will write about their understanding; and some will be held by God in silence. For those who stay, the monastic life is in itself proof that God is real, and that there are deep interior values to life. The newness of one's life can be so fresh and so unparalleled that it is the greatest kind of witness.

Whenever a Christian monk is genuinely called into solitude, that monk goes into deeper silence *not* in order to achieve some satisfaction, however pious or holy. He or she goes in because such a monk has been called, summoned. And who can resist the divine, infinite calling? A genuine monk is convinced that the deeper one goes into solitude the more he or she is in redemptive touch with all people, with all creatures, with all the universe.

QUESTION: Father William, what do you see to be the responsibility of the laity? What can the laity bring to the monastery?

FATHER MCNAMARA: There's a great dance going on between monks and lay people. The monk makes a specific kind of contribution to lay life, and lay people come to the monastery with their viewpoint in order to challenge, provoke, feed, and inspire the monks. So it's a give-and-take relationship. One without the other wouldn't provide as nourishing or as inspiring a situation.

FATHER KEATING: As a monk who has been a member of one of the stricter monastic traditions in Christianity, and who has been on this journey for about forty years, I would just like to focus on a specific issue here, if I may. There is no question that the monastic witness and environment is of transcendent importance to society: the question is whether the structures of monastic life as they now exist in the Christian tradition are the right ones for our time. I see a great need for another kind of monastic commitment, one which would be open-ended and temporary, while still being truly monastic in the quality of its practice. It seems to me that there are presently many Christians who would resonate to the kind of monastic life that is expressed in Zen and Tibetan monasticism. Without denigrating the great value of solitude, I would suggest that an alternation between solitude and social action could be a beneficial rhythm. Incidentally, there are some representatives of the Protestant tradition in our midst, and perhaps after listening to all this talk about monasteries, they will be inspired to start one! If you do, may I suggest that you consider some of the Eastern models, rather than those that have developed and solidified in the West. Our monasteries have great value, but at the same time I think they tend to be stuck in a mind-set that comes from a different time than the one we are now in. (Applause.)

REGGIE RAY: Father Thomas, are you objecting to the idea of a cloistered community in general, or to the notion of a lifetime commitment? You don't object to periods of strict solitude, do you?

FATHER KEATING: Oh no! By no means. Indeed, retreat! (Laughter.) All I'm saying is that perpetual enclosure could be replaced by a system that would make it possible for someone, at a certain period of his or her life, to serve outside the cloister for a time, or even permanently. And I don't wish to imply that the already-existing orders must change; they have their life and they should be allowed to keep it. But I am suggesting that in the Christian religion there needs to be a new kind of structure existing alongside the old ones.

REGGIE RAY: Roshi, I'm wondering how the Zen tradition has traditionally dealt with this issue.

EIDO ROSHI: The Japanese Zen monasteries, especially the Rinzai Zen monasteries, are communities of monks. However, unlike the Christian monasteries, Zen monks are not expected to stay in the monastery the rest of their lives. In fact, there is a sort of unwritten rule that says if a Zen Buddhist monk stays in a monastery more than ten years, either he will become an abbot or something is wrong with him. So, during his training in the monastery, his connection with society is rather limited, so that he can concentrate on his spiritual training. But he is not bound to the monastery for life; rather, he is encouraged to deepen his insight to prepare him to relate to the larger world. Every since Zen Buddhism began coming to this country, and especially during the past twenty or thirty years, we have been trying out what Father Keating has described: a kind of lay monastery. However, as far as I am concerned, a lay monastery should not be a commune. It is still, after all, a monastery consisting of monks and lay dharma brothers and sisters. My monastery, Dai Bosatsu Zendo in upstate New York, is struggling to establish such a monastic community, to meet the spiritual needs of twentieth-century America.

Celibacy I

David Steindl-Rast O.S.B.
William McNamara O.C.D.

BROTHER DAVID: Father William, I understand that in your community there are men and women living together while following a celibate life. Now, that's such a wonderful and unique example to have in the Christian Church today. I think you are the only community doing such a thing. So I would like to hear, first of all, how you got permission to do it . . . (laughter) . . . and secondly, how it's working out.

FATHER MCNAMARA: Yes, I do agree with you, Brother, that this is a most significant aspect of our lives as a community, and I think it may be our most important contribution to the church. When I first spoke to Pope John about it, as I recall I was rather oblique. (Laughter and applause.) I remained that way until the whole thing got going. It was difficult in the beginning. We all proceeded very carefully, because we didn't have any models to go by. We wanted to make sure that our idea would not be spoiled early in our career, but would have a chance to develop into a real and living example. We've now been living this way for twenty-five years, and most of the difficulties are over. As for how it's worked out, well, living with women . . . there are a lot of things I could say. (Laughter.) It's wonderful. I think nothing can take its place. A woman evokes from a man, and a man from a woman, something that is not otherwise evoked. I think it is important that we develop within the monastic tradition this idea of celibate lovers—that we learn how to be highly sexed, and to have warm, intimate, passionate relationships, and yet to be willing to deliberately renounce the genital privileges and pleasures of spousal love. That is the religious celibate expression of love.

BROTHER DAVID: As for the first part of your answer, it has been said that it is much easier in the Roman Catholic Church to get absolution than it is to get permission (laughter), so I think you went about it the right way. But I would like to ask you to explore the second part of your answer a little further. I'm not quite clear why, in your vision, your community renounces genital activities. Is it because you see sexual contact as being basically undesirable, or is it that you want to clearly separate your community from involvement with the householder way of life?

FATHER MCNAMARA: I don't think that a celibate, mixed community would have a chance of survival if it did not adhere strictly to both renunciation of genital privileges as well as renunciation of the conjugal home life. Renunciation really is a deprivation, because both privileges are in themselves quite wonderful, I think. It is a mortification and it is a discipline. But there are wonderful fruits and byproducts that come from that kind of free, deliberate renunciation.

BROTHER DAVID: Could you articulate specifically how these privileges would be detrimental?

FATHER MCNAMARA: In our eremetical lifestyle, although there is a great deal of silence and solitude, there is also a great deal of community life. A genital expression of love would inevitably lead to the kind of possessiveness that rips a community apart with jealousy and rivalry. It has been my experience of humankind, and it is also the revelation of the Bible, that the central sin is jealousy. Right from the beginning, people have either been jealous of God or jealous of one another.

QUESTION (from audience): According to Rumi and other mystical poets, the visual contact between lovers who are spiritually sensitive can supercede and excel all the delights of genital contact. Now, in that case are we really talking about celibacy as renunciation? It is certainly convenient in a monastic situation not to have to have genital contact, but is that really a virtue when people are living and sharing powerful emotional and spiritual lives? Isn't abstinence really a simple accommodation to the realities of monastic life?

FATHER MCNAMARA: In the case of every member of our community, it is a virtue—a heroic virtue, I can assure you. (Laughter.) Granted, in the case of many religious, celibacy has become a convenience and an accommodation, so in that case it wouldn't necessarily be a virtue.

QUESTION: Can you conceive of a monastic model that included married couples and their families? Would that also pose a problem for the core of your community?

FATHER MCNAMARA: No, I don't see that as a problem. In fact, one family has been closely associated with us for a number of years now, and that has been a happy, fruitful arrangement. I hope that more families will also join us. The Celtic monastic life, which is my favorite historical instance of monasticism, took this form. I would like to see our community grow in that direction as well.

QUESTION: Given that married people could also have the monastic experience, do you feel that celibacy is in any way inherently advantageous as an alternative to marriage?

FATHER MCNAMARA: Well, they are different experiences. I wouldn't say that one is better than the other, but each is qualitatively different. One who is celibate does have more independence and more solitude, which creates a certain atmosphere. I suppose I would say that celibacy provides a particular freedom that is not otherwise achieved.

Celibacy II

Tessa Bielecki

Those of us who are celibate have made a choice, and I can say that I not only like being celibate, I love it. Eros is the greatest gift that God has given to us, but this crazy culture we live in tries to tell us that erotic energy has no outlet other than genital intercourse, which is nonsense. Father William (McNamara) defines eros as "a reaching and stretching with every fiber of your body-person for the fullness of life." Sometimes this reaching is expressed as sexuality, but there are a million other ways to express it. Some people choose to express eros through marriage. In the Catholic Church, marriage is a sacrament, because it can help us move toward union with God, which is the final goal of all human striving. But whether we are married or celibate, it is important that we are open to possibilities other than genitality for expressing our passion. Eros can also be directed toward scholarship, the arts, or social reform. In my life, and in the life of most celibates, it is directed toward a mystical life with God. This is what we call sublimation—which is not repression. It is not a stuffing down, but a raising up of this energy. I am always so delighted when I come across the occasional enlightened psychologist who acknowledges such an approach as healthy and normal. The reason that it is healthy is because mysticism is not disguised sex; sex is disguised mysticism.

In the last chapter of *Mystical Passion*, Father William says that, as a society, we are afraid of passion, and he describes the flight from eros into sex. He gives us this definition of eros:

> Eros relates us not only to other persons whom we love, but also the pig we are raising, the house we are building, the car we are driving, the vocation we are following. If we had been sufficiently charged with eros, for instance, we would have participated in a reverent dialogue with our environment which would have precluded the ecological disaster we are now suffering— the catastrophic conditions of our natural world brought on by the petty passions of uninspired and unconcerned hordes of hollow men.[3]

Contemplative Capsule

Thomas Keating O.C.S.O.

It seems to me that anyone in the present audience who is not a monk or nun should forget about aspiring to be one. I say this because of a certain mind-set in the Christian tradition, reinforced by centuries of expectation, which believes that if you want to improve your life, you have to enter a monastic community. But if you think you can only pray effectively in a monastic setting, you have not understood the incredible possibilities of ordinary life. God is just as present in your homes as he is in any monastery. You don't have to go somewhere in search of the Ultimate Mystery.

Anyone who is committed to the spiritual journey is already a monk or nun, in the transcendent sense. We must be clear about this. Otherwise, every time you have a little trouble in daily life, you will say, "I've got to get away and make a retreat." I am not in any way knocking the value of occasional periods of retreat. It is just more important that we develop a discipline that is suitable to the style of life we are actually living. In this way, we will gradually awaken to the Ultimate Mystery within the context and service of our whole response to life.

For a lay person, daily life is the primary practice. It is also true that every human being needs some interior silence in order to nourish the dynamic growth toward communion with the Ultimate Mystery. To make daily life work, we have to find ways of incorporating contemplative prayer into it, because some way of calming the mind and the emotions is the essential prerequisite for sensitizing us to the presence of the Ultimate Mystery in our lives. Even if this presence seems a little opaque in the beginning, it isn't necessarily going to be so in the long run, provided that we can regularly maintain an adequate level of interior silence in our psyche and nervous system. The half-hour or forty-five minute period when we withdraw from activity is the critical time when we affirm the basic values of monastic life: silence, solitude, simplicity of lifestyle, and a discipline of prayer. It is like taking an antibiotic in the form of a capsule. This medicine, of course, will only work if we take the proper dosage. In short, we need a contemplative practice that is carefully planned and adapted to our particular state of life and administered on a regular, daily basis.

When you begin to practice regular periods of silence and solitude, you may run into opposition from your spouse or family. The conflict then arises: how am I to be faithful to the truth of my spiritual journey and at the same time be faithful to my commitment to this other person? This is where you have to be creative. Let us suppose you feel you need two half-hour periods of prayer as a daily minimum. You get the morning session in okay, but in the evening when you come home and start to prepare for your evening session, your wife walks in and says, "What's the matter with you? Have I done something wrong?" She obviously wants some kind of dialogue at this time of the day. Fortunately there are other methods that can provide for such eventualities. One of these is an active prayer. This was a favorite device of the Desert Fathers of fourth-century Christian monasticism. It involves silently repeating a short phrase from the scripture, six to ten syllables in length, over and over. The phrase shouldn't be too long, or you may forget it; and it shouldn't be too short, or it could lead you into interior silence. For an active life, you need something just long enough to effectively compete with the usual tapes that arise from the unconscious in response to the frustration of our emotional programs for happiness. These programs are the equivalent of what in the Hindu frame of reference are referred to as the first three chakras: the instinctual drives for survival and security, affection and esteem, and control and power. These develop in pre-rational life and become increasingly defended in later life when frustrated or denied. By the time we come to the age of reason our emotional programs are so firmly established that, instead of re-assessing their value, we allow reason to be co-opted by them. We are also encouraged by our peer groups and culture to satisfy them; accordingly we rationalize, justify, and glorify them. As a result, when we experience the frustration of needs that are not being met, certain stereotyped tapes or commentaries justifying our emotional programs rise to consciousness.

For instance, suppose you live in the suburbs of a large city. One morning you are running out the door on your way to work when your wife stops you because she wants your help in planning a dinner party for the evening. As the initial frustration turns to anger, a commentary also rises to mind: "How can she be so thoughtless? Doesn't she know I'll be stuck in that rush hour traffic?" Obviously there is a good chance you will say, "To hell with you, darling! I'm going to work." But suppose you have practiced an active prayer, and in the course of the previous six months have worked a particular phrase into your psyche. It could be "Oh God, come to my assistance," (laughter) or "Not my will but thine be done." It really doesn't matter what it is. What matters is that it can serve to maintain the reservoir of interior silence that was built up during prayer.

I know some of you will think, "Monks have nothing else to do all day long but say these silly prayers, but what about us, who have to earn a living and raise a family?" All I can say is, you need to pray more than we do. (Laughter.) You don't always have supportive structures to remind you of the spiritual values of life. Although you may have established a reservoir of interior silence your morning period of prayer, once you hit the street, the water starts to drain out fast. But suppose when you got into your car or walked down the street, you were saying an active prayer over and over to yourself. I'll bet there are several hours in every day when you could be doing this: while you are doing chores, taking a shower, changing diapers, feeling sorry for yourself . . . (laughter) . . . you could be silently working your prayer into your unconscious. It is like Eido Roshi's story about Ummon knocking on the Zen master's door.[4] In this case, you are knocking on God's door. So say it quietly and calmly, and synchronize it with the beat of your heart. The repetition shouldn't be panicky. It is not, "OH GOD COME TO MY ASSISTANCE!" As a matter of fact, he is always coming to our assistance.

What happens when you practice the active prayer—and this is according to the testimony of many lay folks—is that just at the moment when you are dying to get on the road, and you start thinking, "Why does this person only think about herself instead of me?" to your great surprise, up comes the phrase: "Oh God come to my assistance." And this tape has the psychological effect of erasing the previous tape. You find yourself in a neutral space, in which you are free to reconstruct a new value system. Without that active prayer tape you would probably get caught in emotional reactions reinforced by self-justifying thoughts about why you are in the right, why you don't need to apologize to your wife, and other rationalizations that go on forever. Once you have stopped, or at least slowed down, the compulsive tendency to react emotionally, you have freedom. You can then decide what to do in the present moment. The "gift of counsel," which is the Spirit reaching out from a secret place within us, suggests, "Love her! Let her have her way."

I once heard of a woman who had been practicing an active prayer for some time and had successfully worked it into her subconscious. And by the way, you really do have to work at it. You might have to remind yourself with a note stuck on the bathroom mirror or other places around the house. You might have to do a few stupid things, but compared with the other stupid things we do . . . (laughter) . . . this one might actually prove worthwhile in the end.

Anyway, this woman was driving slowly down the road, to avoid a boy who was riding his bicycle ahead of her. Another driver came up behind and wanted to pass. He didn't see the youngster, and so, in a fit of fury, he gave in to his pre-recorded tapes. He stepped on the accelerator, zoomed around her car, rolled down the window, yelled out a string of obscenities, and spat in her face. Of course hurt feelings started to arise, and along with them came the old tapes: "How can someone be so cruel? How can God allow this to happen to me?" But then, all of a sudden, up came her active prayer: "Not my will but thine be done." And it erased the old tapes! Into her heart poured tremendous compassion and forgiveness for this man. Full of joy, she drove off down the road feeling as if someone had just given her a bouquet of roses.

Another practice that is extremely effective for lay folks is what used to be known in Christian tradition as "guarding the heart." You watch for the particular afflictive emotions that you have recognized to be coming from your unconscious motivation and causing you misery. For example, you may have an emotional investment in controlling other people. Now, in every community there are people who are better suited to lead than others. But occasionally some poor soul decides that power really constitutes true happiness. He or she starts climbing the social, political, or ecclesiastical ladder: junior executive, senior executive, president of the United States, the Dalai Lama, the Pope of Rome . . . I don't know where you go after that. At every stage the craving to control will be frustrated, and that will trigger the computerized program of indignation, rage, and the desire for revenge. If you want to control others, you are in competition with four-and-a-half billion other people who are trying to do the same stupid thing. The statistics are against you. There is no hope for success! Obviously such an ambition means that you are programmed for human misery.

If we don't face our emotional programs, our unconscious motivations will go on influencing us for the whole of our lives. Suppose when you were four years old an older sibling came along and swiped your lollipop. Your desire for pleasure was frustrated. Perhaps being a with-drawn sort of person, you ran up to your room, hid under the bed, and screamed in useless rage. Now let us say that fifty years later you were the president of General Motors. On one occasion the board of directors overruled one of your major decisions. Again, your feelings of indigna-tion and withdrawal went off, you climbed into your Leer jet, flew to the Bahamas, and spent a few months on tranquilizers, glaring at the Car-ibbean and feeling sorry for yourself. (Laughter.) Or perhaps instead of president of General Motors, you ended up as abbot of a monastery. At some point you didn't get your way, and you responded with, "It is time for me to take a retreat. I'm going into solitude." At that moment you would be practicing nothing but sheer selfishness. Someone should tell you to get on your knees and ask for the community's forgiveness. In both cases, nothing really changed in fifty years: only the lollipop changed.

In the Christian tradition, taking oneself in hand in order to dis-mantle the false self is called the "practice of virtue." The struggle with the emotions is the first stage of the spiritual journey. We should start by confronting whichever emotional program is strongest in us. There are several ways of doing this. One is to become aware of the principal up-setting emotion in our lives and then notice what event generally sets it off. Each time the particular afflictive emotion goes off, don't rationalize or justify it, but simply acknowledge: "I feel angry . . . sad . . . jealous." You acknowledge the fact of the emotion. Then you might recognize that the reason you lost your temper was an enormous emotional attachment to being the one in control. With that understanding you can release the harmful energy through a deliberate act of the will: "I give up my desire to control."

I once knew a woman who had maintained a three-hour-a-day prac-tice of contemplative prayer for twenty-five years. During this time, she had raised a family of four. She was a highly emotional person, who went through incredible ups and downs. Her temperament reminded me of a harp: if you touch just one string, the whole instrument vibrates. (Laugh-ter.) I often wondered whether she would ever penetrate the deeper lev-els of peace. She kept praying, serving her family, and trying to integrate everything into her spiritual journey. One night she woke up and sud-denly realized that her emotional swings were not the emotions as they really are, but the emotions as they are filtered through the false self system. They were emotional reactions to false values. With great astonishment she understood that she could *be* anger, *be* joy, *be* sadness, without feeling the emotional swings. The right way to experience the emotions is to feel them. Then you can be them insofar as they are appropriate in the present moment. After her realization, this woman found that for the first time in her life she could talk to her son when he had done something wrong and lay down the law without the least shadow of annoyance. She just *was* angry. That is the kind of emotion that no one on the receiving end can resist, because it is absolutely authentic; it isn't coming from the false self system. It is the kind of anger that comes from someone who loves you, and you can't deny its truth.

Another way of maintaining divine union within the context of everyday life is to let go into the present moment. The habit of letting go of thoughts and feelings, which we cultivate in contemplative prayer, is applicable to the whole of life. Before reacting to an irritating noise, or to an interior movement of anger or impatience, you let go of it by paying close attention to what is going on in the present moment. This doesn't mean, practically speaking, that you always renounce your own preferences. It means that your first response is to let go. Then you are free to decide what action to take in light of the circumstances. The point of this practice is to forestall the compulsive habits of our emotional programming. When you accept what someone else wants to do, or some breakdown of your plans, you increase your freedom to discern what actually should be done in the concrete situation. This practice of letting go is one way of bringing the fruits of contemplative prayer into your body. Sometimes you may have to hang onto a chair and grit your teeth in order not to react the way your emotions would like to.

In a monastic environment, the process of releasing unconscious programs begins quickly, because the dynamism of silence and solitude propels one into the night of sense. When two people get married, this process is also triggered, because love makes you vulnerable. There is a tendency for the unconscious to release the dark side of our personality because genuine love reduces the defense mechanisms that hide it from ourselves and others. Therefore, even without contemplative prayer, the night of sense may begin. When this happens, some couples think that there must be something wrong and say, "I guess we just weren't made for each other after all." But that is not necessarily so. It is precisely the genuine love for one another that enables the unloading of the unconscious to begin. In the Christian view, marriage is a great way of going to God. It involves bearing each other's emotional burdens and thus healing them. The personality difficulties that arise in marriage are a sign that things are going well. People who understand what they are committed to in marriage recognize that they are ministering the Ultimate Mystery to each other.

Jesus said that we would find the kingdom of God in ordinary life. However, it is difficult to understand our lives as a way of going to God, and to fulfill our duties which may demand great perseverance and sacrifice, without the regular practice of contemplative prayer. By integrating contemplative prayer with certain practices for times of action, ordinary life becomes a passage into the unknown, where God invites us to entrust ourselves to him completely.

Stretched by Activity, Penetrated by Practice

Loppön Lodrö Dorje

As lay practitioners, our lifestyles are determined in part by the cultural environment we find ourselves in, in part by the teacher and teachings we are attracted to, and in part by personal style or vocation. In the history of the Kagyu lineage of Buddhism, we find a wide variety of responses to the cultural and historical conditions of the time. For example, one of the lineage forefathers, the Indian pandit Naropa, began his spiritual career as a noted scholar and teacher at Nalanda, a large monastic university in northern India. He followed a life of rigorous communal study and practice until the day he suddenly realized that he needed to leave the monastic life in order to fully actualize what he had learned. He went into the jungle in search of the guru Tilopa. Naropa then lived with Tilopa for a number of years, during which time he led the unconventional and uncompromising life of a siddha. Naropa's student Marpa, on the other hand, was a householder. He married, raised seven sons, and was a famous merchant and scholar in Tibet. Marpa managed a farm, and through the agency of one of his first disciples ran a tea, butter, and silk trading business with North Tibet and China. Nevertheless, he also managed to spend sixteen years in India, studying and practicing the dharma with his guru, Naropa, so that he was able to fully transplant the Kagyu lineage in Tibet.

The Vajradhatu sangha, which is under the direction of the Venerable Chögyam Trungpa Rinpoche, is also a continuation of the Kagyu lineage. We are evolving a lifestyle, or container, which is culturally Western and yet which is also based on the inspiration and principles of Mahayana Buddhism. Within that container we cultivate our various meditative disciplines, including Vajrayana practices. The primary concern of Mahayana Buddhism is to bring about benefit for human life. Traditionally, it is said that two things are necessary in order to accomplish this goal: the accumulation of merit and the accumulation of prajna, or wisdom. By translating these two traditional phrases into practical guidelines, we can begin to describe a Western lay lifestyle that is in keeping with the tradition of Mahayana Buddhism.

To say that we should accumulate merit is another way of saying that we should cultivate whatever is positive, constructive, and wholesome in our daily activities, so that we naturally become trustworthy and responsible people. If someone is a pillar of the community, whether it is as a tribal chieftain or as the president of an upstanding, sane corporation, that is a situation of merit. It is not purely accidental that someone has arrived at such a position: it has come about through the cause-and-effect process of discipline, exertion, virtue, and reliability. Obviously, meritorious action may be mixed with other elements, such as military or political astuteness. Nevertheless, we can say that if one acts with the Mahayana motivation of having a genuine concern for others, then that action will have the karmic consequence of bringing about the accumulation of merit. Habitual tendencies will be overcome and something worthwhile will be accomplished.

Merit comes about through such life situations as being involved in the community, running a business, or raising a family. From one point of view, we could feel that such responsibilities are an unwanted imposition on our schedules, but from another point of view they are a source of development. If we are practicing in a lay context, we need to be captured into life involvements. We need to commit ourselves to a variety of situations, some comfortable and some uncomfortable, so that by settling into those commitments we gradually become well-processed. Ego is tamed, because we must necessarily surrender to concerns that go beyond personal preference.

Cultivating prajna, on the other hand, means developing the ability to penetrate activities with insight. In the ordinary sense, this brings about sophistication, so that you might develop a certain expertise about cars or finances, or perhaps a penetrating insight into people's psychology. At the same time, through meditation you also develop a dharmic insight into the egolessness of situations. The role of wisdom is to prevent the merit of one's worldly accomplishments from becoming a source of arrogance and ego-fixation.

The accumulation of merit and the accumulation of prajna go hand in hand, so that we are able to join together our karmic involvements with the profundity of the dharma. Ordinary involvements need to be digested by practice; otherwise there is no way of transcending ego, and there is no way of overcoming habitual karmic patterns. In this way the wisdom we develop in our contemplative practice enables us to transcend the situation of ordinary life. The "good life" may be fine, but we may also have aspirations for greater depth of insight and realization. At the same time, the realization of practice is being constantly applied to, and sharpened by, activity, so that any tendency to dwell in practice can be overcome.

The bodhisattva path is in fact highly demanding. We may often think that our lives would be more workable if we could just find the right happy medium between our commitments to life involvements and to meditation practice, but it is my impression that such a happy medium does not exist. It is as if we are being, in Trungpa Rinpoche's words, stretched out in all directions and then penetrated. We are being stretched because there are seemingly excessive demands on our time and energy, coming from all directions. We have to continually give in to a lot of situations that are personally inconvenient or are more challenging than we had expected. At the same time, we are being penetrated by practice, so that we are not able to just dwell in conventional preoccupations and the self-satisfaction of our good deeds. Our ego investments and particular personal identities are being continually dissolved. I think we often mistake the challenges of such a path for our own shortcomings. But it may be more accurate to say that we are biting off a lot to chew, and what we are experiencing is simply the reality of how hard it is. That impossible situation is the path.

Practically speaking, there are several guidelines for how to balance practice and activity in one's lifestyle. First of all, it is extremely important to establish a clear sense of priorities. Often, instead of directly addressing the question of how to shape our schedule in order to include practice, we allow our time and energy to be shaped by habitual tendencies. Then we say that we don't have time to practice, although in fact everyone could meditate for at least twenty minutes a day. It is also beneficial to integrate periods of intensive practice into our long-term schedules. Retreats bring about an attainment and depth of connection that day-by-day practice does not. However, continuity of practice is still superior to a schedule of no regular meditation at all dotted with occasional intensive spurts. When we regularly alternate meditation and activity we enhance both, and we develop a lifestyle that naturally integrates practice, rather than one that reinforces a habitual schizophrenia between "active" periods and "practice" periods. In general, we need to overcome the dichotomy of regarding formal practice as a state of refuge and inactivity, and daily life as a state of busyness and speed. Formal practice is in fact a dynamic process of opening, and daily life is an opportunity to join energy with meditative stability. If one's body and mind are going in different directions, one's life and one's practice won't be able to effectively nourish each other. Continuity of practice also results in a greater momentum of the practice in our state of being, so that at any given time we are less susceptible to emotional confusions, sleepiness, and other obstacles that may arise.

Of course, there will be times when our schedule is unavoidably taken over by various commitments. In the long term it may be helpful to view our lives from the perspective of rhythm. Sometimes we are in a period of life when we can practice intensively; other times we are in a period that is professionally or domestically intensive, such as when we are developing a new career or starting a family. At these times we may feel nostalgic for our previous practice-intensive days, or we may even give up on our meditation discipline altogether, out of discouragement and frustration. But we should realize that our lives will go through such fluctuations, and that the important thing is to maintain a thread of continuity in one's practice.

Finally, we should remember that devotion to one's lineage and sympathy for others bring about a continuity of awareness in everything we do. As it is said in the Kagyu lineage: "Small devotion makes small practice, middling devotion makes middling practice, and great devotion makes great practice."

Not Enough Time

Reginald Ray
Jack Engler
Tessa Bielecki

REGGIE RAY: I'm sure everyone interested in this dialogue appreciates the importance of the contemplative life. But as a lay person myself, I would suggest that it is actually very difficult to find the time to do serious contemplative practice. We have so many other commitments: our jobs, families, social activities. It is a different story for people in monastic situations. I would therefore like the speakers to address this question: how do we, as lay people, deal with this issue of simply not having enough time?

JACK ENGLER: Speaking from my own experience, both as a former Christian monk and as a Buddhist lay practitioner, I would say that monks don't necessarily have more time than lay people. The real problem is that we always think everything is happening somewhere else. The fact is that monks often get just as busy and distracted as anyone else. They may not watch as much TV, but they find other things to fill their time. In my experience in Christian and Buddhist monasteries, both in this country and in Asia, about five percent of the monks practice a meditative or contemplative path in a serious and sustained way. I would guess that the percentage of lay people who practice in a sustained way is not all that different. It only looks to the layman that the monk has certain advantages, and it only looks to the monk that the layman has certain advantages. That is exactly how we deceive ourselves. No matter who we are, there is never any time. Or, there is plenty of time. It is all a matter of a little flip of the mind. One of my reasons for first going to India was to do field research with a group of Bengali Buddhists who had reputedly attained some stage of enlightenment. Among them was a fifty-six-year-old grandmother who was one of the busiest people I have ever met. She was a large woman, and when she walked into the room, you knew it. She came in, whoosh. In India, a woman who runs the household carries the keys wrapped in the tip of her sari and slung over her shoulder. She was that kind of woman. She and her husband ran one of the biggest bakeries in Calcutta, and they also had six children and sixteen grandchildren. When she had first become interested in meditation she had told the meditation teacher that she couldn't possibly sit still, and furthermore she had no time. The teacher said, "Yes, yes, yes. But start by just sitting five minutes." She did, and then she worked up to six minutes, ten minutes, twelve minutes. She was sitting during the time after the noon meal, when her family took a rest. Then she began sitting at night. Finally she was sitting through the entire night and sleeping maybe one or two hours during the day, and she was just as busy as ever in her daily life. She didn't need as much sleep because her mind was becoming quieter and she was more in harmony. After two years, her mind opened. So I would say that time is not the issue.

MOTHER TESSA: You either have to work less or sleep less. I get up at 5:30 in the morning, and I go to prayer for an hour. Then I have two hours of silence before the official work day begins at nine. I know that during the day I will have ten phone calls to make and literally eighty letters to write. Each morning I have a choice: will I take my time in silence and solitude or will I succumb to the work pressure? I work all day from nine to five. Then there is one hour for communal prayer. And then the evening comes and I have a choice again: am I going to continue working because I am bombarded with requests for appointments and all kinds of business? Those are the kind of temptations I have to resist. Jack is absolutely right. We have to say, day after day, "I believe in my contemplative life and I am going to make the choices that make it possible for me to live that way." Otherwise, we end up blaming all the external circumstances, which are just convenient excuses. I will honestly confess that only in the last year have I really been able to put my foot down about this.

QUESTION (from audience): Obviously we do need to devote a certain amount of time to formal practice, but I think a more important question is, how willing are we to be put on the spot by our lives? I hear you talking about the contemplative life as if it were in contrast to everyday life, and this doesn't seem right to me.

MOTHER TESSA: Yes, that is an important point. In my early years as a contemplative, all I did was work, because we were such a small community and there was so much to be done. One of the things I remember Father William saying to me during that time, which proved to be extremely helpful, was, "No one is an intruder, and nothing is an interruption." That was a useful mantra for me. Another mantra I often use comes from Zorba the Greek, who used to continually ask himself, "What are you doing now, Zorba?" So I always ask myself, "What are you doing now, Tessa?" And in the Garden of Eden, God asks, "Adam, where art thou?" There can be only one answer to that question. It is not an intellectual, verbal answer, but an existential one: a personal, passionate presence to whatever is going on. It is that simple. But still we need to commit ourselves to that presence in our formal practice time. Otherwise we forget, because we get so caught up in everyday business. That is why the two have to go together. And if we get so forgetful, then we have to go on a long retreat. I think we need a certain period each day, and then a more intensive time each year, in order to keep reminding ourselves that this is how we should be living.

JACK ENGLER: This issue often comes up in my work as a therapist. I am reminded in particular of a patient I had last year. Just when I thought I knew where things were going, something would suddenly flip. She would vilify me, screaming at the top of her lungs about what a miserable and useless therapist I was. I think everyone experiences a shock during moments like that, when all our assumptions about who we are and what we are doing are suddenly challenged. Actually, those moments happen to us continually, though perhaps not so dramatically. In essence, the contemplative path involves opening to the invitation to go beyond whatever limiting assumptions we've made about ourselves at any given time. It is a self-emptying process which happens over and over throughout the day. If we allow ourselves to be challenged, to be blown open and catapulted into open space, that is contemplation.

A Way of Living

Tessa Bielecki

We shouldn't even have to ask the question: how do we follow the spiritual path in everyday life? Spirituality should be our most natural, spontaneous, and instinctual human response. But it isn't. So we have to ask why it isn't. The answer involves all the psychophysical problems we experience as a result of having become denatured, desensitized, and de-humanized. Because we live in a noncontemplative society, we need to relearn how we can live a full, human life. Some people think that Buddhist practitioners are at a particular disadvantage because they have to develop a new social context for their spiritual practices, which have been taken from an Eastern cultural environment. However, as a contemplative Christian, I find this culture as foreign as the Buddhists do. For the most part, our culture is Judeo-Christian in name only. Therefore we share with the Buddhists the same task of discovering for ourselves how we can create an environment that will make spirituality an integral part of everyday life.

What are the elements that make an environment "contemplative"? This is a question that concerns me greatly, and one that I have been working on for almost twenty years. In my community, we believe that contemplative living grows out of a lively, human atmosphere, and we have been trying to pinpoint more and more specifically what that means. To begin with, we have found that, to set the stage for contemplative living, we need an environment that is natural, ordered, and balanced. For example, compare the experience of walking into a room and discovering a vase of freshly-cut lilacs on the table with that of walking into the same room and finding a bouquet of plastic flowers. Or compare the experience of going into the kitchen and finding a loaf of bread that has just come out of the oven—with steam still rising from its crust and its aroma filling the room—to going into the same kitchen and finding a plastic bag of "balloon" bread from the supermarket. These are simple little things, but they sharply contrast how naturally we should be living against how artificially we usually live. Our lives are derivative instead of real, plastic instead of primordial. So the first important step in the creation of a contemplative environment is to make it as natural as possible.

Secondly, our environment must be ordered. So often people think that "contemplative" means just hanging out and letting it all happen. In a sense, "letting it all happen" is ultimately what contemplative life is all about, but at least at the beginning, we need to establish order in our environment. We need to live deliberately. Over the years a number of psychologists and counselors, interested in learning what the monastery could teach the marketplace, have come to visit our community. What seemed to strike them the most was the fact that we live an ordered life. We have an horarium, a rule of life. Because certain times of the day are better for specific activities than other times, there is a natural form, shape, and structure to each day, which we acknowledge and then follow. Psychologists have found that order is effective in the context of lay life, as well. I personally think that everyone should have a rule of the day, in the form of an outline for how each day will ideally unfold. That does not mean that we must tightly structure every single moment, but that we at least have a sense of what is most important. You can start by prioritizing your activities, beginning with your spiritual practice. You could look at the day and determine what is the most optimal way to focus on your prayer or meditation, and then build the rest of the day around that. For most people, this usually means getting up earlier or going to bed later. My personal experience, and the experience of hundreds of other people I have spoken with, is that it is better in the long run to get up an hour earlier to do one's practice than to sleep in. Even if there is a certain amount of tiredness during the day, the focus, integration, and recollection that carry over are so crucial that the tiredness isn't really a problem. But when you skip that important session of prayer, even if you have all the energy in the world, you won't have as much chance of creating a contemplative environment for yourself.

Another aspect of planning is to build in "do-nothing times." As Americans we tend to be too methodical and rigid. I am saying this at the same time that I am saying we are too flabby and loose. We are both. In our schedules we can allow "just-be" times when there is absolutely nothing planned, even for only a few minutes. And here is a helpful koan: cut out half of what you are doing and do the other half well. Perhaps you don't need to do so literally, but at least you could sit with this idea and begin to understand what it could mean for your life. I personally have to say this one to myself every single day.

Thirdly, the contemplative environment is balanced. We need physical disciplines for the body, intellectual disciplines for the mind, and meditative disciplines for the spirit. One of my own frustrations is that in many retreat environments I find too much emphasis on spirituality. Of course, we could also overemphasize bodily discipline and become "jocks," or overemphasize mental discipline and become big-headed, but when we place too much emphasis on spiritual discipline, at least in the Christian tradition, we very often end up as pious prigs. Another necessary balance is between work and play. I think one of the greatest obstacles to contemplative living in this culture is the neurotic compulsion to work. We overwork. Now, work in itself is good, and it is an important element in contemplative life: it is not only humanizing and energizing, but it is also a good preparation for contemplation. But if we are neurotically compelled to work, then that is an obstacle. Our work has to be balanced by play, which is an equally crucial dimension of contemplative life, and I think this is one of the most important witnesses that my community brings to monasticism. Monks generally do not play enough. In my community, we set aside one day each week, on Sunday when we celebrate the Sabbath, when we do nothing but play. Some Sundays we play together; some Sundays we play individually. We may go canoeing, play volleyball, or go on a hike. Or it might be more intellectual play: looking at art, listening to music, or reading poetry. One of my favorite Sunday activities is painting with watercolors. I wouldn't necessarily show other people what I paint, but that is just the point. There is no purpose to it. As Eido Roshi says, it is "just this."

I think there is generally tremendous illusion in people's ideas of what it is like to live in a monastery. People who come to visit us are often surprised to discover that the elements of our contemplative environment are not at all foreign to them, and that our problems are also their problems. Perhaps the only real difference is the lack of community support that many lay people encounter when trying to live contemplatively in everyday life. I would agree that it is a real deprivation not to be in some way bonded with other people who share the same ideals and aspirations. Sometimes we are able to put such people in communication with each other, or to offer them some kind of community support. We now have an extended family consisting of people who don't live in residence with us, but who share our ideals and aspirations, and who stay in touch with us through letters and personal visits. We also include a column called "Contemplation for Everyone" in our quarterly magazine, *Desert Call,* where we invite people from all walks of life to write about the obstacles they encounter and the lessons they have learned for overcoming them. Our newsletter, *Nada Network,* is also a forum of exchange between the monastery and the marketplace. Contemplative life is every bit as possible in the marketplace as in the monastery. After all, the contemplative is not a special kind of person, but everyone is—or ought to be—a special kind of contemplative.

Parting

Jack Engler

I was raised a Catholic, and I can't tell you the number of Masses I've attended in my life, including the number I've attended since beginning Buddhist practice. However, I have never experienced a Mass such as the one the Carmelite community celebrated with us here yesterday, which had an extraordinary contemplative spirit.

When I became a Buddhist, I stopped participating in communion, out of respect for the integrity of the Christian community. But yesterday when the communion began, I felt a great dilemma, and I asked Brother David, who was sitting next to me, what he thought I should do. Holding up his hands, close together, he said, "Well, there is this church . . . and then," he said, still holding up his hands, but this time wide apart, "there is *this* Church. You belong to *this* Church!"

So I went up and took communion. And when I came back to my seat I realized that something that had been disconnected in me twenty years ago was reconnected. It was a profound moment of healing, of something coming back together again. In the *Four Quartets*, T. S. Eliot says that the end of all our strivings is to return to the place we started from and to know it for the first time. In some ways, this conference has been that way for me. I have returned to places I started from, and I've known them for the first time.

And so now we all leave. Leaving brings up a lot of feelings. Whether we realize it or not, during the time we've been together we've created a kind of community here. Hopefully each one of us will go back to the practices and traditions that we brought here.

I am reminded of an Indian proverb that asks: What is the best way to find water? Do you dig 100 wells, one foot deep? Or do you dig just one well, and keep going until you hit water? This kind of dialogue shouldn't inspire us to rush out and dig six more wells in addition to the ones we've already dug. Instead, we will recommit ourselves to whatever our particular path is, and we will keep going until we hit water.

I remember when I took leave of my teacher for the last time; it was an extremely painful moment because I had no idea whether I would ever return, or whether I would ever see him again. I could only barely bring myself to go and say goodbye. I was weeping. He embraced me, which was an extraordinary act in a country where physical touch, especially in public, is generally considered unacceptable. And he said, "Where there is love, there is no separation." So we will go back to our lives, and we will dig our wells, and hopefully we will all hit water. In some ways we will be separate, but in other ways we won't be separate at all.

Poem

Keeping Quiet

Now we will count to twelve
and we will all keep still.

For once on the face of the earth,
let's not speak in any language;
let's stop for one second,
and not move our arms so much.

It would be an exotic moment
without rush, without engines;
we would all be together
in a sudden strangeness.

Fishermen in the cold sea
would not harm whales
and the man gathering salt
would look at his hurt hands.

Those who prepare green wars,
wars with gas, wars with fire,
victories with no survivors,
would put on clean clothes
and walk about with their brother
in the shade, doing nothing.

What I want should not be confused
with total inactivity.
Life is what it is about;
I want no truck with death.

If we were not so single-minded
about keeping our lives moving,
and for once could do nothing,
perhaps a huge silence
might interrupt this sadness
of never understanding ourselves
and of threatening ourselves with death.
Perhaps the earth can teach us
as when everything seems dead
and later proves to be alive.

Now I'll count up to twelve
and you keep quiet and I will go.

PABLO NERUDA[5]

Chapter 10: Notes
1. Epigraph: "Cat's Yawn" in *The World of Zen*, ed. Nancy Wilson Ross, p. 35.
2. Epigraph: *Meditations with Meister Eckhart*, trans. Matthew Fox (Santa Fe, N.M.: Bear & Co., 1983), p. 116.
3. William McNamara, *Mystical Passion: Spirituality for a Bored Society* (New Jersey: Paulist Press, 1977), p. 119.
4. See "Twentieth-Century Buddha-Nature," in Chapter 2.
5. From *Extravagaria* by Pablo Neruda, translated by Alastair Reid. English translation copyright 1969, 1970, 1972, 1974 by Alastair Reid. Reprinted by permission of Farrar, Straus and Giroux, Inc.

Profiles

Tenshin Anderson

Harold ("Reb") Anderson was born in Mississippi in 1943, and then moved with his family to Minneapolis, Minnesota. He studied at the University of Minnesota, graduating with a bachelor's degree in mathematics and a master's degree in psychology. During college he became interested in Zen and tried to form a sitting group, but was unsuccessful. Reb went to San Francisco to look for a teacher and there met Shunryu Suzuki Roshi, in January 1968. He has been intensively involved in the study and practice of the Soto Zen tradition since that time. In 1982 he received dharma transmission from Richard Baker Roshi, and in January 1986 he became abbot of Zen Center in San Francisco.

Sister Benedetta

Sister Benedetta was "born and bred" as a member of the Anglican Church of Canada. She grew up in Toronto and in 1940, at age seventeen, she became a postulant (candidate) in the Community of Sisters of the Church, a mixed order founded in London in 1870. Dedicating her life to God in this way seemed a natural and fitting response to the social climate of the time, which was pervaded by the wartime values of sacrifice and dedication. In 1945 she spent one year in England, working in the slums of London; she returned again in 1953 and worked for two years in the order's financial offices. From 1955 to 1972 Sister Benedetta taught in an Ontario private school for girls, serving as the principal between 1962 and 1972. She was elected Provincial Superior of Canada and held that office until 1981. Sister Benedetta holds a bachelor's degree in sociology from the University of Toronto and a master's of divinity from the Toronto School of Theology. She was ordained into the priesthood in 1986 and is now engaged in parish ministry in the diocese of Niagara in Ontario. She was well-schooled in Ignatian meditation during the early years of her training and has been practicing centering prayer since the late 1960's. She first became involved in the Christian-Buddhist dialogue through an invitation to participate in the conference hosted by the Nalanda Foundation in Toronto in 1984.

Tessa Bielecki

Tessa was born a Connecticut Yankee of Polish peasant stock. Like many girls, she grew up reading beauty magazines, keeping movie star scrapbooks, and assuming that she would eventually marry and raise children. She entered Trinity College in Washington, D. C. with a major in Russian and the intention of pursuing a career in linguistics or diplomacy. During her junior year, Tessa attended a student retreat led by Father William McNamara. Upon meeting him, she was struck by his "holiness and integrity" and recognized him to be "a remarkable spiritual leader. . . . I knew intuitively and immediately where my vocation lay." Nevertheless, Father McNamara encouraged her to finish college and then to work for one year. She did so, leaving to join Father McNamara and the forming Spiritual Life Institute, then situated in the desert of Arizona, at age twenty-two. Since then, her life has been dedicated to building and nurturing the Carmelite community that has evolved under Father McNamara's spiritual direction. Her leadership role has given her the title of Mother Abbess. As an "apostolic hermit" with a zest for spiritual adventure, Mother Tessa now leaves the hermitage for several weeks each year to speak at contemplative retreats, workshops, and conferences.

Lodrö Dorje

Lodrö Dorje (literally "Indestructible Intellect") is the Tibetan name that was given to Eric Holm when he formally took Refuge Vows and became a Buddhist. Eric grew up in Dubuque, Iowa on the campus of the Wartburg Lutheran Seminary, of which his father was president. When Eric entered college he began pre-theological training with the aspiration of becoming a Lutheran minister. Some time during his second year, he suddenly realized that, in spite of his training, he had nothing to tell people about the spiritual life. Feeling a mixture of intense disappointment and freedom, he changed his major to science and began reading books on Eastern mysticism and meditation. He was attracted both to the devotional literature of Hindu bhakti yoga and to the precision and clarity of Buddhist sutras. He also read the songs and life story of Milarepa and felt a strong affinity to the Tibetan tradition. In 1971, Eric dropped out of graduate school and began looking for a teacher. He heard Kunga

Dawa, a student of the Venerable Chögyam Trungpa Rinpoche, speak in New York City and was impressed by this Westerner's straightforwardness and lack of spiritual jargon. He inquired about his teacher and was directed to Tail of the Tiger (now Karme-Chöling) in Vermont. There he met Trungpa Rinpoche and began to practice meditation. In 1976, Trungpa Rinpoche empowered Lodrö Dorje as the Loppön, or head master, of practice and study for the Vajradhatu community. That same year, Lodrö Dorje and a few other students formed the Nalanda Translation Committee under Trungpa Rinpoche's direction. The Committee translates Tibetan Vajrayana texts and liturgies into English. As Loppön of Three Yana Studies, Lodrö Dorje continues to formulate and oversee education and meditation programs within the Vajradhatu community, and in 1985 he was given the added title of "Dorje" Loppön as further confirmation of this role. He lives with his wife and son in Boulder, Colorado.

Jack Engler

Jack Engler grew up in an Irish Carmelite Mission parish in northern New Jersey. From the beginning, he was attracted to the contemplative side of religion, even though the tradition he found himself in didn't encourage or foster that interest. He studied English literature at the University of Notre Dame and then, after graduating with a bachelor's degree, entered the Abbey of Gesthemeni in the fall of 1961, at age twenty-two. His novice master was Thomas Merton, who at that time was going through a period of disillusionment with his own life at Gesthemeni. In the winter of the following year, Merton advised Jack that the Trappist life was not for him, and that he should leave in order to go to Europe and pursue graduate studies. Jack felt he could not understand Merton's personal bitterness, nor his conclusion about his own vocation; nevertheless, he reluctantly followed his advice and set off for Europe. He studied theology and Biblical exegesis at the Universities of Munich and Oxford and became trained as a "Wissenschaftler" (scientist) of religion. After seven years in Europe, he found that his interest in the academic pursuit of religious truth as well as his interest in his own religious tradition had dried up. He returned home in 1969 and threw himself into social and political activism. He taught in southern schools under the Ford Foundation-Title III Project and became involved in the desegregation movement. For a number of years he was in a spiritual limbo. Out of that period came the decision to take up the spiritual quest once more, but this time to do so through an understanding of mind. He entered a Ph.D. program in religion and psychological studies at the University of Chicago. He encountered the Buddhist tradition for the first time and felt that it offered the possibility of combining his personal and academic interests. In 1975, Jack went to India and Burma on a Fulbright Research Fellowship and for two years studied and practiced vipassana meditation in the lineage of the Venerable Mahasi Sayadaw under Mahasi Sayadaw himself, Anagarika Munindra, and Sri Mati Nani Baruna. Feeling that he had finally found what he had been looking for for twenty-five years, he returned to the United States with the conviction to pursue spirituality in a more experiential way and to work more directly to alleviate human suffering. He left the academic life and began clinical training as a psychologist at the Menninger Foundation, McLean Hospital, and the Yale Psychiatric Institute. He also became involved with the Insight Meditation Society in Barre, Massachusetts, and has been on its teaching staff since that time. He is now Clinical Director of the Lawrence Schiff Psychiatric Day Treatment Center at the Cambridge Hospital and also teaches, supervises, and consults in the Harvard Medical School, specializing in the treatment of chronic major mental illness (psychosis, schizophrenia, and severe borderline disturbances). Jack is also well-known for his writing on cross-cultural systems of psychotherapy. He has served on the board of directors and as president at IMS and also teaches at the Cambridge Insight Meditation Center. He is editor, with Ken Wilbur and Dan Brown, of *Transformations of Consciousness: Conventional and Contemplative Perspectives on Development* (Boston: Shambhala, 1986).

Joseph Goldstein

Joseph grew up in the Catskills region of New York. He entered Columbia University as a philosophy major, motivated by a desire to understand mind. His studies, however, left his curiosity unfulfilled. In the academic milieu he found little inquiry into the mind itself: instead the inquiry was into what various people had *said* about mind. After graduating with a bachelor's degree, he joined the Peace Corps and in 1965 went to Thailand. There he began going to Buddhist discussion groups. When Joseph first received meditation instruction, he was extremely excited by this new discovery and invited his friends to come over and watch him meditate (they often didn't stay long, he adds). When he returned to America, he tried to continue the practice on his own, but soon decided to go back to Asia to find a teacher. In Bodh-Gaya, India he met the Burmese Theravada master Anagarika Sri Munindra and was immediately attracted to his teaching style, which was simple, to the point, and without excessive cultural trappings. From that time on, Joseph practiced consistently and diligently, experiencing "plenty of struggles, but no doubt" about the value of the practice. Except for a few intermittent trips back to America, Joseph stayed in India until 1974, sometimes practicing vipassana meditation for months at a time. During his last year there he began teaching under Munindra-ji's guidance. In 1975 he founded, along with Jack Kornfield, the Insight Meditation Society in Barre, Massachusetts. Since then he has participated in and led intensive practice sessions at Barre and around the world. He is the author of the inspirational book on vipassana meditation, *The Experience of Insight: A Simple and Direct Guide to Buddhist Meditation.*

Thomas Hopko

Thomas Hopko was born in Endicott, New York and raised in the tradition of the Eastern Orthodox Church. His educational achievements include a bachelor's degree in Russian studies from Fordham University, a master of divinity from St. Vladimir's Seminary, a master's degree in philosophy from Duquesne University, and a Ph.D. in theology from Fordham University. Father Hopko was ordained into the priesthood of the Orthodox Church in 1963 and served as a parish priest from that time until 1983. He is presently an associate professor of dogmatic theology at St. Vladimir's Seminary. He is also a member of the Faith and Order Commission of the World Council of Churches and the Orthodox Theological Society of America. He lectures widely; has written many articles and a number of books, including *All the Fulness of God, The Spirit of God: Christian Spirituality East and West,* and a four-volume handbook of *The Orthodox Faith*; and cares for a family of five children and one grandchild.

Thomas Keating

Thomas Keating was born in New York City in 1923 and raised as a Roman Catholic. He was educated in New York at Deerfield Academy in Massachusetts, and then at Yale, where he experienced a call to enter the Cistercian Order. He subsequently transferred to Fordham University; he graduated in 1943. In January of the following year he entered Our Lady of the Valley, a Cistercian monastery in Rhode Island. When the monastery burned to the ground, he moved with the community to Saint Joseph's Abbey in Spencer, Massachusetts, where he served as the novice master from 1954 to 1958. Between 1958 and 1961, he helped to found Saint Benedict's Monastery in Snowmass, Colorado, where he served as its first superior. In 1961, he was elected abbot of Saint Joseph's Abbey in Spencer, Massachusetts. After twenty years of office at Saint Joseph's, Father Keating retired and returned to Saint Benedict's, where he now resides. Occasionally he leads intensive retreats in centering prayer, both at the monastery and in cities around the country. Recently he established a contemplative community in West Cornwall, Connecticut, which regularly hosts retreats and introductory workshops. Father Keating has been active in interreligious dialogue for a number of years and is chairman of the North American Board of East-West Dialogue. In 1984, he invited a group of representatives from the world's religions (the "Snowmass Group") to come together annually for the purpose of exploring issues related to the common spiritual journey. Father Keating's published books include *Crisis of Faith, Heart of the World,* and *Open Mind, Open Heart.*

The Dalai Lama

His Holiness Tenzin Gyatso was enthroned as the Fourteenth Dalai Lama (literally "Ocean of Wisdom") in 1940, at age six. The Dalai Lamas are the spiritual heads of the Gelugpa school of Tibetan Buddhism, and they are considered to be emanations of Avalokiteshvara, the bodhisattva of compassion. Since the mid-seventeenth century, they have also been the political leaders of Tibet, with succession occurring through reincarnation. Tenzin Gyatso was born in a small village in the province of Amdo, near the Tibetan-Chinese border. When he was two years old, a search party arrived from Lhasa and identified him to be the child seen in a vision by the previous Dalai Lama's regent. He was taken to Lhasa and trained as the spiritual and political leader of the Tibetan people. In 1950, when the Dalai Lama was sixteen, the Chinese army entered Tibet. For nine years, he tried to negotiate a peaceful understanding with the Chinese government, until finally, in 1959, the increasingly volatile political atmosphere and repressive Communist policy toward Buddhism forced the Dalai Lama to flee Tibet. He took refuge in India and assumed leadership of the government-in-exile in Dharamsala, India. He now teaches and lectures widely and has become known around the world as a great statesman and humanitarian. His books include *The Opening of the Wisdom Eye; Kindness, Clarity, and Insight;* and the autobiography *My Land and My People.*

Judith Lief

Judy Lief grew up in Decorah, Iowa as a member of the Congregational Church. She went to Luther College and then began graduate studies in sociology and Asian Studies at Columbia University. She went to India on a Fulbright Scholarship, but it was not until she was back in New York, where she met the Venerable Chögyam Trungpa Rinpoche in 1971, that she began to practice and study Buddhist meditation. In 1972 she moved to Boulder, Colorado and from 1975 to 1980 she was the head of Vajradhatu's editorial office. In 1980 she was appointed dean of Naropa Institute. Between 1980 and 1984 she led the Institute through a critical growing phase, establishing it as a recognized "contemplative college" of the arts and humanities. Judy has also been a teacher and administrator at three Vajradhatu seminaries and has led a number of seminars and courses in Buddhist meditation and the *Tibetan Book of the Dead.* At the end of 1984 she moved to Halifax, Nova Scotia with her husband and two daughters, and she is now director of the newly-founded Naropa Institute of Canada.

William McNamara

William McNamara was born in Providence, Rhode Island on Valentine's Day, 1926. Influenced by his eighth-grade teacher's admiration for John of the Cross and Teresa of Avila, he became a Discalced Carmelite monk in 1944, at age eighteen, and was ordained a priest in 1951. He received his bachelor's degree in theology and philosophy from the Catholic University of America and a master's in education and psychology from Boston College. He founded *Spiritual Life Magazine* in 1955 and was its editor until 1962. With a mandate from Pope John XXIII, in 1960 Father McNamara founded the Spiritual Life Institute, a small monastic community of men and women who live according to the primitive Carmelite ideal. His aim was to create a contemplative environment that would feed the personal and existential needs of spiritually-inclined people from all walks of life. During his prolific career as a spiritual director, Father McNamara has traveled and lectured widely; recently, however, he spends most of his time in solitude at Nada Hermitage in Crestone, Colorado or Nova Nada in Kemptville, Nova Scotia. His books include *Earthy Mysticism, The Art of Being Human,* and *Christian Mysticism.*

Reginald Ray

Reginald Ray grew up in Darien, Conneticut as a devoted Episcopalian. During childhood, he also had recurrent and compelling dreams about Tibet. He later pursued undergraduate studies at Williams College in Massachusetts, and then, after his second year, set off to visit Asia. He received meditation instruction in a Japanese Zen temple at age nineteen. He traveled through Southeast Asia, India, and Nepal, but then fell ill and had to return home. Reggie subsequently graduated from Williams with a bachelor's degree in religions and went to the University of Chicago to continue his studies. He became interested in Jungian psychology and worked closely with June Singer. In 1970, Reggie heard a lecture by Kunga Dawa, a Western student of the Venerable Chögyam Trungpa Rinpoche, and soon afterward went to Karme-Chöling. Upon meeting Trungpa Rinpoche, he felt " . . . no question that this was the teacher I had been looking for for twenty-eight years." He expressed a desire to leave university in order to pursue meditation wholeheartedly, but Trungpa Rinpoche encouraged him to stay and complete his academic studies. He did so, graduating with a Ph.D. in the history of religions. After teaching at Indiana University for one year, he moved to Boulder, Colorado in 1974 to organize and then chair the Naropa Institute Buddhist Studies Department. Reggie continues his administrative and teaching responsibilities at Naropa Institute, and he is also an active member of the Nalanda Translation Committee. He lives in Boulder, Colorado with his wife and two daughters.

Eido Shimano

Eido Tai Shimano was born in Tokyo in 1932. His ancestors on both sides of the family were all of samurai stock. Because of this, and because of the cultural climate of prewar Japan, his early years were spent in a military-style environment, both at home and at school. There was also a Buddhist element to this environment: when he was conceived, for example, his mother was chanting the Heart Sutra. Of course (Eido Roshi adds) he did not know this at the time. He himself had learned the Heart Sutra by the age of nine. After 1945, everything around him changed: the samurai tradition, the values of Japanese culture—even the Buddhist element changed. As a young adolescent, all of this disoriented him greatly, and his confusion continued for a number of years, until he started to realize that there was one value that didn't change: that of the Buddhist teachings. He was ordained as a Zen monk in 1952 and was trained in the Rinzai tradition at Ryutaku-ji monastery in Mishima under Soen Nakagawa Roshi. He studied at the University of Hawaii from 1960 to 1964. In 1972 he received dharma transmission from Soen Roshi and became abbot of New York Zendo Shobo-ji. Eido Roshi is a founder, along with honorary cofounders Nyogen Senzaki and Soen Roshi, of Dai Bosatsu Zendo Kongo-ji, a Zen monastery in rural New York. Since his arrival in the West, Eido Roshi has been actively devoted to the transmission of buddha-dharma from East to West. He is the author of *Golden Wind: Zen Talks*.

Tai Situpa

The title "Tai Situ" was first given to Choji Gyaltsen, a disciple of the fifth Karmapa, by the Chinese emperor Tai-Ming in the early fifteenth century. This was the beginning of the Tai Situ line of incarnations, of which the present Tai Situpa, Pema Donyö Nyinche Wangpo, is the twelfth. He was born in Tibet in 1954 and recognized as a *tulku*, or reincarnation, of the Situ lineage by His Holiness Karmapa and His Holiness the Dalai Lama at the age of eighteen months. When he was five years old, he fled Tibet under the care of the Karmapa, to settle and train with him at Rumtek Monastery in Sikkim. With the death of the sixteenth Karmapa, and in anticipation of the seventeenth Karmapa's arrival and empowerment, Situ Rinpoche has assumed temporary responsibility, along with three other appointed regents, for the spiritual leadership of the Kagyu School of Tibetan Buddhism. He has also been active in developing community projects to assist Tibetan refugees in India; in teaching Mahayana and Vajrayana Buddhism to both Tibetan and Western students; and in establishing Maitreya Institute, a series of Western-based educational centers for East-West studies. In 1976, he re-established the seat of the Situpas at Sherab Ling in northern India, where he now resides. He is the author of *Way to Go: Sowing the Seed of Buddha.*

David Steindl-Rast

Born in Vienna, Austria, Brother David was raised in the Catholic tradition. As he was coming into his teens, the Nazis occupied Austria and began persecuting the church. As a result, the adolescent rebelliousness that is often directed against the established religious and cultural values was in this case directed against Nazi ideology. The Catholic priests, who were often heroic in their resistance and courage, became role models and drove young idealists such as David deeper into the Christian faith. In college, he studied art, anthropology, and psychology. He earned degrees from the Vienna Academy of Fine Arts and the Psychological Institute and received a Ph.D. degree in experimental psychology from the University of Vienna. David was attracted to the monastic life through the Rule of Saint Benedict, which to him embodied spirituality in its least diluted form. He spent a number of years searching for a monastic community that lived according to the Rule, until 1953, when he joined the newly-founded Benedictine Monastery of Mount Savior in the Finger Lakes region of New York. After twelve years of monastic training, he received permission to explore Zen Buddhism, which he then did under the guidance of Hakuun Yasutani Roshi, Shunryu Suzuki Roshi, Soen Nakagawa Roshi, and Eido Shimano Roshi. In 1968, he cofounded the Center for Spiritual Studies, which brought together members of the Hindu, Buddhist, Jewish, and Christian faiths. He has lectured worldwide on the topics of contemplative renewal, interreligious dialogue, and world peace. During the present period of his life, Brother David spends about three months each year traveling and teaching; the remaining time he spends in hiding in a monastic hermitage. He is the author of *A Listening Heart* and *Gratefulness, the Heart of Prayer.*

George Timko

Father Timko was raised in the Slavonic tradition of the Orthodox Church of America. As a young man, he was an active participant in the church; however, since he was English-speaking, the gospel and liturgy, which were entirely in the Slavonic language, were inaccessible to him. At age twenty-five, he experienced an awakening through reading the gospel and felt a strong inner pull to go to seminary. He attended St. Vladimir's Seminary in New York, where Father George Florovsky introduced him to the *Philokalia*, a compilation of writings of the early Fathers. He was ordained into the priesthood when he was thirty years old. His first parish assignments were in Marblehead, Ohio and Whitestone, Long Island. He developed a rigorous personal discipline based on the instructions of the early Fathers. Often when he spoke out of that experience, he was accused of having "Buddhist tendencies." This provoked his curiosity, and he turned to Buddhist texts to find out what was "Buddhist" about his experience and understanding of how the mind works. He also began practicing hatha yoga, first for health reasons, and later as a way to complement Christian prayer and meditation with a self-awareness discipline. Through yoga, he learned that it was possible to let the effort and struggle of the will relax through non-effort. Father Timko is now a member of the interreligious Snowmass Group founded by Father Thomas Keating in 1984. He is married, has five children and four grandchildren, and is currently a parish priest in Buffalo, New York.

Chögyam Trungpa

The Venerable Chögyam Trungpa Rinpoche was born in eastern Tibet in 1939. He was recognized at infancy, through a vision by His Holiness the Gyalwa Karmapa, to be the eleventh incarnation in the line of Trungpas, who traditionally oversaw the Kagyu monasteries in the district of Surmang. He began his spiritual training when he was five years old and was ordained as a novice monk when he was eight. Through his root guru, Jamgon Kongtrul of Sechen, and also through the teachings and empowerments he received from His Holiness Dingo Khyentse Rinpoche and others, he inherited the orally-transmitted lineages of the Kagyu and Nyingma schools of Vajrayana Buddhism. Trungpa Rinpoche left Tibet after the Communist takeover in 1959. After three years in India, he went to England to study comparative religions, psychology, and fine arts at Oxford University. He appreciated the inquisitiveness of Western mind and the dignity of British culture and felt increasingly convinced that his vocation was to find a way to bring the essence of the Buddhist teachings to the West. He also felt ambivalent, however, about how he could do so—how he could bridge the cultural distance and penetrate the Western tendency of superficial fascination toward Eastern spirituality. His ambivalence mounted, finally reaching a point of crisis: one day while driving his car in Northumberland, he blacked out, smashing through the front of a joke shop. When he regained consciousness, he realized he could "no longer attempt to preserve any privacy . . . any special identity or legitimacy." He determined to give up his monk's robes and monastic vows and plunge into the culture with which he felt so compelled to communicate. He married a young Englishwoman and in 1970 they moved to the United States. In the seventeen years after his arrival in North America, Trungpa Rinpoche, with the help of a growing community of students, established an international network of Buddhist meditation centers (Vajradhatu), a secular meditation program (Shambhala Training), an education system based on contemplative principles (The Naropa Institute, the Vidya School, and Alaya Preschool), a number of community service organizations, the Nalanda Translation Committee, and several dharma art groups. His books include the autobiography *Born in Tibet; Meditation in Action; Cutting Through Spiritual Materialism; The Myth of Freedom;* two books of poetry, *Mudra* and *First Thought, Best Thought; Glimpses of Abhidharma,* and *Shambhala: The Sacred Path of the Warrior.* Trungpa Rinpoche died in Halifax, Nova Scotia on April 4, 1987 at the age of forty-seven.

John Yungblut

John Yungblut was born and raised in Dayton, Kentucky. He graduated from Harvard College and then went on to do graduate study in theology at Harvard Divinity School and the Episcopal Divinity School in Cambridge, Massachusetts. He was an Episcopalian parish priest for twenty years, until 1960, when he became a member of the Religious Society of Friends (Quakers). During the 1960's he was director of the Quaker House in Atlanta, working closely with Martin Luther King and the civil rights movement. He has been director of the International Student House in Washington, D. C.; Director of Studies at Pendle Hill in Wallingford, Pennsylvania; and is currently Director of both the Guild Spiritual Studies in Rye, New York and Touchstone Farm in Lincoln, Virginia. He lives at Touchstone with his wife, Penelope. For the last twenty-five years he has been a student of the writings of C. G. Jung and Teilhard de Chardin. He aspires to be an apologist for the mystical heritage in Christianity, updated by Jung's myth of the psyche and Teilhard's myth of cosmogenesis (a universe still being born). He is the author of *Rediscovering Prayer, Rediscovering the Christ,* and *Discovering God Within.*

Directory

The reader wishing to pursue an interest in contemplative retreats or in ongoing contemplative communities is encouraged to investigate and explore local networks and resources. Beyond that, some periodicals feature listings of workshops and seminars across the country. The *National Catholic Register,* for example, publishes an extensive calendar of upcoming programs twice a year (Write to *National Catholic Register,* P.O. Box 281, Kansas City, MO 64141 and ask for their "Fall and Winter Listing" or their "Summer Listing"). To tap into the Buddhist network, *The Vajradhatu Sun* (1345 Spruce Street, Boulder CO 80302) lists and advertises major programs and events. Also, each issue of *Spring Wind,* a quarterly journal published by the Zen Buddhist Temple of Toronto (46 Gwynne Avenue, Toronto, Ontario M6K 2C3, Canada), includes a calendar of upcoming events sponsored by various Shinshu, Theravada, Zen, and Tibetan Buddhist centers in North America.

For the readers who have a specific interest in one or more of the communities affiliated with the contributors to this book, following is a list of their retreat centers and study programs.

Affiliated Communities and Programs
A. Retreat Centers

Contemplative Outreach Community

This Christian community of men and women, situated in the Berkshire Mountains of northwest Connecticut, is under the direction of Father Thomas Keating. The daily schedule includes contemplative prayer, work, and solitude. Guests are welcome for a day, week, or longer. The community regularly hosts centering prayer weekend programs and seven- or eight-day intensives.

> Contemplative Outreach Community
> R. D. Box 330
> West Cornwall CT 06796
> (203) 672-0091

Insight Meditation Society

The IMS retreat center in Barre, Massachusetts hosts vipassana meditation retreats. Group retreat programs, which include meditation instruction and dharma talks by visiting and resident teachers (including Joseph Goldstein and Jack Engler), are available to both beginners and experienced practitioners. Programs vary in length from two days to three months.

> Insight Meditation Society
> Pleasant Street
> Barre MA 01005
> (617) 355-4378

Karma Triyana Dharmachakra

KTD is a traditional Tibetan Buddhist monastery founded by H. H. the XVIth Gyalwa Karmapa. It is open to lay practitioners for retreats and special programs. Kagyu lineage holders who reside in India (such as Situ Rinpoche) often conduct teaching programs at KTD during their visits to North America. The newsletter *Densal* publishes dharma talks and news of upcoming events.

> Karma Triyana Dharmachakra
> 352 Mead Mountain Road
> Woodstock NY 12498
> (914) 679-2487

Spiritual Life Institute

Founded by Father William McNamara in 1960, the SLI is a small monastic community of Carmelite hermits. Its two retreat centers—Nada Hermitage in southern Colorado and Nova Nada near Kemptville, Nova Scotia—welcome Christian and non-Christian retreatants. Visitors may choose either to remain in solitude or to participate in the community life of the residents. SLI publishes *Desert Call,* a quarterly magazine, and *Nada Network,* an informal newsletter which serves the extended lay community. Two cassette programs, "Christian Humanism: A Cassette Retreat" by Father William McNamara and "Prayer and Intimacy: Transforming Erotic Energy" by Mother Tessa Bielecki, are also available.

Nada Hermitage
The Spiritual Life Institute
Crestone CO 81131
(303) 256-4778

Touchstone Farm

Touchstone Farm, the residence of John and Penelope Yungblut, is located forty-five miles west of Washington, D.C. John and Penelope conduct "quiet days," seminars, and retreats following the tradition of Quaker spirituality and incorporating the depth psychology of C. G. Jung and the evolutionary perspective of Teilhard de Chardin.

Touchstone, Inc.
Box 23
Lincoln VA 22078
(703) 338-7879

Vajradhatu

Vajradhatu is the network of Buddhist meditation and study centers under the direction of the Venerable Chögyam Trungpa Rinpoche. Its two main retreat centers are Rocky Mountain Dharma Center in northern Colorado and Karme-Choling in northern Vermont. Both centers host four-week dathuns (group meditation programs), one-week meditation intensives, a variety of special practice-study programs, and solitary retreats. Vajradhatu publishes *The Vajradhatu Sun,* a bimonthly Buddhist newspaper.

Rocky Mountain Dharma Center
Red Feather Lakes CO 80545
(303) 881-2530

Karme-Choling
Barnet VT 05821
(802) 633-2384

Zen Center

The abbot of Zen Center, Tenshin Reb Anderson, is a dharma heir of Zen Center's founder, Suzuki Roshi. Green Gulch Farm in Marin County offers a residency program as well as regular one-day sittings and seven-day sesshins. The Tassajara Zen Mountain Center, located near Carmel Valley, offers two ninety-day practice periods between September and May. Applicants to these more extensive programs are expected to have at least one and a half years of prior practice experience. Zen Center publishes *Wind Bell.*

> Zen Center
> 300 Page Street
> San Francisco CA 94102
> (415) 863-3136

The Zen Studies Society

Eido Tai Shimano Roshi is the abbot of Dai Bosatsu Zendo, a mountain monastery for lay people situated in the Catskill Mountains 140 miles northwest of New York City. Dai Bosatsu Zendo invites interested people from all faiths to participate in a Zen way of life. The ongoing schedule includes zazen, dokusan, work, and study. The spring and autumn schedule each include three week-long sesshins.

> Dai Bosatsu Zendo Kongo-ji
> Beecher Lake, HCR 1, Box 80
> Lew Beach NY 12753
> (914) 439-4566

B. Study Programs

Maitreya Institute

H. E. the Tai Situpa Rinpoche began Maitreya Institute in 1984 as a forum for East-West studies. The Institute, presently based in Honolulu and San Francisco, hosts lectures, workshops, and classes in the healing arts, psychology, meditation, interreligious dialogue, and the arts.

> Maitreya Institute
> 3315 Sacramento Street, Suite 622
> San Francisco CA 94113
> (415) 781-5590

The Naropa Institute

Naropa Institute is a contemplative college (i.e. based on the principles and experience of meditation) centered in Boulder, Colorado.

Founded in 1974 by the Venerable Chögyam Trungpa Rinpoche, the Institute offers accredited undergraduate degree and certificate programs in movement studies, writing and poetics, Buddhist and Western psychology, the psychology of health and healing, Buddhist studies, book arts, music, and psychophysical studies; and graduate degree programs in contemplative psychotherapy, dance therapy, and Buddhist studies. The Summer Institute hosts workshops, intensives, and conferences (including the annual conference on Christian and Buddhist Meditation). The Naropa Institute of Canada, established in Halifax, Nova Scotia in 1985, is a younger sister of the Naropa Institute in Colorado.

> The Naropa Institute
> 2130 Arapahoe Avenue
> Boulder CO 80302
> (303) 444-0202

> The Naropa Institute of Canada
> 1084 Tower Road
> Halifax, Nova Scotia
> Canada B3H 2Y5
> (902) 422-2940

St. Vladimir's Seminary Summer Institute

The annual Liturgical Institute provides pastors, musicians, educators, and church workers with the opportunity to widen their horizons, improve their skills, and deepen the understanding of their vocational responsibilities in the Orthodox Church. The Summer Institute takes the form of an intensive one-week program of lectures, discussions, and liturgical services.

> St. Vladimir's Seminary Summer Institute
> 575 Scarsdale Road
> Crestwood NY 10707
> (914) 961-8313

Vajradhatu

Urban Vajradhatu centers in the United States, Canada, and Europe offer ongoing evening and weekend courses in Buddhist psychology and meditation. Local addresses can be obtained from Vajradhatu, or by looking in the phone book under "Dharmadhatu" or "Dharma Study Group."

> Vajradhatu
> 1345 Spruce Street
> Boulder CO 80302
> (303) 444-0190

Zen Center

Classes are offered quarterly at Hosshinji (Beginner's Mind Temple) in San Francisco, ranging from basic courses in Buddhism to advanced topics.

> Zen Center
> 300 Page Street
> San Francisco CA 94102
> (415) 863-3136

Zen Studies Society

Every Thursday evening the New York Zendo hosts a public meeting, with zazen instruction and practice for beginners and a talk by Eido Roshi, a guest speaker, or senior student. From Monday to Friday there are regular zazen practice programs.

> New York Zendo Shobo-ji
> 223 East 67th Street
> New York NY 10021-6087
> (212) 861-3333

Select Bibliography

Christian

The recent renewal of interest in Christian mysticism and contemplative prayer has led to the retranslation and republication of many of the ancient classics (Paulist Press' Classics of Western Spirituality series, for example), as well as to the appearance of a large number of books on spiritual direction by contemporary writers. The following list is a selection only, intended to open the door and indicate a direction. Many of the titles in this and the following section are self-explanatory; some are annotated with brief descriptive summaries or relevant notes about the author.

Anonymous. *Meditations on the Tarot: A Journey into Christian Hermeticism.* Warwick, N.Y.: Amity House, 1986.
This book, with its apparently esoteric subject matter, turns out to be a collection of accessible, insightful meditations.

Arseniev, Nicholas. *Mysticism and the Eastern Church.* Crestwood, N.Y.: St. Vladimir's Seminary Press, 1979.

Bacovin, Helen, trans. *The Way of a Pilgrim and The Pilgrim Continues His Way.* Garden City, N.Y.: Doubleday & Co., Image Books, 1978.
The journal of an anonymous nineteenth-century Russian peasant whose one pressing question was, how does one pray constantly?

Chariton, Igumen of Valaam. *The Art of Prayer.* Translated by E. Kadloubovsky & E. M. Palmer. London: Faber & Faber, 1966.
A collection of Orthodox texts on prayer.

Clissold, Stephen. *St. Teresa of Avila.* New York: Seabury Press, 1982.

Cunningham, Lawrence S. *The Catholic Heritage.* New York: Crossroad, 1983.

Finley, James. *The Awakening Call.* Notre Dame, Indiana: Ave Maria Press, 1985.

———*Merton's Palace of Nowhere.* Notre Dame, Indiana: Ave Maria Press, 1978.
James Finley writes out of his experience as a former novice under Thomas Merton at the Abbey of Gesthemeni and as a contemporary spiritual director in his own right.

Hopko, Thomas. *All the Fulness of God.* Crestwood, N.Y.: St. Vladimir's Seminary Press, 1982.
Essays on the theology of the Orthodox Church, ecumenicism, "Children and Holy Communion," and "Orthodoxy and the American Spirit."

John of the Cross, Saint. *The Collected Works of St. John of the Cross.* Translated by Kieran Kavanaugh and Otilio Rodriguez. Washington: Inst. of Carmelite Studies, 1964.

Johnston, William. *The Wounded Stag: Christian Mysticism Today.* New York: Harper & Row, 1984.

————Ed. *The Cloud of Unknowing and The Book of Privy Counseling.* Garden City, N.Y.: Doubleday & Co., Image Books, 1973.
Now classics in the tradition of Western mysticism, these two essays on contemplative prayer are by an anonymous fourteenth-century English writer. This edition has been translated into modern English and introduced by Father Johnston. In his words, "All thoughts, all concepts, all images must be buried beneath a cloud of forgetting, while our naked love must rise upward toward God hidden in the cloud of unkowing."

Kadloubovsky, E. and Palmer, G. E., trans. *Writings from the Philokalia on Prayer of the Heart.* London & Boston: Faber & Faber, 1951.

Keating, Thomas. *The Crisis of Faith.* Petersham, Mass.: St. Bede's Pubns., 1979.

————*The Heart of the World: An Introduction to Contemplative Christianity.* New York: Crossroad, 1981.

————*Open Mind, Open Heart.* Warwick, N.Y.: Amity House, 1986.

————Pennington, Basil; and Clarke, Thomas. *Finding Grace at the Center.* Petersham, Mass.: St. Bede's Pubns., 1979.
A collection of essays on "centering prayer," a renewal of the traditional prayer which leads to contemplation, along with a description of its historical context.

Lawrence of the Resurrection, Brother. *The Practice of the Presence of God.* Ramsey, N.J.: Paulist Press, 1978.
A collection of conversations, letters, and spiritual maxims by a lay brother of the seventeenth century, whose prayer involved the simple practice of being continually in the presence of God.

Lossky, Vladimir. *The Mystical Theology of the Eastern Church.* Crestwood, N.Y.: St. Vladimir's Seminary Press, 1978.
Lossky (1903-1958) was a Russian lay theologian.

McNamara, William. *Christian Mysticism: A Psychotheology.* Chicago: Franciscan Herald Press, 1981.
"This practical book zeroes in on the simplest and truest way for people in the West to become mystics without really trying: by immersion in the Incarnational worldliness of the Christian Way." (Spiritual Life Inst. catalogue)

———*Earthy Mysticism: Contemplation and the Life of Passionate Presence.* New York: Crossroad, 1983.
"The sacred and sacramental nature of the flesh grew in the Western world and reached its peak in the body of Jesus who became the Christ. Matter matters, events affect us profoundly, creatures link us to the Creator. Therefore Western mysticism is notoriously earthy." (Spiritual Life Inst. catalogue)

Merton, Thomas. *New Seeds of Contemplation.* New York: New Directions, 1972.
A collection of personal reflections. This, along with the autobiography, Seven Storey Mountain, are Merton's most widely-read works. All of his other writings are also recommended as further reading.

Meyendorff, John. *St. Gregory Palamas and Orthodox Spirituality.* Crestwood, N.Y.: St. Vladimir's Seminary Press.
Father Meyendorff is presently dean of St. Vladimir's Seminary.

A Monk of the Eastern Church. *Orthodox Spirituality: An Outline of the Orthodox Ascetical & Mystical Tradition.* Crestwood, N.Y.: St. Vladimir's Seminary Press, 1978.
An "unpretentious little book . . . long recognized as a trusty guide for those wishing to explore the Orthodox ascetical and mystical tradition." (SVS catalogue)

Nemeck, Francis and Coombs, Marie Theresa. *Contemplation.* Wilmington, Del.: Michael Glazier, Inc., 1980.
Spiritual direction for contemplative prayer, integrating historical writings into a systematic guide to the signposts along the way.

Nolan, Albert. *Jesus Before Christianity.* Maryknoll, N.Y.: Orbis Books, 1978.

Palmer, G. E. H.; Sherrard, Philip; and Ware, Kallistos trans. *The Philokalia,* Vol. 1. London & Boston: Faber and Faber, 1979.
The Philokalia *is a compilation of writings from the early Fathers, and is an important source of spiritual direction for the Orthodox Church. Volume One includes the Fathers of the fourth to eighth centuries and therefore represents a heritage common to both the Orthodox and Catholic traditions. Evagrius of Pontus's* Texts on Prayer *is in this volume.*

Pennington, M. Basil; Jones, Alan; and Booth, Mark. *The Living Testament: The Essential Writings of Christianity Since the Bible.* San Francisco: Harper & Row, 1985.

Seventy-two excerpts from the writings of Western Christianity, chronologically arranged. A key at the back of the book provides short but helpful notes on the historical context of each entry.

Schmemann, Alexander. *For the Life of the World: Sacraments and Orthodoxy.* Crestwood, N.Y.: St. Vladimir's Seminary Press, 1973.
Father Schmemann (1921-1983) served as dean of St. Vladimir's Orthodox Seminary for twenty-one years. He was a prolific writer and well-known throughout the world as a spokesman for the Orthodox Church. This is his most popular book.

Scupoli, Lorenzo. *Unseen Warfare.* Translated by E. Kadloubovsky and G. E. H. Palmer. Crestwood, N.Y.: St. Vladimir's Seminary Press, 1978.
Written in the sixteenth century by a Catholic priest, this book was later translated and edited in the eighteenth century by the Greek Orthodox Nicodemus of Mount Athos and again in the nineteenth century by Theophan the Recluse. It became a classic in the tradition of "ascetic theology": how to discipline the mind and purify the heart. It also includes instructions on the Jesus prayer.

Steele, Douglas V., ed. *Quaker Spirituality: Selected Writings.* Ramsey, N.J.: Paulist Press, 1984.

Steindl-Rast, David. *Gratefulness, The Heart of Prayer.* Ramsey, N.J.: Paulist Press, 1984.
Brother David describes "gratefulness" as the thread of continuity that runs through all aspects of a life lived in contemplative awareness.

———*A Listening Heart.* New York: Crossroad, 1984.

Teilhard de Chardin, Pierre. *The Divine Milieu.* New York: Harper & Row, 1968.
As scientist, philosopher, and Jesuit priest, Teilhard de Chardin asserts divinity to be inseparable from the world of matter and eloquently expresses a "simultaneous love of God and the world."

Thérèse of Lisieux, Saint. *Story of a Soul: The Autobiography of St. Thérèse of Lisieux.* Translated by John Clarke. Washington: Inst. of Carmelite Studies, 1976.
Saint Thérèse (1873-1897), sometimes called the "Little Flower," was a Carmelite nun who taught that sanctity is to be gained through continual self-denial in the "little" circumstances of everyday life. She is one of the most popular of the modern saints.

Thornton, Martin. *Spiritual Direction.* Cambridge, Mass: Cowley Pubns., 1984.
Thornton writes out of the tradition of English spirituality, which has its own distinctive flavor.

Ulanov, Ann and Barry. *Primary Speech: A Psychology of Prayer.* Atlanta: John Knox Press, 1982.

The psychological implications and processes of prayer: prayer as self-awareness, self-acceptance, and transformation; prayer as an intimately personal act of devotion.

Underhill, Evelyn. *Mysticism.* New York: E. P. Dutton, 1961.

Vasileios, Archimandrite. *Hymn of Entry: Liturgy and Life in the Orthodox Church,* translated by Elizabeth Briere. Crestwood, N.Y.: St. Vladimir's Seminary Press, 1984.
Father Vasileios is regarded as the pioneer of the movement which led to the modern revival of monasticism on Mount Athos. In this book he affirms that liturgy is the true theology, in that it expresses the essence of the Church's mystical life.

Ward, Benedicta, trans. *The Sayings of the Desert Fathers: The Alphabetical Collection.* Kalamazoo, Mich.: Cistercian Pubns., 1975.
Stories and sayings of the early Fathers, chiefly those of fourth- and fifth-century Egypt.

Ware, Archimandrite Kallistos. The Orthodox Way. Crestwood, N.Y.: St. Vladimir's Seminary Press, 1979.
An introduction to the basic doctrines and principles of the Orthodox way.

Buddhist

The Buddhist teachings have been brought to the West by Eastern masters and English-speaking translators. Thus many early books on Buddhism, though translated into English, are imbedded in the context of a foreign culture and therefore are seemingly inappropriate to the Western reader, while many others have been distorted by the filter of Western language, preconception, and scholastic "objectivity." Although this list is not comprehensive, the following books have been selected because they hopefully provide an accessible and reliable introduction to the Buddhist traditions represented by the contributors to this book.

Aitken, Robert. *Taking the Path of Zen.* Berkeley: North Point Press, 1982.

Aronson, Harvey B. *Love and Sympathy in Theravada Buddhism.* Delhi: Motilal Banarsidass, 1980.

Cleary, Thomas, ed. and trans. *Timeless Spring: A Soto Zen Anthology.* New York: Weatherhill, 1980.
Articles on the history, philosophy, and methods of the Soto school of Zen Buddhism, by the classical masters. Soto is one of the two major lineages of Japanese Zen (the other

being Rinzai). Soto Zen was carried to Japan by Dogen Zenji in the thirteenth century (see the following entry) and then to North America by the late Suzuki Roshi, founder of Zen Center in San Francisco.

Cook, Francis. *How to Raise an Ox: Zen Practice as Taught in Zen Master Dogen's Shobogenzo.* Los Angeles: Center Pubns., 1978.
Teachings by Dogen Zenji on the practice of Zen meditation, along with introductory essays by the translator.

Dalai Lama, Tenzin Gyatso, the Fourteenth. *Kindness, Clarity, and Insight.* Trans. and ed. Jeffrey Hopkins. Ithaca, New York: Snow Lion Pubns., 1984.
Twenty articles that are based on the Dalai Lama's lecture tours in the United States and Canada between 1979 and 1981.

Fields, Rick. *How the Swans Came to the Lake: A Narrative History of Buddhism in America.* Boston: Shambhala, 1981.
A comprehensive, anecdotal introduction to the "cast of characters" that has brought Buddhism to America.

Goldstein, Joseph. *The Experience of Insight: A Simple and Direct Guide to Buddhist Meditation.* Boston: Shambhala, 1983.

Kato, Bunno; Tamura, Yoshiro; and Miyasaka, Kojiro; trans. *The Threefold Lotus Sutra.* New York: Weatherhill, 1975.
A collection of three sutras (teachings of the Buddha) which are central texts of Chinese and Japanese Mahayana traditions.

King, Winston L. *Theravada Meditation.* University Park: Pennsylvania State Univ. Press, 1980.

Kornfield, Jack and Breiter, Paul, eds. *A Still Forest Pond: The Insight Meditation of Achaan Chah.* Wheaton, Ill.: The Theosophical Publ. House, 1985.
Spirited teachings on the practice of Theravada meditation by the Thai vipassana master who was the primary teacher of Jack Kornfield, cofounder of the Insight Meditation Society.

Nhat Hanh, Tich. *The Miracle of Mindfulness.* Boston: Beacon Press, 1976.
Tich Nhat Hanh is a spokesman for Buddhist practice and ethics in the world peace movement. He teaches "engaged Buddhism": the application of mindfulness and compassion to social issues.

Nalanda Translation Committee, trans. *The Rain of Wisdom.* Boston: Shambhala, 1980.
A collection of dohas (songs of realization) from the Kagyu lineage of Tibetan Buddhism, translated into English under the direction of Chögyam Trungpa Rinpoche.

Nyanaponika, Thera. *The Heart of Buddhist Meditation.* New York: Samuel Weiser, 1973.
A classic description of Theravada satipatthana (mindfulness) meditation.

Rahula, Walpola. *What the Buddha Taught.* New York: Grove Press, 1974.
A comprehensive introduction to the Four Noble Truths, the Buddhist views of ego and egolessness, and Theravada meditation.

Ross, Nancy Wilson, ed. *The World of Zen: An East-West Anthology.* New York: Vintage Books, Random House, 1960.
A compilation of Zen (particularly Rinzai) teachings, as well as both Eastern and Western examples of artistic, social, and everyday-life applications of Zen.

Sekida, Katsuki. *Zen Training: Methods and Philosophy.* New York: Weatherhill, 1975.

Senzaki, Nyogen; Nakagawa, Soen; and Shimano, Eido. *Namu Dai Bosa: A Transmission of Zen Buddhism to America.* New York: Theatre Arts Books, 1976.
This book documents the founding of Eido Roshi's monastic center, Dai Bosatsu Zendo. It also includes talks on the Rinzai tradition of Zen by Eido Roshi; Nyogen Senzaki, a pioneer of American Zen; and Soen Roshi, Eido Roshi's teacher. Available from Dai Bosatsu Zendo (see "The Zen Studies Society" in the Directory).

Shantideva. *A Guide to the Bodhisattva's Way of Life.* Translated by Stephen Batchelor. Ithaca, N.Y.: Snow Lion Pubns., 1979.
An eighth-century classic of Indian Mahayana Buddhism, outlining the virtues and methods of cultivating bodhichitta, the wish to achieve buddhahood for the sake of all beings.

Shimano, Eido Tai. *Golden Wind: Zen Talks.* Tokyo: Japan Publications, 1979.
Although now out of print, this book is worth looking for in your local Zen center library.

Situpa, Khentin Tai. *Way to Go: Sowing the Seed of Buddha.* Edited by Ken Holmes. Eskdalemuir, Scotland: Kagyu Samye Ling.
A commentary on the principles and methods of the Tibetan Mahayana path.

Suzuki, Shunryu. *Zen Mind, Beginner's Mind.* New York: Weatherhill, 1970.
Based on talks by the founder of Zen Center in San Francisco, this book has become a "meditation manual" and inspirational guide for Western Buddhist practitioners of all sects.

Tendzin, Ösel. *Buddha in the Palm of Your Hand.* Boston: Shambhala, 1982.
Ösel Tendzin is the dharma heir of Chögyam Trungpa Rinpoche. Using the Western

idiom, this book outlines the path of meditation as it has been taught by Kagyu lineage holders of the Tibetan tradition.

Trungpa, Chögyam. *Cutting Through Spiritual Materialism.* Boston: Shambhala, 1973.
A description of the "confusion, misunderstanding, and expectation" that the aspirant, and particularly the Western aspirant, brings to the spiritual path, followed by a description of the essential teachings of the Tibetan Buddhist path.

————*Journey Without Goal: The Tantric Wisdom of the Buddha.* Boston: Shambhala, 1985.
The tantric (Vajrayana) journey, described in experiential terms.

————*The Myth of Freedom.* Boston: Shambhala, 1976.
The application of Buddhist psychology to meditation practice, including a discussion of the six styles ("realms") of self-deception, the Buddhist approach to working with emotions, meditation-in-action, and the guru principle.

Dialogue

A comprehensive, though slightly dated, bibliography on Christian-Buddhist dialogue can be found in Joseph Spae's book, *Buddhist-Christian Empathy* (see below). Also, the annotated "Christian-Buddhist Encounter: A Select Bibliography," compiled by David G. Hackett in 1979, is still available from the New Religious Movements Librarian, Graduate Theological Union Library, 2400 Ridge Road, Berkeley, California 94709. For recent articles and book reviews the reader is also directed to the journal *Buddhist-Christian Studies,* edited by David W. Chappell and published annually by the East-West Religions Project, University of Hawaii, 2530 Dole Street, Honolulu, Hawaii 96822.

Amore, Roy C. *Two Masters, One Message: The Lives and Teachings of Gautama and Jesus.* Nashville: Abingdon, 1978.

Cobb, John B. *Beyond Dialogue: Toward a Mutual Transformation of Christianity and Buddhism.* Philadelphia: Fortress Press, 1982.
John Cobb articulates the Christian theological and historical context for dialogue, emphasizing the need to move beyond superficial dialogue and work toward the goal of "mutual transformation."

Dumoulin, Heinrich. *Christianity Meets Buddhism.* Translated by John C. Maraldo. LaSalle, Ill.: Open Court, 1974.

Graham, Dom Aelred. *Conversations: Christian and Buddhist. Encounters in Japan.* New York: Harcourt, Brace & World, 1968.
Edited transcripts of a Benedictine abbot's conversations with Japanese Buddhists.

Ingram, Paul O. and Streng, Frederick, eds. *Buddhist-Christian Dialogue: Mutual Renewal and Transformation.* Honolulu: Univ. of Hawaii Press, 1986.

Johnston, William. *The Inner Eye of Love: Mysticism and Religion.* San Francisco: Harper & Row, 1982.

———*The Mirror Mind: Spirituality and Transformation.* San Francisco: Harper & Row, 1981.

———*The Still Point: Reflections on Zen and Christian Mysticism.* San Francisco: Harper & Row, 1970.
William Johnston, an Irish Jesuit priest, is an important contributor to the field of contemplative dialogue. He writes out of his experience as a Zen practitioner and former director of the Institute of Oriental Religions and professor of Religious Studies at Sophia University in Japan.

King, Winston. *Buddhism and Christianity: Some Bridges of Understanding.* Philadelphia: Westminster Press, 1962.
Compares Theravada Buddhist and Christian concepts of God, love, guilt, suffering, prayer and meditation, the conquest of self, grace, and faith.

LaSalle, H. M. Enomiya. *Zen Meditation for Christians.* Translated by John C. Maraldo. LaSalle, Ill.: Open Court, 1974.

Merton, Thomas. *The Asian Journal.* Edited by Naomi Burton, Patrick Hart, and James Laughlin. New York: New Directions, 1973.

Rockefeller, Steven C., ed. *The Christ and the Bodhisattva.* Albany, N. Y.: SUNY Press, 1986.
This collection of talks is based on a symposium held at Middlebury College in 1984. Contributors include: David Steindl-Rast, the Dalai Lama, Robert Thurman, and Luis Gomez.

Spae, Joseph. *Buddhist-Christian Empathy.* Chicago: Chicago Institute of Theology and Culture, 1980.

Suzuki, D. T. *Mysticism: Christian and Buddhist.* Westport, Conn.: Greenwood, 1976.

Waldenfels, Hans. *Absolute Nothingness: Foundations for a Buddhist-Christian Encounter.* Translated by James W. Heisig. Ramsey, N.J.: Paulist Press, 1980.
A philosophical and theological comparison, with a particular focus on the issue of being versus nonbeing.